293

Short Flights

Short Flights

///////////.

Barbara Probst Solomon

///////////.

THE VIKING PRESS

NEW YORK

First published in 1983 by The Viking Press
40 West 23rd Street, New York, N.Y. 10010
Published simultaneously in Canada by
Penguin Books Canada Limited

Library of Congress Cataloging in Publication Data
    Solomon, Barbara Probst.
    Short flights.
1. Solomon, Barbara Probst.
2. Journalists—United States—Biography.   I. Title.
PN4874.S575A34   1983   070'.92'4   [B]   82-17360
ISBN 0-670-33053-1

Selections from this book previously appeared in *The New York Review of Books* and *Present Tense.*

Grateful acknowledgment is made to the following for permission to reprint copyrighted material:
George Borchardt Inc.: excerpt from the introduction to *Ogro* by Barbara Probst Solomon; Houghton Mifflin Company: excerpt from *Spanish Prelude* by Jenny Ballou, copyright 1937, copyright renewed © 1965 by Jenny Ballou; *The New Republic:* "Reporting from Portugal: The Divided Junta," October 1974 issue, copyright © 1974 by The New Republic, Inc.; North Point Press: *Italian Journey, 1786–1788,* copyright © 1982 by J. W. Goethe, translated by W. H. Auden and Elizabeth Mayer; Warner Bros. Inc.: lyrics from "Blues in the Night" by Johnny Mercer and Harold Arlen, copyright 1941 (renewed) by Warner Bros. Inc.

Author's Note
What follows is my best recollection of the people, events, places, and experiences as I perceived them. The names of certain people are so well known that their actual names are necessarily used, but the names and some of the characteristics of the other people described have been changed to preserve an anonymity that they wish to retain.

I would like to thank the National Endowment for the Arts for a grant which made the writing of part of this book possible.

Set in CRT Garamond
Printed in the United States of America

For my father,

J. Anthony Probst,

1896–1975

and

For my mother,

Frances Kurke Probst

But, after all, my one wish has been to see this country at any cost and, were I to be dragged to Rome on Ixion's wheel, I should not utter a single word of complaint.

—Johann Wolfgang Von Goethe,
Italian Journey (1786–1788)

Contents

I

*Of These
Many Games*

1

Face facts—I've always had a tenuous relation to the Grand Design. Let Woody Allen claim *Casablanca*, I'm keeping *Pepe Le Moko*. French and American version, small details count. Gabin matters more than Boyer. Take the way I meet Juan.

In 1974 he visits me in my place; it is one of those dry, early January days, full of New York crisp *lumière*. You get a good corner view of Central Park through the big, old-fashioned windows of my West Side apartment. Well, first we sniff around each other. Talk about the old Spanish gang in Paris. Franco. My political pieces on Spain. The new zapped-up Spanish Communist Party. (The expression "Euro-Communism" hadn't yet caught on in early 1974. So we just said "zapped-up.") But despite the flashy international chitchat, I have the feeling, as I stare into Juan's cool blue Spanish eyes, that I have stumbled across a Gabin man. Ostensibly Juan has come carrying news of my Spanish friends in Paris. But Juan lets clues slip as to his true nature. His new novel is set in Tangier. Juan starts conversations about Noam Chomsky, linguistics, the fate of the fancy French magazine *Tel Quel*, but soon his conversation meanders; lapsing he says: "Did you know during World War II Tangier was the biggest spy center in Europe?"

Did I know? How could Juan believe I have so little grasp of the historic essentials? As in Charles Boyer, as in Hedy Lamarr. Not to mention Dietrich and Cooper in Von Sternberg's *Morocco*. A plump, young, Germanic Dietrich belting out to the café crowd in Tangier— "Who vill buy mein apples?" Who bought her apples? Why, Cooper, as that brave Foreign Legionnaire, sitting in a hot café, watching a hatted Dietrich fling her black maribou in his direction. It is unimportant that Juan was born in Barcelona, and me in St. Mark's Hospital (now torn down) over by St. Mark's Place on East Tenth Street in Manhattan. We are both members of one of the first generations to have grown up with an international childhood code memory. Our dream was the movies, our idiom was English—star language, Hollywood's poetry.

All right, in an earlier life, at the age of eight or nine, Juan was Jean Gabin. So who am I? Always an optimistic dreamer, age, I tell myself, is not the bad news it used to be. True, I have two daughters in college. Back in the 1960s I was thought too young to have become a widow. But that was a decade ago. Still, it is in style for a woman to be well into her forties. So what is erotic but a style of engaging people? No matter what happens, I reassure myself, as I pour us both coffee in my large Central Park West living room, remember, Ingrid, Rita, and Lauren were stars while you were still a kid taking in the double features at the RKO off Lexington and Eighty-sixth Street. So, if Juan is Jean Gabin on the move, then I *am* just Pepe Le Moko's New York fix.

At the beginning of World War II, my brother and I still lived in our parents' old apartment, at the corner of Ninety-fifth Street and Fifth Avenue. Later we moved downtown to Sixty-sixth Street. Those were the last days of the Depression; when I was a child and walked over toward Lexington, there was a certain sadness that clung to some of the streets in the city. We weren't yet called Barbara and Mark. Janet and Clara, my mother's two younger sisters, had been brought in to take care of us during my mother's long absences. Clara, the younger, had high cheekbones, natural thick honey-colored hair; she jiggled her buttocks as she walked, and she wore small, tilted, brown velour berets, carelessly knotted "skins" around her neck; she worked as a young decorator in Macy's Little Shop, talked about someone called Elsie de Wolfe, and brought my older brother and me bags of books from Macy's Red Star Book Club. Macy's had a book war; they undercut other bookstores. A happy thief, I waited for Clara to arrive each month with the brown parcels stuffed with new books. Janet, my other aunt, was a natural white blonde; she wore toques, smiled easily; frequently she touched and kissed my brother and me. Mickey was black-haired like my mother, I was dirty blonde like my aunts.

In those days we were called Bunny and Mickey. (The family's Jewish identity went largely unnoticed until some time after World War

II. I don't think as children we were very Jewish. We became vaguely more so after being grownups.) If you leaned at a certain uncomfortable angle out of our living room double window, you could catch a view of a slice of Central Park, which included a piece of the reservoir. I liked to watch good-looking men and women galloping on sleek horses just beneath the dam on the bridle path. My bedroom window had a back view over the brownstones. One June evening, during the time my mother lived in Europe (up until the beginning of the Second World War) a burglar catwalked from the roof of the adjoining brownstone into an apartment opposite ours. I watched from my room while the police ran into the apartment and the thief hung from a ledge opposite me. I could have thrown a heavy object against his head and he would have fallen seven flights to the ground. But I didn't, and he leapt across to a townhouse roof, and despite the police with their whistles and sticks, he got away. I wanted to think he was Dillinger, the biggest gangster of them all.

"The routine; Mickey and Bunny, do your routine," our two young aunts begged while we all waited for *the* telephone call, the mysterious long distance (through pipes in the sea?) from my mother in Europe. My brother smashed my father's gray fedora on his head and Clara's velvet beret on me. Clara would turn Dixieland jazz on the Victrola, Mickey whirled me about; we did our routine, mimicking, dancing, acting, laughing, while Clara and Janet applauded us. "Again! More!" Mickey fed me the lines while I invented new pieces of dialogue. "My name is Miss Murphy, I have come from Minneapolis to see the World's Fair—"

Mickey, three years older, a nervous, kinetic kid with spendthrift energy and an introverted imagination, leaned against me, stroked my neck and hugged me; he hissed into the dull-red, early-evening, living room light, "My name be Pepe Le Moko and I will take you to ze Casbahhhhhhhh!"

"Oh no, no, not that. You are Jack Armstrong—you have come to take me to the World's Fair—to Coney Island—O Luna Park, O Jones Beach!"

"I be Pepe Le Moko, and I leef in ze Casbahhhhhhhh."

In the Gabin version of *Pepe Le Moko,* Gabin, the exiled gangster, forgotten in the Arab quarters of Algiers, stares into Mireille Balin's eyes, and reflected in her irises, poor, lonely Gabin sees the boulevards and plane trees of Paris.

"I be Pepe Le Moko. You come with me to the Casbah!" Mickey mimicked.

While we waited for the telephone call from Europe, Janet and Clara and Mickey and I danced to Victrola music.

> *My momma done tol' me*
> *When I was in pigtails,*
> *My momma done tol' me, hon . . .*

We whirled in circles on the polished parquet floors; Mickey held me at the waist.

> *A man is a two-faced,*
> *a worrisome thing,*
> *Who'll leave you to sing*
> *The blu-es in the night.*

Juan talks until ten that night. Later, we move into the kitchen. When I first came to the neighborhood (my younger daughter, Maria, had just been born and we had outgrown our Village walk-up), the old West Side apartments were a drug on the market. Fear of Puerto Ricans. But neighborhood Spanish, since I spoke the language, didn't scare me. Seduced by the enormous space, the high ceilings, and the great view, I persuaded Harold to rent the place. For $200 a month we got ourselves a big barn and a great bargain. In the late 1960s, after his death, when the market was low, I bought it. Took $25,000 of a $30,000 insurance policy he had left me, and with terror in my heart (it was my first business investment) I bought it outright. Now the neighborhood has become classy again. So, in terms of space, I live in style.

Juan talks about New York as though the city is a great Byzantine bazaar. While he converses, he eats the warmed-over boeuf bourguignon I have heated for him. Slight of build, he seems able to pack it away. I get the feeling he suffers from that European alarm concerning American food. Will he be forced to eat a plate of turkey, heated jam, and banana Jell-O? Relieved that the bread is firm, the wine all right, and the cheese at room temperature, he relaxes. My attitude concerning European men always has been: serve them three perfect meals a day; keep the steam heat shut off, bottled water in the refrigerator, and the blinds drawn tight across the windows at night. After that, I expect them to clue into my needs. Well, there is one more thing. Never ask too many questions.

I notice that his intelligent, orphaned blue eyes blink at the sound of the Mozart Sonata in D Major coming from my hi-fi. He asks me if he can play the record a second time, the music overwhelms him. During dinner, he mentions that his mother was killed in a German bombing raid in Barcelona. Which made his conservative upper-class family very anti-German.

Although we have met only once before, in Paris in 1959, we gab with the familiarity of people who share a common past. We know the same crowd. My first big love, from my student days in Paris, was Spanish. He was an anthropologist. (In his thirties he was killed in a jeep accident in the desert in Iran.) In a small creaky country like Spain, cultural news travels slow, writers and artists hold their positions for a longer spell than we do. In Spain, with luck, one could stay on top of the cultural heap for fifty years. In America, with luck, one might hold on for fifty weeks. Paco Benet, my dead ex-boyfriend, has a brother, who is also a Spanish novelist named Juan. I notice Juan Goytisolo likes the double identification.

When I ask him to turn on the front burner on the stove, I need boiled water for our tea, he rears back as though in the presence of a major gas explosion. I think about Barcelona, the fire bombings, his dead mother, and I take the matches from him and light the burner myself.

Back in the living room, he drinks the hot tea and inquires, politely, "I hear you are *en ménage* with a baseball player?"

So he has made inquiries. "Sportswriter—not baseball player. We decided to stay together through Christmas and a New Year's Eve party. He left two weeks ago; I have his red baseball cap, and sometimes his teenage son from his first marriage. My daughters are away in college."

American habits baffle Europeans. Juan seems even more puzzled when I point out that prior to the sportswriter, I had been friendly with a man who spent most of his time sailing.

"I somehow don't connect you to baseball players or sailors."

"Well then, neither did I—life's full of accidents. But fresh air isn't the worst fate for a woman. Sometimes I think there simply isn't enough fresh air in modern novels."

"Is that why you found yourself a baseball player and a sailor?"

I think about that for a while, then I walk over to the phonograph and put another Mozart on the player.

"For myself," he says, "I don't have American sports hobbies." He pauses. "I'm just a solid city walker."

2

I am the child of an emotional trio that endured for half a century. My mother had a bad postpartum depression when Mickey was born and couldn't take care of him for the first year. A young German girl, Marte, was brought over from Magdeburg in north Prussia to take care of my brother, and by the time I was born, the three of them— my mother, Marte, and my father—were permanently locked into a triangle that had little to do with either my brother or myself. In my earliest memories, I was, quite simply, Marte's child. We babbled together in broken English laced with German, she dressed and fed me, we walked together along Madison Avenue or in Central Park, and in the early grades of school, Marte tried to do my homework with me. She learned to spell in English while she carefully monitored me. I was an American child who learned first-grade arithmetic in German. *Eins, zwei, drei, vier, fünf.* Marte smashed my heart early by threatening to leave Mickey and me forever. She did take trips back to Germany, but when I was older, I finally learned that she always came back. Marte and my mother traveled at different times. When Marte was in Europe, my mother was at home. When Marte was in America, my mother restlessly and nervously traveled through Europe, a habit that continued until the beginning of World War II. In those days, doctors still prescribed sea voyages for female emotional disturbances. At first I yearned to carve out of my askew family a picture-book story. Four of us: a mother, father, brother, and sister. But if I gave myself two parents—what would I do with Marte, who had raised me? There she was, an unclaimed extra. I would window-gaze, spending hours trying to fathom what went on with those three adults. Marte wanted to be mother to Mickey and me, that was clear. Marte liked my father, that was clear. Mickey, my friends, and I whispered about the odd relationship and wondered. I felt my father wanted my mother. He was disappointed at her rejection of him, put out at her failure to notice she had produced two children. His behavior fluctuated. Occasionally, on a Sunday morning he would mutter how he was both mother and father—and suddenly he would swoop us up, ignoring Marte's predictions that we would become spoiled rotten kids, and take us to play baseball in Central Park, to movies at the old Roxy or Capitol (both had floor shows), and then to Chinatown for Sunday dinner. Everything for my energetic father was play; he liked being a smart lawyer, living in the center of things, courting his son and daughter, but when we had to be home on school nights, his attention to us slowed down. Spending time in the apartment bored him. I sensed he felt an emptiness—there was only Marte, Mickey, and me at home.

During the week my father rarely came in until one or two a.m. I would lie awake waiting to hear the sound of his key in the door, listening to his walk as he came down the long hallway toward his bedroom, and I always wondered what mysterious delights had kept him out so late. I had a vivid imagination, I was curious. The secrets of adult life seemed delicious.

In the evening, while we were supposedly doing homework, Mickey and I lay legs sprawled on the thick gray living room carpet with the radio turned high; Jack Armstrong and the Lone Ranger were our favorites. (When I was sick I got the daytime soaps—*Our Gal Sunday, Helen Trent,* can a widow of thirty-five find love and happiness?) Marte would mutter: *"Die Kinde, die Kinde."* Or went around singing German songs and predicting in a loud voice the terrible fate that awaited Mickey and me: "With him out to four in the morning and her away." Meanwhile, sprawled on the floor, we read whatever sexy books we could find in the bookcase. *Companionate Marriage,* Anatole France's *Revolt of the Angels,* and *Thaïs,* and *The Love Songs of Ovid.* We devoured the dirty pictures in *Casanova's Memoirs.* On the flyleaf was stamped, in purple, SOLD AT RETAIL BY MACY'S. PRIVATELY PRINTED BY THE EXOTICA CLUB 1930. Stacked high in piles near our two prone bodies were *The Saturday Evening Post, National Geographic, Collier's, The New Republic, The Nation, Vogue, The New York Post,* and *PM.* My parents were never home, but they subscribed to everything.

When I was very young, I got into the habit of figuring out my mother. On those scattered, sweet-smelling spring days, when the evenings in New York were long, sometimes we would stroll along Fifth Avenue, over to the Seventy-second Street mall. I had figured out her secret. My mother was afraid. She feared being with me and Mickey.

She was terrified that if she walked with us along the street, something bad would happen to us all. She had to maneuver so that Marte, or my father, or her two younger sisters took care of us, because of her being scared. So, on the rare occasions I was alone with her, I held her hand tightly, and would slowly explain the world to her. I repeated (as my teachers did in school) what I saw, indeed what we saw: the trees, the horses; I steered her over to Madison Avenue, where there were places we could stop. I kept saying the obvious. "Now we are approaching Ninetieth Street. It's warm today. It will be hotter next month."

The two of us had odd conversations. She was fond of certain small shops along Madison; we would stop and browse. She had a fine eye; together we bought interesting bric-a-brac, upholstery material. Sometimes she purchased blouses and skirts in one of the smaller stores and when I sensed her becoming nervous—a look of surprised unsteadiness would come into her eyes—I would accompany her home. When she wasn't frightened she would make extremely intelligent observations. But she was always, emotionally, the child of our family. The outings with me I perceived as being meant for her.

When Marte walked with me, I was the child. Just as my mother was unsteady in her psyche, as we conquered the streets of New York, Marte, the immigrant, was unsteady in language. After school she would go with me to Yorkville (Germantown) and she would buy me toys. She got me hoops, jump ropes, a weathervane made of a gilt-edged piece of cardboard with a little boy yodeler whose pants changed to violet before rainy weather, a diary with a lock, a small gold heart to wear around my neck with my initials, a set of jacks, and white dickies with *Bobbie* embroidered in red. I was Marte's American girl.

I tried to "see" my mother. I loved hearing about the family past. My great-grandparents were Polish Jews. They came from a small border town between Danzig and Königsberg. According to my aunts, my great-grandfather was a scholarly man who did nothing but piously read the Talmud, while my great-grandmother supported the family by smuggling liquor beneath her skirts, driving her horse and wagon across the German border. So, I deduced, on my mother's side, we descended from pious smugglers. My grandfather's older brothers had been fishermen. After they were lost at sea in the Gulf of Danzig (a great family tragedy), my grandfather and grandmother, pretending to be brother and sister, in 1890, at the age of sixteen, emigrated to the United States. My grandfather brought nothing with him except mild religion. He was unnostalgic about what he had left behind. My grandmother carried three very good copper pots. They hang now in my kitchen, my inheritance. When I get discouraged at night, I walk out into the kitchen, turn on the lights, feel the burnished metal. She traveled across the Atlantic with three pots and made it, so what's with you? The saucepans are my courage. Pot courage.

Unencumbered, and with a natural gift and flair for making a handsome suit or fur-trimmed coat, my grandfather prospered moderately by designing for fashionable stores, and he soon opened his own factory. He rapidly moved his young family to the upper Nineties on Madison, and within a short time established many of his greenhorn relatives in small apartments on the same block. My grandfather allowed only English to be spoken, while my grandmother learned about American desserts (Jell-O) from her German-Jewish neighbors. The family destiny was already pointed to assimilation. In my generation none of my grandfather's grandsons married Jewish women, although my grandfather never recognized that he was a cog in the ecumenical wheel. In deference to a promise made to my great-grandmother, he kept up with the Jewish God.

The next mover in assimilation was to be my black-haired "beautiful witch" of a rebel mother. In 1913 Frances Kurke came home from school and noticed the enormous amount of work connected with changing dishes for Passover. So she took the freshly washed Passover dishes and smashed them on the floor. She told me she had a gentle mother and got off scot-free. Dizzy with success, her next act of rebellion was to surreptitiously fry herself a hamburger, which she put between two halves of roll generously smeared with fresh butter. She then calmly devoured her non-kosher sandwich, which was the most delicious food she had ever eaten. That night, she went to sleep expecting God to punish her. As he never appeared, she soon realized God wouldn't be bothering her, so she continued making her wonderful hamburger and butter sandwiches. In 1921, when she met my father, he added lobsters and Christmases to her aesthetic life. Later, on her own, my mother found another God named D. H. Lawrence.

Despite my mother's abstract devotion to D. H. Lawrence—and her great feminine beauty, she was an extraordinarily shy woman. Clearly she irritated my virile father by not wishing to have anything "physical" with him. All physical acts repelled my mother; she avoided touching either my brother or myself.

As a child, I tried to piece together the puzzle—her prudishness concerning physical functions seemed at odds with her outspoken devotion to Lawrence and her habit of surrounding herself with drawings of the nude body. Occasionally my mother would have what was then called a spell. Her balance would go off; then, in a few moments, after someone gave her spirits of ammonia, she would be all right.

I sensed my mother's troubles were connected to her own mother's death. She had seen her die of a seizure of some sort, which had caused cardiac failure. But whenever I asked my mother what disease her mother had died of, she would vaguely reply that her mother had borne too many children. I tried to cut through her mistiness. "Mother, what did your mother die of? Mother, people die of something, a disease. Your mother died of a bad heart. Mother, you don't die of having too many children when your youngest child is already eleven. Mother, your mother had a maid, and went away to the country in the summer. Mother, did your mother have *epilepsy?* Mother, your mother had diamond bracelets and fur coats; you have the jewelry, and we have pictures of her. All dressed up in furs." Occasionally my mother would answer, "The doctors told her not to have more children. Then she went ahead and had Janet and Clara."

"Mother," I reasoned, "children can't kill a mother years after childbirth. Your mother was just *sick*." But no matter how pragmatic I sounded, my mother's mood fluctuations continued to startle me. One morning she seemed very happy. She had been out the previous evening to a party with my father. I was glad to see her so vivacious. "We went to this art ball," she half-whispered to me, while she brushed her hair, seated in front of the dressing table in a pale-blue slip. "It was such a funny party." She laughed. "Well, everyone wore costumes. Some of the women dressed as men—and some men wore women's evening dresses." My mother giggled. "I had to go to the bathroom, and there was this woman in the dressing room; she was wearing a black silk top hat. She said I was beautiful and didn't at all have what she called a New York accent."

I stared at my mother. (I was about eleven now.) Her face and neck had flushed as she described her encounter, and for the first time I had seen my mother enthusiastic. Her odd description of her female conquest was our first and last sexual conversation. Groping about through the maze of adult relations surrounding me, I finally grasped, in an inchoate way, that Marte was there not just for Mickey and me, and not only because of her yearning for my father (who in turn, seemed to lust after my uninterested mother), but because of my

mother's need of her. I understood that the three of them were together for the long haul. I ceased trying to rearrange, trying to understand, and I went my own way. Later, when I went to high school, my
home-room teacher, fishing, asked if my parents were divorced because
no one came to school for my reports.

"No, ma'am, we all live together."

"At Sixty-sixth Street and Madison? What an odd neighborhood to
bring up children."

"We used to live up in the Nineties, but my father likes walking to
work."

"And you? How do you visit your friends?"

"I walk, or take the Madison Avenue bus. Or Lex. If it's late, a
taxi."

"And do you have enough money for, just like that, a taxi?"

Her question startled me. "Well, yes. I take what I need."

"From where?"

"The pot in the hall—that's what it's meant for."

"Don't you have an allowance?"

I stared at her. "We use the hall pot. I take what other girls in the
class get. That's fair."

"Oh." She coughed slightly. Finally she got to the point. Why
didn't my mother show up for school reports?

After a long pause I said, "Well, sometimes my mother gets sad."
Miss Hill dug around until she got herself invited to dinner at our
house. Marte sat with us. Lewis, a man who came each afternoon to
clean windows and polish silver, served a dull, somewhat overcooked
meal. My father charmed Miss Hill; my mother was reserved. Neither
of them apologized for not having come for the parent-teacher conference. Miss Hill murmured some compliments about my talents. My
mother suddenly looked up. "Barbara knows everything," she said
flatly. "She just does."

When I started high school, I also sent my mother off to art classes,
and it was the start of a better existence for both of us. Unexpectedly,
and little by little, she developed into an extraordinarily original artist.
But the family confusions made me wonder about myself. Who
would I end up liking? At night, I stared at myself in the mirror near
my bed as though my reflection was of another woman. I tried kissing
my own arms, and breasts, to test myself. But then I flopped down in
bed, and whispered, Ah am you-hurs, Rhett, Ah am yo-hurs. Scarlett
wha-ants you, Oh, Re-hett, dah-lin.

Years later, after I was grown up, my mother locked herself in the bathroom; she wanted us all to go away. I refused my father's request to "handle it."

"Daddy," I said, nervous, "I can't." But my mother wouldn't leave her locked space. We were huddled in the living room, and then suddenly I went to the telephone and called the outside world for help with an urgency that would have awakened the dead, and I didn't get off the telephone until an analyst promised to come right over. My father was too unnerved by my mother's behavior to do anything, so the doctor entered my mother's room, me pointing the way. After a while, my mother came out into her bedroom and sat on her bed, while the doctor drew a chair up close to her, and he also sat down. They talked a long time. Finally my father and I (we waited outside in the hall during most of the talk) came back in. The doctor had asked my mother, "If I find you a therapist to visit several times a week—would you be afraid?"

My mother shook her head.

"Then what are you afraid of?"

"Of me," she whispered. "Only me." I looked up at my father; he said nothing. After that my mother went regularly to a doctor whom the specialist recommended. Between art school and the visits to the doctor her morale seemed to improve. At that time my parents also had their big place in Connecticut, which my mother filled with her sisters, stray orphans, an odd assortment of help, and her women friends from the art school. Meanwhile, Marte ran the city place, which was where my father mostly lived. At times, when my mother was in a good mood, we seemed almost like sisters. My mother's troubles kept her looking amazingly young; she was girlish, fey.

Just before my seventeenth birthday, my father sent the two of us to the fur district. His accountant knew of a good man. As the great-granddaughter of those pious smugglers from the Polish-German border near the Baltic Sea, and the granddaughter of a man who did okay in America due to a quick eye and light hand with few yards of wool, I shared with my mother a great sense of the visual. We both knew what to do with colors, what bric-a-brac in a junk shop to buy, where a seam was needed, and how to imagine a bolt of cloth into a fantastic dress. My mother and the furrier took seriously my suggestions for the sleeves and collar of her wild-mink coat. The two of us bent our heads together and agreed that the lining should be toffee-colored silk, to blend with the caramel cashmere skirts and sweaters she wore most days with a dark-brown scarf knotted at her neck. Mental troubles aren't static or frozen—some years are better than others. "Well," said my mother, "if I get wild mink, then you are entitled to something, too."

"What do I get?" By this time I was graduating high school.

"Beaver," she said, "a full-length sheared beaver." The furrier nodded approvingly. "And what does Grannie get?" (My grandfather had remarried before I was born.)

"Black Persian."

"What about gray Persian? Or brown?" I suggested, always wanting to be different.

"No, I think, for the life she leads, Grannie would be happier with black"—my mother paused—"we'll take the three coats up to Poppa, when they are ready, and see what he thinks of them." My mother, despite D. H. Lawrence, transvestite galas, and nervous breakdowns, still wanted her old man's stern approval. My grandfather knew the real stuff from the junk; he had a way of pulling and breathing on the material. The copper-pot courage, I got from my mother's Polish side. My father's people, a bunch of wild, high-living Viennese, were quite another story.

It is 1974.

I walk across the park; the old WASP East Sixties of my childhood, severe, elegant, puritanical, at times housing oddly careless kinds of people, has given way to jet-set chic. The avenue, overstuffed with French and Italian boutiques, has discreetly begun to advertise post-Christmas sales. Behind the façades of Yves Saint Laurent and Ungaro, I feel the ghostly presence of Liberty Music Shops, Womrath bookstores, German ladies who owned frumpy lingerie shops, and my teenage self. At that time, all the gut energies of my childhood went into making that trio *not be. Nolo esse.* Later, a sharp sense of rage motored me away from home, across the Atlantic—toward Europe. And now? A woman in her forties, with two daughters in college—I walk slowly toward my parents' home. My father is dying, and the main point is, the three of them have to be kept together. They cling to one another, aging survivors from another time.

My father is flat broke, and it is hard to keep them going in their apartment in the Sixties, although they have lived there so long, their rents haven't kept pace with the new prices in the neighborhood. When he was a young man my father, in his energetic way, made fortunes. But in the 1960s, when he was getting old, and was crippled with Parkinson's and had lapses in judgment and memory, he kept control of the reins in his nineteenth-century top-dog way; he overexpanded at a time when money was short—didn't understand that younger wheeler-dealers were coming up behind him, and that the banks didn't see him as a young whiz with a long future ahead. Now he is an old man with ten diseases. "Why, Bunny," he says, "why, Bunny." He speaks careful, well-modulated, slightly Victorian English—a tone an ambitious boy, son of down-and-out Jewish Austrians with a murky marital history, might affect. (Did my grandmother ever legally divorce her first husband?)

Fragile now, and spindly-legged, his eyes have the look of intelligent wonderment reminiscent of a yellowed photograph of him in an oval frame on the corner living room table. He was the type of lonely young man, son of poor bourgeois Viennese who thought they were better than the other immigrants and, consequently, kept themselves aloof. Who, in his fast rise up, took time out to learn—in that careful English—all of Shakespeare and Milton. When he was young he collected rare books of English poetry; my father thought himself a sport. "Why, Bunny," he says, the voice and mind remaining intact, commenting, as though he were still the big power, "the women have just been terrific. Your mother, especially your mother, has really come into her own. She's been just fine to me. She's really taken hold, your mother has. And Marte's been steady." He bestows compliments as a means of regaining his sense of self. In the palmy days my father needed to pick up every restaurant check, a man of a certain time in New York. "And the women the hospital has been sending over are very competent. Very good help."

Does he know the people who come over come from the social agencies? Not a question I will ask.

He reaches over to his bookcase, his hands shake, but by himself, he locates two books; he knows exactly which shelf to go for. "You have two lovely daughters," He shows me the books, one for each. "The Coleridge, and a young girl would like Christina Rossetti." He points to the back spine. "Here, there's a letter tucked in. A letter written by Christina Rossetti. I got hold of this one in '27, before the Crash."

I take the books and sit down in the lounge chair facing my father's desk. We never talk head on—a failure of my family. My babbling covers much reticence. I feel bad. He's going to die without my having remarried. He doesn't know what's going to happen to any of us. He has never commented on my life. That wouldn't be his way. When my daughters were younger and I'd go away on brief vacations, I would have to leave an address. So clearly he knew I had affairs. Once, after I had made a trip to the Virgin Islands, he asked a few polite questions. "Oh, you went sailing. Lovely. What type of craft?" Then he paused, groping for the right words. "Was your host pleasant?"

Now, confined to his room, he has invented a project for himself. My father wants to solve New York City's traffic problems. He tells me he has thought hard about the city, and he means these eighty pages—which a woman from the social agency has typed for him—to be his last statement, his gift to the city. Neither of my parents mentions, ever, what they have lost. Instead they have projects. "Now, Bunny"—he gives me the sheaves of paper—"now, Bunny, I want you to forget you are my daughter. I want your opinion—as a professional writer. Be tough with me now. Ruthless."

I take the papers and stare at him. What does he think of me, of my life? Did he know me? One New York evening, the first Juan I knew, Juan Benet, came into town. The two of us laughed about the old days when we were kids back in Paris, and we stopped, on the way to dinner, to see my folks. When he realized who Juan Benet was, his expression suddenly changed. Like he was startled, like he suddenly remembered that Juan's brother had been my first boyfriend. And about the jeep accident in the desert. Then I saw the unexpected look of pain on my father's face, though Juan and I were laughing, and I heard him say, "Why, Juan, I knew Paco—he was—so *nice.*" Suddenly I realized, My father *knows* who matters to me, he knows me.

My mother calls, I take the papers from my father and go down the hallway to her bedroom; there I admire the collages she is making. Her sense of design is very keen. "Do read his traffic plan this week. Marte is in her room; you know she waits for you. Marte," she yells, "Barbara's coming to see you"; then she pulls me over to her small sofa. "Here, I have something for you . . ." Abruptly she throws a pearl ring on the table. "Try it on—see if it fits."

I slip it on; the ring looks vaguely familiar. I look at her questioningly.

"When you sold the diamond out of your engagement ring, you left just the setting; it looked like a mouth where a tooth had been pulled. See, you don't even remember it," she laughs. "Finally, I knew what to do with it. I just ripped a round button off one of my blouses and pasted it in with Krazy Glue. All your friends will think it's just one more of your heirlooms. The more you use it"—she waves her arms in the air—"the realer it will become."

I stare at her. I take the ring from my mother, the papers and the Coleridge and Rossetti from my father, and slowly I walk down the hall. Then I knock on Marte's door. "Marte," I say, "I'm here." I pause. "I'm home for lunch."

3

Tolla is waiting for me in the living room. She knows I mean to put her in a book; I've mentioned it to her. Like my daffy parents, I have my own projects for prosperity. I have one diary I dump odd facts in.

SURVIVAL KIT FOR WOMEN ALONE
Explain the importance of Tolla in your life.
Explain she was a temporary secretary who came to you to help sort out mess after husband died.
Explain the terrible money panics when children were small.

I put in it odd scraps of information that might be handy for women who have to survive on their own. Tolla complains; she has no desire to be included.

"Nonsense, Tolla. Every woman on her own with no bucks needs a friend."

The first Saturday afternoon of each month Tolla comes to my apartment. The next three hours are entirely for me. We don't speculate if my fancy family has money tucked away (they don't), or if I am neurotically anxious about money. We just face facts. Tolla pulls out the files marked BILLS, and we deal with the truth in front of us. Together. Tolla pays what she can—and when there is no money, she stalls. Left to myself, I would continue to panic, leave the stuff unopened, and live in permanent dread. We air every last detail. What to do about taxes, what gets deducted. What I can afford. Why don't those occasional writer's jobs in universities in Buffalo and Boston pay more?

I go in the kitchen, make coffee for the two of us.

"Tolla, I didn't want you to open all the mail—you should have waited until I got here."

"What are you planning to do with the bills? Frame them? Pickle them?" Tolla abruptly changes the subject. "Say, where is your roomie—the sports journalist? His typewriter is missing."

"We've amicably parted."

"*Amicably?* What kind of language is that? I've never heard you use such words about a guy you were hooked on. So, you got bored?"

"Well, we were different from one another—"

"I should hope so—he is a marrier, though."

"Frequently."

"But you were so worried what it would be like with the girls gone—what are you going to do now?"

I walk over to the window and look across to the park, twisting my ersatz pearl-and-diamond ring. "Christ, Tolla. Maybe I don't want to inherit two new sets of kids. Yesterday I went for a walk, then I stayed downtown and went swimming from six until eight at night—I always used to be home at dinnertime, or guilty about it. I think, now, I just want to be for a while. Tolla, I wasn't the greatest of wives, I was mildly unfaithful. But when I became a widow, as I had some men in the background who were already part of my life, the next phase was made easier. I mean, it was less abrupt to sleep with men I had already known. Now, I'm not making judgments, one way or the other, I would just like to examine what happened as a *fact*. Like those bills are a *fact*."

"Are you going to put that in your survival kit?"

"Maybe. Now I just want to jot things down. And think about what it all means."

Tolla looks at me. Then she puts back the checkbooks and bills for the next month.

After she leaves, I putter in the apartment and go for a swim. The pool at the Barbizon remains open until nine.

When Juan comes to dinner the second time, I decide not to use the kitchen. Instead, I bring two trays into the living room. With the girls away the apartment has a new shape. I notice the skyline from the living room window. I have prepared odd bits and pieces of smorgasbord food, the type of meal you only make for two people. Maybe I am Nora of *A Doll's House* in reverse. All these years I have been out in the world, trying to make the pieces work. Now I am on my own, and in some perverse way, I seem to have turned around, opened the door of my own house, and walked back inside.

SURVIVAL KIT FOR WOMEN ALONE

Major failure of women's movement: in initial phase didn't emphasize enough economic liberation. Sexual liberation as primary goal presupposes that financial needs have been met. By whom? Who meets family needs?

   medical expenses
   schools
   legal fees
   psychiatric fees (mental health)
   care for aging parents

These have been my bondage: services which a sophisticated economy would provide. The women's movement did it ass backward; they try to legislate orgasms, which are a private matter, and ignore social programming, a public matter.

My kit is filled with helpful hints. Nobody should be expected to function like a superwoman. In settling estate, could lawyer's fees have been avoided? How much fee reduction could you have achieved by having employed part-time help (secretary and accountant) to figure out what was owed the government?

How much of what seemed complex was due to monetary panic? Emotional loss creating economic chaos?

Do professionals take advantage of crisis situations?

Should have insisted on nailing lawyer down to a fee in advance.

Okay, you are forgetting your bad state when you consulted lawyers. One week after your husband's death you weren't a reasonable person.

Plan A

A temporary, total support system for survivors of sudden tragedy. If victims can be *instantly* given outside help, they will be freer to figure out reasonable future solutions. Need not be overwhelmed. Should be able to reach out for help. Oh, paradise!

By the time February's sour, wet-smelling days have begun to give way to clearer, lighter weather, Juan Goytisolo and I have become friends. We now have a habit of eating together, either at my place or out.

I have begun another novel. I consider my books novels, even though I sometimes use real names. Why should a roman à clef be more of a "novel" than a book that splices in authentic names the way artists make collages? Isn't *Ma Jolie* a painting? Are Flemish portraits less good because we know the names of some of the burghers and their wives?

The roman à clef stinks of eighteenth-century monarchy, snide court gossip, sexual scandals, and gross caricature. It is a convention of mechanically changing names merely to create a thin disguise, while its real purpose is to nail down some embarrassing characteristic or set of circumstances so that the readers can guess who is being destroyed. What has this to do with imagination? At the end of the twentieth century, at a time when sexual news is no longer the real news, why bother with this creaky, mean stuff?

I snap the ends off the string beans for Juan's supper and listen to rock 'n' roll on the kitchen transistor. Isn't the novel really just some sort of first-class news of the outer world laced with stuff about the inner self? Now, what is it about this endeavor that makes so many experts firmly announce its imminent demise? Is this fair?

Considering that high authority has deemed it kaput, I find it odd that such a suspiciously large number of groups are so energetically seizing the territory. Sociologists have for a long time claimed it as their slice of the pie; then there are those who wish to use novels as casebooks for psychoanalysis. Others want them to be handmaidens to human progress or mental hygiene. Political groups, porn fans, and linguistics professors are all horning in—a big crowd for a dead art.

As snapping string beans is repetitive work, I debate the confused motives of novelists. Why are the novelists I admire such klutzes when it comes to progressive ideology? Why are so many of the best downright reactionaries? Do I really want Dostoevsky or Tolstoy shaping my future with their private obsessions? Why weren't these men more clear-minded?

I write little about my daughters. Here is an immediate distortion.

Carla and Maria are central to my life, but I rarely mention them in print. I am superstitious. My gut instinct has always been to leave the kids some room.

Nor have I written any graphic sex scenes about their father.

Chores: I spend sixty percent of my time doing uninteresting tasks. But I don't want to bore the reader. Which makes for distortion. My protagonists' lives take on an unreal excitement. Still, a novel with too many errands would be cumbersome.

Not in Book
Strobe lights. (I don't think there are any strobe lights in this novel.)

Not in Book
belladonna eye drops
handmade sachets
condoms
real Picasso
Porsche cars
sleeping pills
Fig Newtons
Coney Island (as it used to be)
friends (so many are left out)
~~shame~~ — YES, IN
snakes

When Juan walks in, shoulders hunched, smelling of damp newsprint (he carries *Le Monde* rolled under his arm), wet wool and windy rain, he instantly finds, lying on my living room desk, his tortoiseshell glasses, left by mistake after his visit last week. He has begun, slowly, silently, and with economic grace, to take possession of the territory. While I (on the surface verbally bouncing from subject to subject), giving him no signal of recognition, have slowly begun to acquiesce.

You're a con artist in the kitchen, I tell myself, as I make a production of deftly steaming the string beans *al dente* and then rapidly sautéeing them in olive oil, garlic, and prosciutto, while Juan watches, seated at the round J. P. Brunner butcher-block kitchen table, listening to a Judy Collins tape on the cassette machine I keep on the table. I serve him a plate of the string beans, to be followed by gray Dover sole with lots of lemon wedges, and salad and fresh strawberries in

Lillet. A fake and a fraud. Have you no shame? All those years you ran a family in this apartment—husband, two daughters, with an *au pair* girl to help out; when it was for real, three meals a day, three boring meals a day, did you set foot in this kitchen? You ordered vast quantities of stuff from Macy's freezer plan, and lugged huge shopping carts full of provisions from Sloan's on Columbus; the family got Seabrook Farms frozen string beans topped with one pat of butter, a touch of pepper, and that was that. No gray sole, no prosciutto. Now that you are cooking three, maybe four meals a week, you can afford to putter. In those days, you leapt out of bed at seven in the morning, you made a frantic dive for the bathroom before Harold steamed it up with his long showering time, you screamed orders to the children and the *au pair* girl, you made a quick list of things to be done in the house, and from nine to nine-thirty telephoned errands, then you went into your bedroom, slammed the door, and started to write.

We are two middle-aged people in good health and on vacation—in a manner of speaking. My husband dead, daughters at college. Juan has left behind a wife in Paris, twenty-year mark. No, I didn't spend my married years flip-flopping green beans in ham, but then I doubt Juan played Judy Collins country music on a cassette machine during supper those twenty years in Paris. We are doing a small amount of gentle lying to make each of us sound more interesting to the other.

Juan wants to publish a short article on censorship inside Spain and asks me to help him translate. After dinner, I walk over to the table in the living room, and I type an English version while he reads his piece aloud; sometimes he speaks in French, sometimes in Spanish. Soon we are dealing casually with three languages. He leans over my shoulder to read what I have done, then he continues in French. I am sensitive to the timbre of a voice. I respond to the sound of language and the visual look of things. Juan is now speaking entirely in French, and my writing speeds up. I seem able to anticipate the flow of his ideas; I feel on familiar ground. His accent in French—upper-class Barcelonian— his mix of French and slangy Spanish argot has an almost hypnotic effect on me. He sounds like Paco. Juan talks on, unaware of my hypersensitivity to his voice: suddenly I blurt out from some deep place in my past the name of a late-nineteenth-century Spanish poet—wildly, furiously romantic, writing at a time romanticism already was kneeling in the grave, done for. "Gustavo Bécquer," I say. "Oh, how I went for him, at seventeen as a schoolgirl in Paris—I read all his stuff."

Now, why do I think about Bécquer? I pull myself together, concentrate on the Smith-Corona keyboard. "Well, if I read him now, I'd find him Christ-awful . . . wouldn't I?"

"No," Juan disagrees. "You could still read him. Cernuda liked Bécquer. You were right to have liked him. He's not just schoolgirl-romantic, a superb taste—"

"He's not a name that comes up in cocktail conversation often in New York City . . ." Often? More like never in a quarter of a century.

Juan climbs up the bamboo bookcase ladder and pulls a dusty copy of Spanish verse off one of the top shelves. We find, in the Spanish Oxford, a page or two of Bécquer. The pages smell of mold. I am disappointed. I shake my head. "There was another poem . . . in my head I hear another poem . . ."

Juan keeps speaking in his hypnotic French-Spanish, and, as I smell the wet wool of his jacket I see myself as I was then, or as I now think I was, walking down the rue Vaugirard, the dampness of the street choking my chest. I never liked Parisians, but that is beside the point. I lived there young.

4

After Juan leaves I try again to find the other Bécquer poem, but it isn't in the Spanish Oxford. Or if it is there, I no longer recognize it. I suddenly recall something quite different, my time as a patient in a New York analyst's office in the mid-fifties. My analyst liked my marriage.

Harold had almost a decade on me, and was a brainy, obsessive law professor. We bedded together, produced children, misunderstood, strove, wounded, and sulked. A marriage of two people, living high on neurosis, that the analysts, those days, felt they could grab like a horse's bit between their hybrid Freudian teeth. What Schultzer impressed upon me was: "This isn't one of your symbiotic affairs. You don't fool me, Barbara; you entangle men in your narcissism, in your need for symbiosis—now here—finally, we see a core of health." He favored the schoolteacher "we."

Schultzer saw me as a strong-minded woman paradoxically too much in pursuit of ephemeral goals. "You think life is sitting gabbing in a European café?" He was nosey about our marriage; he even checked me out with Harold. While ostensibly telephoning him to inquire about my recovery from winter flu, he got Harold's okay on our marital sex life. Once Schultzer knew that worked between Harold and me, there was no persuading him that some of my real wants weren't being met. "A Harvard *magna cum laude* who loves you?" (As Schultzer was surprised that I had fallen into this healthy marriage, he framed that statement as a question.)

"Look, I'll settle for less love and more time spent together. The trouble is, we share no common frame of reference. You overrate sex, Dr. Schultzer; do you think once that's on the up-and-up—no pun intended—there can be no loneliness?"

"A law professor and a young woman novelist. A fine difference of interests. Here, you will adjust to your being two different people. He goes off to his life, you to your own. No symbiosis. Independence, and separate definitions for each of you."

"Look, Schultzer, I need someone to gab with. Maybe that's the way I am. I can't make love to the typewriter. All day long, write, write, write. I want a friend."

"You want a *playmate*."

"I want to talk."

"What can't you talk about?"

I disgusted myself with the spoiled-female wail rising from the deepest sources of my being. "Dr. Schultzer, I am a very lonely young woman. Why does such a perfect marriage leave me feeling faceless and bereft? Very well, my Harvard husband loves me. Maybe I am not a woman who needs so much love, but believe me, I need a friend. We were not meant to die of aloneness; no, don't tell me again how well I function—that is not the core of health, or if it is, I leave you the core, I want the apple. Something juicier. After a movie, walking along Fifty-ninth Street with Harold, if I say casually, 'My God, what a romantic schoolgirl I was when I lived in Paris. Reading poets like Bécquer,' he goes silent and becomes angry, because what I have mentioned isn't a Harvard reference. Dr. Schultzer, I have begun to feel that everything I experienced before marrying happened only in my *imagination*."

"So—who is Bécquer?" Schultzer challenged. "You think it's so goddamned essential that every little thought that passes through your brain—which has been overexposed, anyway, to the wrong countries—is met with some response? With recognition? In addition, you have strange reading habits. You want a husband, or a professor of comparative literature?"

"Dr. Schultzer—come off it. Do you fancy hanging out with a bunch of people who, each time you gab about Freud, ask you, 'Who, what, when?' "

I sparred with Schultzer because he evaded the source of my sadness. I loved Harold, but a sense of urgent intimacy was missing from our marriage. What Schultzer defined as "symbiosis"—that rare moment when sex, friendship, the writing life, fun, politics, high and low ideas were fused—happened only twice to me. The first time was those student days in Paris with Paco. Then, when I was thirty-two and living in Chicago with Harold, who was teaching law school, I fell in love with a Chicago-born writer my own age, and I left my marriage and ran toward the experience, not waiting to find out whether some Chicago Freudian would label me, yet a second time, on the road to unhealthy love. Those lovely, sleepy days and nights of putting it all together—the sex, the intelligence, the friendship—felt to me as though I had walked through paradise.

5

After Juan Goytisolo publishes his censorship piece in the Book Ends of *The New York Times Book Review*, he tells me, over the telephone, that two of his women graduate students have recognized my name as his translator. Valerie and Ann-Jo want to take us out to dinner—is it okay? The women teach at Staten Island CUNY.

The following week, undaunted at the long trip in from New Jersey, they meet us at an Italian restaurant in the West Forties. As soon as the four of us are seated, the women make it clear that I, as the woman writer, am the star of the evening.

Valerie's natural red hair is piled on her head in a Renoir washerwoman knot; the turn-of-the-century hairdo accents her late-twentieth-century getup of tight jeans and a khaki-colored lumberjacket. She moves her long, tapered, painted nails with grace. She seems aware of her good neck and good hands and uses these parts of her body in such a way as to appear to be giving great gifts to the onlooker. Despite the sharp difference in physical style—Ann-Jo is a smaller, drier woman; she dresses in the monotones favored in small stores popular in New England college towns—the two women act like twin sisters who have chosen to take their still somewhat young parents out to dinner. Tonight is Mother's Day.

I have always thought I was good at claiming center stage for myself, but under the steady spotlight created by Valerie and Ann-Jo, I become aware how much easier it is for me to defer slightly to Juan.

Meanwhile, Juan, who is one of those quiet, almost monosyllabic men whose aggression is protected from mass view by his orphan's tough-shy veneer (what sensible person gives her heart to a successful orphan) switches gears. In his timid way, he is used to finding himself on the center of the stage. It is a role in which he is at home. It takes a certain amount of energy and swift drive to have become top of the heap among the Spaniards writing in Paris. The French tolerate no wilting lilies when they are passing out goodies from the literary cookie jar. But allowing me to flower in the limelight in front of his two female admirers is part of Juan's American jaunt. He is a modern *Quijote* traveling a new turf. A tip of the hat in the direction of the liberation of the female sex is as much a part of the American scenery as Soho, cable television, Norman Mailer, country music, and the Kennedy assassinations. Juan approaches his new role with the same gusto that the French did when they first discovered the possibilities of blue jeans.

Valerie and Ann-Jo have put themselves on a first-name basis with the characters in my book *Arriving Where We Started.* (So, why, if you want so much privacy, do you write memoirs?)

Valerie leans closer to me. "How are the children doing?"

I am unnerved. "Children?"

"Carla and Maria," she continues in easy, confidential intimacy.

"Oh, fine. Both in college now."

"They got over their father's death? How awful. Your husband was so young."

"What did you do next?" Ann-Jo asks. She is the more concrete of the two women, Valerie the romantic.

"Next?" I pause; direct questions undo me. I am bad at thinking up short answers. I hesitate. Few marriages, these days, which last fourteen years, as did mine, are lived through in total fidelity. What could I say? I slept with old friends? Juan seems to be enjoying my dialogue with Valerie and Ann-Jo. He also seems curious to hear my answer. I am very bad at saying the obvious. I always leave out the sympathy-getting sentence "I suffered" and tend to leap ahead to a more interesting emotion.

"Well, a year later I found this widower, Daniel Heltzer. He had a fantastic sailboat, so we sailed in places like the Virgin Islands. That is, he sailed and I learned about the boat. He was rich, so he had time to do things like walking in the country. I think, after tragedy, fresh air picks you up."

"You—who in your youth helped rescue prisoners from concentration camps in Franco Spain; who, together with Paco Benet, why, helped form the Spanish Resistance, who became this great heroine—you went off with a man who was merely rich?"

"Well, he was a left-wing millionaire," I reply lamely. Now, why am I apologizing? My answers have come out sounding flip. But once you board a wrong train, in these sorts of debates, there is a tendency to stay on it. "Look I am doing this notebook—Survival Kit."

"—Is that a new book you are working on?" Ann-Jo asks.

"No, just notes I am jotting down. I emphasize the importance of fresh air for widows. One of the problems of getting to be a widow, if there's been a long illness, is that, physically, it gets to be exhausting. The looks can go fast. Now, for a woman over thirty-five it is very self-preserving to get in a few vacations. You want me to make kind, heroic gestures? How could I have done all that—bring up my own children, pay the bills, keep the show afloat—if I had gone off with a poor man with three more children? What gives you the right to demand I live up to such high ideals—indeed, *your* ideals, not mine. You live in New Jersey, where there is fresh air; I live in the city, and I needed to get away."

Oh, God, I think, are we feminists just the newest group in a long line of optimists who believe if we tinker long enough the world can get fixed up? We still believe a pot of gold's to be won. But the journey is all we truly possess, and you might as well do that in some sort of style and grace. Which, when you are on your own and short of cash, is difficult. Suddenly I start to laugh, a crazy non sequitur has leapt into my head. "Ann-Jo, you want to know why so many articles are done about writers at work? You never read stuff about writers at play. That's because of the lousy advances."

Abruptly Juan roars with laughter. He had seemed confused by Ann-Jo and Valerie's objections to the left-wing millionaire. Ann-Jo and Valerie, both on an academic payroll, fail to see the joke. "Life," I continue, "is much better seen as a bouillabaisse for which you are given mediocre ingredients that you have to improve upon. Now, Ann-Jo, I don't mean to fault you, but you are being tight-assed about my position on vacations. My husband was lax in that area, but he gave me other things, a marriage I much needed, two daughters, a stability I wanted in those first uncertain years. After he died, no men seemed in a hurry to marry me. I guess they came under the category of lovers—a dopey word. Well, my lovers gave me vacations. So priorities got evened out, over the long run."

Ann-Jo is patting her spumoni down into a soup with the bottom side of her spoon; it now resembles a child's tapioca pudding. She sucks the ice cream soup into a tunnel she has made with her lips. She looks puzzled.

"Look, Ann-Jo,"—I have another go at it—"writers make lousy progressives. Always you'll find them leaning over the white clothesline of fresh new ideas, staring like a bunch of Moonies backward into paradise, which is all writers truly want—" (When I mention paradise, Juan swiftly looks up at me, this time in a different way, then casually he places his arm around the back of my chair.)

"Now, this looking backward—it's an essential conservative trait. Take revolution—by the time writers get their teeth into the subject, it's a revolution that has failed. For the revolution that will work you have to go to the prophets, not the novelists. No, don't confuse the novel with profiles on mental health. The human mind is still too dark, dank, and atavistic for such a countdown."

Valerie's translucent skin flushes from a mixture of Soave wine and instinctive exuberance. "But I still find your book exciting. When you arrived in Madrid at eighteen, I said, Ann-Jo, that's you and me arriving in Madrid as American students. Why, I *became* you."

I look at Valerie, startled. She continues, "Although the time reference was different—Ann-Jo and I identified mostly with you in America and Spain. I ignored the German part, as I never went there."

"But how could you take Germany out of my book? I lived in Germany only two and a half years after the gas ovens went out of business. How could you cut away such an essential part of my psyche?"

"Well, that Germany has nothing to do with Ann-Jo and me—of course, even the Spanish past was a little different. Like your falling in love with Paco Benet, a hero of the Resistance, and the two of you going back into Spain to get his friends out—awful that he died so young in that jeep accident in the desert."

"Paco Benet? Who was Paco Benet?" Juan asks.

"Juan, you haven't read her book? What kind of machismo crap is this?"

"Look, I'll improve. I'll read the book right away. Who is this Paco Benet who was killed in a jeep accident in the desert? Which desert?"

"In Iran. He was Juan Benet's brother, only a year older than Juan. By the way, Barbara, how *are* Juan and Nuria . . . and Paco's mother, Doña Teresa?" Ann-Jo continues, chatty, disconcerting me by being on first-name terms with the people I had written about in my book.

"Oh, Juan and Nuria Benet are doing just fine," I answer uneasily.

"We have a grant to go to Spain this summer. We mean to be the first feminists to contact the new women's movement growing secretly under Franco—a real *coup*," Ann-Jo adds. "Of course, up until now, I've always been solidly Goytisolo. Valerie has bounced about more, she's done the Latin American theater. Why, you get your hands on a solid work like *Count Julian*"—Ann-Jo smacks her cream-frothed lips—"you get in there right behind Julian's head, into the gut of Goytisolo, the sado-masochism, the graphic, sometimes I feel I can't let go—that I *am* him. Marvelous discipline, breaking through, *cracking* Goytisolo . . ."

Nervously I look at Juan; he receives the gory news with aplomb. His eyes have taken on a contented, blank look; a man who has accepted his fate as one of the chosen of Spanish *belles lettres*.

"But Valerie is right—I shouldn't get overly identified with the Goytisolo camp. Could become a Johnny-one-note." Ann-Jo lays out her plan, blandly unaware of the alarm lighting Juan's effulgent blue eyes. (I am not sure Ann-Jo knows Juan is real.) "So," she continues, "although Juan is *my* perch, I said to Valerie, Well, now we have a chance to meet her through Goytisolo, and meeting Solomon is as good as meeting Juan Benet, we'll be landing a big fish, the King of Madrid—" Ann-Jo snaps open her lucite clipboard. I close my eyes slightly, and remember a button in a Soho bookstore: PROUST IS A YENTA. "Juan Benet's address? Oh, and Barbara, if you could write him some brief note explaining that Valerie and I are friends of yours?"

Juan and I exchange nervous glances. We've been had. Shamelessly flattered and gobbled up by these two academic swifties, had by our own greed, our own urge to wrestle readers from the silence out there, pluck a response from an appreciative audience. Dutifully I write out

Juan Benet's address, unwilling to confront my needy desire to make friends with all possible readers. Especially as their authentic enthusiasm for me shows through.

By making me the steady and sole object of this evening's desire, the two younger women have set a certain static in motion; electricity crackles around the four of us. My daughters are far away in other cities along the Eastern coastline, and suddenly I feel that I must appear to be bathed in some high eroticized light. Even I feel its heat. Juan, jolted out of his customary male position at center stage, has been forced to hear news of my life throughout the evening. As though not quite realizing why I seem so suddenly valuable, or where the sparks are coming from, or who has turned him on, Juan reaches for the back of my neck; by absentmindedly stroking it, he points out to Valerie and Ann-Jo he has had prior dibs on me.

When the four of us go outside, it is thundering in New York City's theater district. "Down with Franco," Ann-Jo and Valerie yell, opening their umbrellas. "Now, Juan—remember, we read *Count Julian*; it is your turn to read *her* book." Then Valerie and Ann-Jo aim their umbrellas toward the noisy yellowish sky and run toward the Port Authority, whose night buses will carry these two women, like twin sisters, with all their dreams of Europe and modern literature, back to the New Jersey darkness. Juan kisses me a fervent good night through the window of the taxi he hailed for me. He will continue by subway to Washington Square. I watch him walk away, shoulders hunched in an arc against the rain; despite the force with which the women threw the evening my way, it is clear Juan is the person they meant to grab.

6

By early March 1974, the early whiffs of spring air convince me that my unconscious is in mint Freudian condition. In my earlier life I wasted so much strength wrestling with a wild child beating against a weak, impaled adult that now I've developed a habitual tic, during calm respites, of reverting to natural optimism. It is on such a peaceful morning that Juan Benet's sister, Marisol, telephones me from Madrid to tell me that Nuria has killed herself. She jumped out of the window onto the back garden of the Benets' home in El Viso, a suburban part of Madrid that had been built up just before the Spanish Republic.

When I put down the telephone, I realized that sweet, even-tempered Marisol has always been the one to give me the bad news. It was Marisol who telephoned me in 1966, to tell me that her brother Paco was dead in a jeep accident. A car crash, Iraqi bandits, foul play, murder, suicide—who knew? To this day, Marisol queries me on my opinion. But with Iran, ninety guesses.

Now Nuria. I walk around the house. For maybe an hour I putter. Suddenly I get it, Nuria, Marisol said, is dead. When I telephone Inez Callahan, and say in a flat voice that everything is fine but Inez might want to know that, by the way, our old friend Nuria has jumped out of a window and is dead, Inez immediately suggests we meet for a drink after she finishes work. Inez and I go back to the age of eight, our lives, since then, have continually run on parallel courses. We have the advantage of being able to read with ease each other's code language. Inez always points out that as soon as she hears me mutter the phrase "Oh, fine, fine," she figures, *tiens,* another catastrophe.

When we meet at the Stanhope, opposite the Metropolitan, we both feel the need to dilute Nuria's suicide.

"Say," I ask Inez, "so how's your love life?"

"Okay, okay—this week." My childhood friendship with Inez was due to Theresa Munz, a fey woman friend of our mothers', who designed sexy, expensive underwear for fancy department stores. Theresa Munz, according to family legend, was intelligent, lovely-looking, refused to marry, was somebody's mistress, and during the Depression took many boats to Europe. As a kid my fantasy was that after she bought silk lingerie in Paris she went from café to café being lovely and intelligent. Like Marguerite Gautier she needed to pay her dues for such fun and she died appropriately young. One of her sisters had no children and liked to invite Inez and me to her house for lunch. On a Manhattan winter afternoon in 1940, when Inez and I discovered we had a mutual talent for slipping through the turnstile of the Lexington Avenue Eighty-sixth Street subway stop without paying the nickel, our taste for fine larceny cemented our friendship.

Inez's folks were from Warsaw, her old man went to Paris during the 1920s to become an artist. Later, when the Depression hit, her parents migrated to New York. In the shuffle Inez got left with her maternal grandparents, who by then had migrated to Haifa. Inez had rickets, and the desert sun and oranges were thought to be a good short cure. There was no money for Inez's passage to New York, so she got stuck, like a moldering crate of blood oranges, in a desert kibbutz. She was four years old when a visiting rabbi from Cleveland finally brought her via the Cunard Line to America. On Inez's living room wall hangs a photo of her sitting on the steps of a Haifa doorstoop, shoulders hunched, looking big-eyed and wistful; her sorrowful expression reminds me of the sad, skinny children in the Adopt a Foreign Orphan charities. It made a strange sort of sense that Inez should marry a passport official. Who else had such divine power to reunite her at will with those feckless parents? It also made another kind of sense that when Inez had had enough—Joe was a sweet, steady sort of Irishman—she left him.

But now, sitting in the Stanhope, Inez is pensive. Despite the jaunty boutique clothes and the jagged Sassoon haircut, her bronze-colored large eyes still have an orphan appeal that inevitably draws men to her. She has a good figure and a heart-shaped face, with clear, translucent skin and high cheekbones, the last two items a mama's gift from Warsaw. "My mother is still muttering dark innuendos at what happens to women who sleep with men. Can you imagine? At my age? And in the 1970s—me, a *nafka?*"

I like Inez's mother, Mrs. Zucker. Several years after Nuria's death I would try to give her some good news just before her husband dies. "Say," I report, "Jacques is mentioned in *World of Our Fathers*, palling around with Soutine." Her reaction is original. One week later, she telephones me back, furious. She has read the book. "Who is this Irving Howe? My Jacques did not go to Paris to discover his identity. He went there because he luffs beau-ty. My Jacques nevair paint ethnic. Oh, it was terrible during the Depression in New York for the artists. With those dumb Bolsheviks grabbing all the jobs—ethnic this, ethnic that, such barbarians! But for people like Jacques, who loved beauty and Trotsky—there were no WPA jobs, no money. Who is this Mr. Howe, who gets it all backside up?"

"Mrs. Zucker—Nina—look, don't take it so negatively. Howe didn't mean it the way you took it. A footnote in history, even one backside up, is more than most of us can claim. No, Mrs. Zucker, you must recognize that history is just one more closed corporation and who gets in the club depends on who has the right connections."

"Barbara, *écoute-moi,* I'll give you the right story about what happened during the war to Soutine." If I would have had my wits about me, I would go right over to the Zucker place facing the Museum of

Natural History, drink some hot tea served in tall glasses by Nina, and get the poop on Soutine, his doctor, his death, the Germans, Paris, and his well-connected mistress, who apparently knew how to handle the situation. But rarely do we have our wits about us, and we are always jotting down the wrong information. For Nina Zucker it was all right for Soutine to have a mistress, okay for Theresa Munz to have been a mistress (after all, she died young of cancer). But when it came to *die kinde,* fooey on mistressing. Inez and I were intended to have a more boring and financially satisfying fate.

"The awful thing about Nuria," Inez observes wistfully, "is that she was a fish out of water in that Spanish leftist ambience they've been living in since Juan had success as a writer."

I nod at Inez in silent agreement. Nuria's face blanks in my head. Always happens to me after a death of someone I count on. Slowly, around the edges, her body returns in parts. In 1968 her leather-gloved hand on the wheel of her sports car; she was wearing a raincoat that day. Made a point of driving me to Chinchón, which has a small square, the perfect tiny *plaza de toros,* the flock of birds rising, to me, in the rain, more beautiful than Venice, I remember that. She wanted to distract me from my *tragedia.* You will love always Paco and Harold, she insisted. I defiantly answered that enough time had passed—I wanted to live with a new man, someone I didn't yet know. "That's not necessary. You have your children."

Then she drove me to a town where Cervantes had lived. But his house was locked. I think it had to do with the rain; the caretaker was away. Nuria's father had been a Catalan novelist. His name also may have been Juan.

Her parents had divorced and died, I was told, when she was quite young. She grew up in Buenos Aires, child of exiles, returning to Spain in the late forties, a pretty, sad-eyed girl given to inexplicable depressions. She had no money and went to work in a Madrid department store. Juan fell in love with Nuria, who was a few years older than he. After several years passed they got married.

Sometimes Nuria made me feel that she lived in suspended time. She clung to childhood illusions about her native Catalonia and Spain before the war; I think she always wanted to reach this prior, magical "good Spain."

Ironically, her depression worsened after she had more contact with Catalonia. What had those chic children of industrialists in common with her Orwellian fantasies? But who could have persuaded Nuria that Orwell doesn't live in Catalonia anymore? Nuria, with her tweed skirts, her ideas on progressive education, her dislike of Fascists and the Catholic Church, her attention to vitamins, good medical care, and piano lessons for the children, was too straight to understand flashy radicals. No, Nuria would have been far better off as the wife of a Harvard professor, living in a rambling house in Concord, Massachusetts. In a New England atmosphere Nuria's lovely mourning for the Spanish Republic never would have been questioned; her innate seriousness and liberal bent would have been put to good civic use.

"I *told* Nuria," I say to Inez almost petulantly, "not to be thrown off balance by that Spanish bullshiteria—"

"Well, that awful cackle, *'hjah hjah'* "—Inez imitates the mean Spanish laughter—"is hard on the soul." She pauses, her bronze pupils darkening as she gazes at me. "Nuria loved you," she says simply.

I look out of the restaurant at the late-afternoon March sky streaked with sheaves of wheat the color of wet plum. Those sleepy, sweet, lovely Madrid days I had spent with Juan and Nuria are done for, part of my life over, ended when Nuria jumped out of the top-floor window.

With Nuria gone, I no longer have a center in Madrid. I bite my lip. If I went back—where would I go? In '68, when I reported on the Madrid version of the May uprisings in Paris, I lived in Nuria and Juan Benet's home in Madrid. I never questioned being there, just taking the gift of their home for granted. In the early mornings I'd leave with my notebook for the university city, full of optimism. I was going to watch the revolution. It was Nuria who would get me moving. "The university city is occupied," she would tell me over breakfast, "Barbara, hurry, so you can get locked in with the rest of them—you'll have a better story." Nuria, wanting to make sure that I wouldn't get trampled between opposing forces—the police with their sticks and dogs and the students with their pamphlets and new ideas—would pack me off in her car and instruct the driver and her youngest son to park near enough to the "trouble" so that they could, if needed, rescue me. Later, when I get back to her home, I would sit on a high wooden stool in her kitchen, and she and her children would listen while I recounted the day's political adventures. Nuria listened *hard;* after I had told my stories over a few times, and assimilated her reactions, *"les événements"* became real.

I frown. "Inezka, I feel I no longer know anybody in Madrid."

She looks up at me, stirring her Campari-and-soda. "Yes, you do—you know everybody you always have known." She stares at me. "Just one person is dead—Nuria."

I glance outside the west window of the Stanhope bar, the air is so cold, as people hurry by outside on Fifth, smoke rings form, the streetlight catching the round, dusty shadows of their wet breaths. Some of what we are remembering remains unsaid, it is the way two old friends think together. Across the street the Metropolitan glows in the night, the newly scrubbed façade and the lit fountains pale light in the dusk, New York's answer to *son et lumière*. I think about Juan Benet's troubles. I have a soft spot for types whose mates die in murky circumstances where one is left permanently unsettled, never sure of who did what to whom.

II

Chicago

7

The winter before Jack Kennedy was killed we were living in Chicago. Harold was a visiting professor at the Law School, and we had sublet a house on Dorchester Avenue in Hyde Park for ourselves and the kids; I was in my early thirties, he in his late. And our malaise with America had not yet been converted into action against the Viet Nam War. That year Harold had his first heart attack. The onset of his illness had a stealthy, covert quality. He first had what the doctors call a "silent attack." This must have happened months before, and it showed up in a cardiogram during a routine checkup given Harold by a Chicago internist. The doctor summoned me to his office. We were just temporary in the city, the doctor was a stranger. So, he said, very matter of fact, in view of the fact that Harold had turned out to have so much wrong with him, the outcome seemed uncertain. He paused and said, offhand, "He could die quite young, you never know."

The timing was rotten. We were both needy then. I was ablaze in a sea of narcissism, my slant on life was very literary; all that writing kept me isolated, in a private world where I was making love to a typewriter and—oh yes, sex. I had had one minor affair during our marriage (going then into its tenth year); sex, children, and novels were what I cared about in 1963. Harold and I had perhaps lived too close, and we were grating on each other's nerves. God, what a time! All that tension and misery of being made to feel we had to stay in love forever—it was all, then, forever. I was, indeed, a creature of the fifties. In the sad atmosphere of the marital bedroom of our Chicago sublet we had already begun to talk separation by the time the doctor informed me, in his circuitous way, uncomfortable with the message he was handing out, that things were very bad.

For a while I made an attempt to "do something." But my relations, at that time, with my own family were tenuous. No, they were never mean or judgmental, but the messages we sent to one another were oblique; they lived in New York, while we had become mobile academics, gypsies, restlessly traveling to new university towns between the East Coast and California.

The only member of my family who kept in touch, who visited us, was Marte. I didn't want Marte trailing after me. Harold and I weren't getting along, and I preferred no witnesses. But Marte persisted: she had raised me, single-handedly; she felt now it was her North German duty to follow us. And come she did, by way of TWA, Pan Am, American Airlines, and Delta, accompanying her family of academic gypsies across the American topography; she felt my daughters were her grandchildren, it was them she wanted to protect.

When Marte returned to New York from Chicago—a month after the doctor gave me the report on Harold—she muttered to my folks that I was not all right, nothing had seemed in order to her, but then Marte always muttered and always saw the gloomy side of life.

Harold was in a fury. Mad at life, at himself, at me. He had been a great runner; now he couldn't sprint anymore. "I can't race," he kept saying. After the kids went to sleep on the second floor of our rented Dorchester house, Harold and I talked with one another, in the quiet of our Dorchester Avenue living room. He told me not to change my plans. Before the report about his heart I had wanted to take the kids back the following year to our apartment in New York; I had wanted to go home to think things over, touch a familiar base.

"It does seem," Harold commented, irritated, "for a woman who did so much traveling young, one would think you would have gotten better adapted to being mobile. Well, knowing you, you'd probably have preferred Europe to Chicago."

"Can't we all go back to New York? I would rather you saw our own doctors," I said plaintively.

"I have a job in Chicago, law career, remember? Oh, Christ, everything we do has to be on your terms—your wacko New York analysts, always handing me such unreal prescriptions. Your wife needs total security and total freedom. Who ever heard of such nuttiness? Or would you mind sending me a calendar, pointing out which day it is, total love or total freedom? Just so I can figure out what's up."

"I just feel we'd all be better off back in New York—"

"In my next marriage," he exploded, "I'm going to marry a woman several years older than me—no more of this waiting for someone to grow up. GROW UP!"

"I'm going to get older soon enough," I said dully. "Each year, I'll be one year more—"

When I was alone, during the day, oh, the failure I felt! It was a time in my life when I still half-believed in magic. Like, you walk on the left side of the street, this future will happen, you walk on the right side, another future will occur. I collected Chinese restaurant fortune cookies and through their misspelled prophecies I gazed into my future. Each decision seemed fraught with major implications—you make one wrong turn, you've screwed up your life. I used my "magic" against myself. If I hadn't published a novel, Harold wouldn't have gotten sick. If I hadn't had that one affair; if, if. I heard his anger while, silently, I went about straightening the three-story Dorchester brownstone; I had already walked my daughters over to the Chicago Lab School. I rearranged in my head the mean messages I was getting from him. Why can't our lives resemble the books I had devoured? A husband or a wife is dying, the two partners spend the time struggling together, tragedy is alleviated by the triumph of unity and love that radiates from the marriage, and the dying partner is filled with appreciation for his mate. The husband admonishes his wife to go forth, to make a new life; reluctantly the young wife acquiesces. I walked through the three-story house, absentmindedly collecting the debris of a family, while in my head I painted sentences out of storybooks. Barbara darling, well, we had ten years . . . ten good years . . . now I want you to go on . . . I want you to go on. I put my hands over my ears, as though to ward off the terrible screams of inchoate, accusatory rage.

I've fucked the duck, mucked up. Those were the days of magic pacts, bargains with life, with gods in whose existence I didn't believe. One of those pacts had been the perfect father for my unborn children. I didn't marry a writer, an idle charmer, a drinker, a macho unfaithful, a café revolutionary. When I came home from Europe, home to New York, I felt a gap in my life. I had spent my school years in Europe, which meant I had never gone out as a "grownup" with an American man.

Harold lived in Greenwich Village, he was my first American "date." Tall, with crinkly black hair like an Algerian, intelligent, almond-shaped hazel eyes—he wore those tweed New Englandy jackets that do nothing for WASPS but are a great foil for gypsyish-looking

Jewish men. He was fun, I was attracted to him, and at the same time, he was *substantial*. Even the name "Solomon" sounded good for the father of my future children. Harvard, the law, *magna cum laude,* a healthy psyche; oh, he was meant to last forever. My magical pact with the gods was that I was going to choose wisely a loving man to father our children—and for being "good"—ah, this was my magical pact, the gods would reward me by not inflicting pain on our children.

So what had gone wrong? So why was he dying when we had barely had a chance to start? When the doctor gave me the report, I felt as though his words had robbed the children of some part of their rightful future. I couldn't bear the thought of their suffering. Meanwhile, Harold inveighed against the doctor. He wanted no mention of his illness. When I reached to take a case of beer cans from him for a dinner party (we went on as though nothing had happened), he yelled at me for grabbing the crate from him. "You are killing me, telling me I'm a cripple, a cripple!"

And in my head I rearranged the messages, and I told myself I was good. Until, slowly, I found I wanted less and less to see people. Talking made me tired. It was hard in the mornings now to get up. Then the messages in my head became jumbled. Sometimes I would be washing dishes, and suddenly I would hear the words, Kill yourself, kill yourself.

I consulted a psychiatrist. In Chicago. He was a stranger. I went a few times. I was very silent. Because I was afraid. Afraid one day I would blurt out those sentences, Kill yourself, kill yourself, and he wouldn't react. Or he would laugh at me. Or say nothing. If he said nothing, I would have walked out of that office and felt obliged to do it. Once I had said it aloud. So I held on; one part of me was trying hard to hold on, I wanted to do what was right for my children. And I said nothing. And I was silent. He said little to me, one day I walked out, and I didn't make any more appointments. Harold telephoned him, but the doctor said the patient had to do the calling. But I didn't. Because I was afraid. How did I know he would hear me?

But nothing remains unchanged—not even nuttiness. My own bout with being crazy got jolted by Clancy Sigal, an American writer who had gone to England during the McCarthy witch-hunt and was making his first trip home. This was in 1963. Kennedy was in, the McCarthy era was out. He wrote me that he would be passing through

Chicago, which had been his hometown, and could we meet. Clancy mentioned that he had read a novel and some essays of mine that had been published in a Socialist magazine in England. He liked what he read, and he wrote that it was good to find an American who was a Socialist. Here I was, on Dorchester Avenue, wanting to be dead—and Clancy Sigal was inquiring into whether I was a Socialist. It is very hard to think of dying when a macho male loads you down with Socialist principles.

When I left America at the end of high school, New York still had the gaiety of having been a major town during World War II, the metropolis of the free world, full of the noise of high ideals, leftist politics, and refugee European cultural panache, the final palmy Roosevelt days. When I returned home, I found another America, quiet, conformist, sunk into the gloom of McCarthyism; what could you expect with Eisenhower as President? I docked at Pier 50, a young stranger in my own country. I was wearing too much good French perfume, my head was too stuffed with *la philo* and Merleau-Ponty, my manners too formal, my stance too aloof. Oh, how lonely I was! I promised myself, if ever an American came back home after a long stay abroad, I would give him the friendliest welcome, I would be so *understanding*. Now, with monumental bad timing, just as I was busy doing away with myself, Clancy Sigal wrote this letter calling me a Socialist, and asking for *his* welcome back.

I wrote him a brief note, giving him my telephone number. I wondered what he would be like. I had just read his novel *Going Away* and thought him a wonderful writer. Then one afternoon the telephone rang and I heard this English-American transatlantic accent: "Mrs. Solomon? This is Clancy Sigal, I've just pulled into Chicago. Could we, uh, meet for a spot of tea?"

I wanted desperately to talk to him, to connect. But I was very tired. I had nothing to say. I felt his urgency over the phone, sensed his anxiety at being a stranger back on home ground.

Suddenly I heard my own voice (I was a stranger to what my voice, those days, was saying) become cutting, my old Eastern Seaboard, private-school drawl becoming more pronounced. "Well, today won't do. I have to go down to the Loop—to select a wig, and afterward I am taking my daughters to the ballet."

There was a silence at the other end; finally he said, "Am I speaking to Barbara Solomon? The writer?"

"Yes."

"A wig. I'm sorry, have you been ill?"

"Oh, no. Wigs are very fashionable this year. In Rome, Paris, New York—haven't they caught on yet in London?"

"Well, I was afraid America might be in bad shape—but this is ridiculous, wigs on the left!" He slammed down the phone.

I put down the receiver and walked upstairs to the room I used as a study. The house we'd sublet was decorated in nondescript Swedish modern and make-do Sears serviceable. On the gritty, 1940s cream-colored walls were poorly done prints of French Impressionists. Clancy Sigal's phantom voice receded from my consciousness, quickly forgotten. I had lost the power of speech. Words were of no use. I had become inchoate. In the lower desk drawer I rummaged until I found the bottle. Each day I popped another sleeping pill into the secret cache, a hidden safeguard against the onslaughts of pain. By that time, I didn't know where the nameless suffering was coming from. As howling a hurt as the most terrible physical torture. But no matter how I juggled, I couldn't make myself believe my non-being would be good for the children. Among the scores of pacts I had made with the fates was the promise not to do to my children what was done to me. MUST NEVER ABANDON THEM. MUST STAY WITH THEM. So, although I kept filling the cache, I also hung on.

Several days later a postcard arrived from Clancy Sigal. *Dear Mrs. Solomon: I hope your wig fits. Clancy Sigal.* His directness startled me. I thumbtacked the card to the corkboard near the typewriter. I hadn't used the Royal much these past months. If I wrote a new novel, I thought superstitiously, this time, no doubt, the whole human race would develop cancer. Sneeze, and you give polio to the world!

In my head I fought with him. An Upper West Side, New York, address was on the postcard. I decided to answer him. Impulsively I rummaged around in Nietzsche, searching for a putdown answer. I came up with something from *Beyond Good and Evil* that referred to façades, disguises, and the use of masks. So, who do you think you are? [I wrote back argumentatively]. Kerouac of the left? Crashing into other people's homes and lives—have you no feeling for the inherent mysteries? [What any of this had to do with his statement "Lady, I hope your wig fits" wasn't clear to me even then, but I rambled on.] Wigs have been popular at certain crucial moments in history. Marie Antoinette wore one, just before she said, "Let them eat cake" and she and Louis XVI had their heads chopped off. George Washington wore a wig, and during his time we had a revolution which meant kaput for England. When we wear masks, who knows what is happening? Perhaps nothing, perhaps one has lost one's own soul. As Nietzsche put it: Every philosophy hides another philosophy; every meaning is also a concealment; every word is also a mask.

I sent off the letter, like a message enclosed in a bottle bobbing in a rough sea; I expected nothing back. I continued filling the bottle in my desk, each night one more pill. During the day, whenever I left the house, I took the bottle with me. I was afraid the nameless pain would overwhelm me and I would be stranded with no handy aid with which to escape into oblivion. It was full-time work to keep fighting against the commands inside my head. I was tired now. But each day I went to the mailbox. I was playing Russian roulette. *Wait an extra week. Perhaps that writer will respond. Give him two weeks. Hang on until then.*

Eight days later a letter arrived from him. I tore open the envelope and read: "Dear Mrs. Solomon: I think we may be soul mates. But don't *gridzhing* the big-boy philosophers. When I read your letter, I got this wacky idea in my head you might need me—Don't mind me, whenever I think somebody needs me, I know I'm in one of my off-the-deep-end phases. Don't be put out. But, on the chance, I am taking a Greyhound bus back to Chicago in four days, and maybe we can start all over again. I will be staying on the South Side. With old friends. Clancy Sigal."

I blinked. He sounded terrific. I was also amazed. He had decoded the message—but how? I wanted desperately to meet him. I suddenly glanced at my reflection in the mirror—I was all grayed out. The black cashmere sweater I'd been wearing had a dank, musty odor to it. I opened the door of my bedroom closet. In previous phases I had been a classy dresser, but during these past years, traveling from campus to campus across America, I had neglected to buy clothes. I didn't seem to need anything beyond a warm coat, some baggy skirts, some old sweaters. What would I wear? What did he think I looked like? Hulda, the twice-a-week cleaning woman (this was her full day) seemed surprised—she had only known me this year—at hearing me telephone for a taxi to take me to downtown Chicago. I didn't know my way around the city, so I headed for the obvious, Marshall Field's.

The city seemed crowded with people. I asked the driver to go by the Lakeshore Drive and down along Michigan. He asked, "Why there?" I said, "Well, I am paying and it is pretty near the lake, and I just want to look."

I went to the place with the European imports, the most expensive bunk in the store. Rapidly I separated the good stuff from the mediocre. The dormant part of me, granddaughter of a good New York Jewish coat designer, daughter of an artistic mother, my own previous flair with clothes, surfaced. I picked out a lemon-yellow French silk dress. The top was V-necked and fitted; the skirt fanned out in pencil pleats. Good for a figure that goes in and out—wide-hipped, busty. Flat no place. The French put darts in the right places, my grandfather's voice returned; I fingered the fabric, inspected the seaming. Suppose Clancy Sigal wants to talk to me more than one time? I can't spend days in one lemon-colored silk dress. I scooped up three more things, all brightly colored. A bottle-green suit, a plum tweed, a plaid skirt, and a red sweater. I wanted to be rid of my black wool skirt, color of mourning, with the smell of death sticking to it. I held the yellow silk up to my face. Here I was, inspecting expensive apparel while a perfectly good husband, who, in other phases of our marriage, loved me profoundly, was spending his day at the university teaching, the two of us acting as though it were nothing out of the ordinary that he would probably die young.

On the way out I picked up a pair of spike black patent pumps, sheer stockings, a large size of Givenchy's Le De, and a new brand of sooty mascara. Back in my house on Dorchester, I bathed myself constantly, trying to scrub off the smell of death, the anxiety, the stale sourness of fear. The day before Clancy Sigal was due in, I washed my hair, brushing with swift strokes until the dullness was gone, and my long, slightly waved, light-brown hair began to gleam. I even rinsed it in chamomile tea, which was what Marte had done during my childhood.

Clancy finally telephoned. This time he made sure there were no further verbal mistakes. He said rapidly, "Tomorrow I will come by your house at one, for lunch, okay?"

I said yes and managed not to blurt out any strange remarks.

Hulda came to clean that day. I stuck my head out of the upstairs window, peering around the corner like a child waiting to discover who was approaching. But how inelegant! Quickly I ducked back inside.

At ten minutes before one, Daisy Schmulke, the wife of a sociology professor (the woman prowled Dorchester Avenue), with her fine nose for hanky-panky, rang the bell and Hulda let her in. Right after, in came Clancy Sigal. It wasn't the beginning I had hoped for; Hulda and Daisy Schmulke bumping into Clancy Sigal, who looked fine and handsome in his battle-fatigue jacket and blue jeans. The three of them huddled together in the entry hall, watching me from below. I slowly walked down the staircase. Daisy took in the patent-leather spike heels, the yellow silk dress; her nostrils quivered, she sniffed Le De. In either ear I was pinned by yellow-diamond studs, given to me, way back, by my father. I wore them without apology. Granted, my getup was blatant for a late winter morning in Hyde Park. What could I do to make him stay? After lunch, suppose he vanished? His hair was dark, but vaguely he reminded me of Paco.

"Clancy Sigal here."

"—Daisy Schmulke. Not *the* Mr. Sigal? Why, yes, of course, Clancy Sigal. You know my husband's work? *The Forgotten Poor of Rural Texas up to the Kennedy Years?* Penguin did the English edition." Daisy blew her nose and continued, "Barbara, a summer dress, short sleeves, while all of Chicago is dripping green mucus, real flu snot weather— my, you're looking good. I almost didn't recognize you—" She went at it nonstop. After I got her out of the house, Clancy Sigal and I sized each other up. "Why, you have nice long hair—you're not wearing a wig?" he asked anxiously.

I laughed. "So, so what does *gridzhing,* mean?" He looked like a pensive, nice-featured Jewish intellectual with a touch of good news from the Beatles added to his stance. Smart eyes and a good British haircut.

"Yiddish—for 'don't pick it to death.' " We were both fumbling, looking for an easy way to talk to one another. "Lunch," he said abruptly. "I'm starved—maybe I could just help? Where's the kitchen?"

The refrigerator was empty. My small supply of emotional energy had gone into getting properly dressed. I had forgotten he would need to be fed. Clancy Sigal walked in front of me; he stared at the empty white shelves. "Oh, *Skippy* peanut butter. My favorite, the lumpy kind. After living in England, peanut butter is a real treat. And Kraft strawberry jam." He reached for the two jars and rapidly spread the jelly and peanut butter on slices of Pepperidge whole wheat he found in a corner of the refrigerator. I meant to apologize. Abruptly I put my hands to my ears. There was no anger in his voice, he was making things easier for me. I boiled us some water for instant, which I poured into a silver coffeepot that I had brought with me to Chicago. It was a wedding present. My movements were slow, his rapid. I felt his lack of anger, and suddenly I compared it to the terrible noise, the recriminations I had been shutting out, hearing nothing, nothing in preference to that sound. When people insist they love you but continually make a snapping din inside your head, *do* they?

I put the sandwiches on a tray that I brought into the narrow living room, which faced Dorchester Avenue; the sun streamed in through the bay window shutters, making geometric designs on the living room rug. *"Clancy?"* I questioned.

"Clarence Darrow—try going through public school on *that*. My folks were Socialists,"—he paused. "Mrs. Solomon, your own work has this strange, covert quality, what you might call obliquely political. Well, I read your stuff in England, just before leaving, and I was—"

"I am a writer," I said, interrupting him.

He seemed startled. "Yes, I know you're a writer—that's why I am here, why we are having this discussion." After I told him how much I liked *Going Away*, he inquired if my folks were Socialists.

"No—my father was a Wilsonian Republican."

"Wrong again, Sigal," he chastised himself, "not even a Roosevelt admirer in the family? Somehow," he continued, "I had the impression we might have come from the same background, I thought, well, maybe I'm a few years older than you, but something about the way you wrote struck me as *familiar*. There's no indignation left in American writers now, our generation is so—damned *quiet*."

ANOTHER AMERICAN EXPATRIATE RETURNS. I am remembering the day my boat docked at Pier 50. The smell of Crêpe de Chine I wore, going back home, turning on the tap, warm steam poured forth over my hands; in postwar Europe we had no hot water. I had tried to recapture the easygoing days of my high school world. But New York had changed. The Rosenbergs were to be electrocuted. America was so still. Or was it me who was different? I had returned from Europe, friends commented, someone else.

Help him, he is groping, come home a stranger. "In your book you mentioned the AYD—American Youth for Democracy. I belonged, during high school."

"Sooo—out of the Young Communists League, gee, I didn't know we had such lookers in the Party then." He made a point of throwing a compliment.

"Well, for two weeks—then I decided too much folk dancing and potato chips . . ."

I knew Clancy Sigal's story, he went to England in order not to testify.

"Were you hit? By the McCarthy era?"

"Personally? Who, me? No—I just ignored it. I was never much interested in becoming a Communist or a Socialist."

He frowned. "Funny, your writing has so much political passion . . ."

"I didn't say I didn't *care,*" I replied, defensive. "I just meant that nobody was looking for me. Maybe I was too young. Or maybe two weeks in the AYD didn't count." I paused. "My husband's from that other decade. I think he was a member of some cell in Harvard; it was all before my time, and he doesn't talk about it much. But he left Washington in the early 1950s and he didn't teach until a few years ago. Harold was in private law practice, so we weren't much affected." I hesitated; it was 1963, things were just beginning to loosen up. Should I have mentioned that Harold had been CP? I was annoyed with myself for blurting it out. Years before I had been more circumspect. My first analyst wanted me to tell him everything about my marriage—why, if Harold had wanted to be a law professor, had he made no move toward becoming connected with a university? I never answered. Now, in two minutes, I had told it all to Clancy Sigal.

"You ask too many questions." I walked back and forth the length of the living room. "What can you learn by barging into other people's lives, asking questions, then zoom, off to other cities? Take my house, you will walk out that door after lunch and say, So, Barbara and Harold Solomon are one of those university couples with a couple of kids, who go for 1950s Swedish modern. A typical American marriage. But you would be wrong. Because this isn't our house, we don't live in Chicago, we are just camping out here, that's only one detail—"

"A lot of people got hurt during the McCarthy era, Mrs. Solomon. Probably including your own husband; you strike me as amazingly casual—"

"Look—I am sick of saying *mea culpa, mea culpa,* because I was never a Socialist or Communist." I amazed myself by my own ability to attack. "*Mea culpa* because I didn't suffer during the Depression, *mea culpa* because I'm Jewish and don't know all the right words like *gridzhing*. Okay, maybe Yiddish can be a warm language—but a lot of that stuff, childhood and egg creams and easy Jewish sayings isn't used as *gemütlichkeit*. That folksy Yiddish can also be used as a weapon against those who never knew the idiom, particularly against middle- and upper-class Jews. And I'm sorry if my attitude concerning the McCarthy era impresses you as cold, I'm telling you the truth. I didn't suffer, even though other people did. I am sorry I am not a Marxist, an ideologue—although I do have my views."

"What are your views?"

"Well, if I had to choose, I suppose I rather admire James Madison and Emma Goldman—"

Clancy Sigal choked on his second peanut-butter-and-jelly sandwich. "Well, I must say, you are original. Although, with thought processes like yours, it must get lonely for you. I mean, I think I could travel from coast to coast and not find one joiner for your combination of Emma Goldman and James Madison. It's . . . it's unique."

"There is nothing odd about it. I've thought a lot about them. Both had the good sense to mistrust organized central government. Madison predicted the ills of modern society, he was no utopian like the Communists—why, the Communists are such shmucks, they never posed the question: So who will run the show?"

"You got to Emma, love, through Orwell?" Clancy Sigal asked in a politely chilly voice.

"No, love. Please stop calling me Mrs. Solomon and love—we're not in England. This is ye olde Chicago."

"You *are* argumentative. I wouldn't want to be married to you."

"You're not. I am. Married."

"My, my—when I came into the house, and you walked down those stairs, looking very Anna Karenina, I thought you were going to turn out to be a much softer woman . . ."

"Anna Karenina?" Did he know? Had he guessed? "You want me to kill myself, you want me to be dead," I answered very rapidly. "Well, you are quite wrong."

Clancy got up; now he paced the small living room. "I want you to be dead? Now where did you get such a daft idea?"

"You called me Anna Karenina. She ended up on the railroad tracks. You call that a positive future?"

Clancy was staring at the stiletto, black patent, four-inch heels; nervously, without thinking, I was kicking my foot back and forth. "Anna Karenina? Oh, now—I was merely throwing a compliment your way, saying you are a pretty married woman, the mother of several children. Look, I always *adored* Anna—"

"Well, I never thought much of Vronsky," I retorted sharply.

"Okay, okay. Let's change the subject. You read much English literature? The contemporary stuff?"

"I like some of the plays—*Epitaph for George Dillon*—but the novels; well, they're comic, but very obsessed with class. Now it's the lower instead of the upper, but basically the novelists are using the same technique about a different social stratum." I paused. "Look, I know the Europeans, the French, overdo their dependence on phenomenology, but the English novel would have more bounce if they *played* with more things, well, like phenomenology."

Sigal stared at me. "May I have another peanut-butter sandwich?" I walked back into the kitchen.

He followed me. I slapped the spread on more bread. "Ma'am," he said, "you sure do get off a flashy sentence."

"You are contemptuous of people."

"I am not—I just went to a different church, where I come from we never got in the habit of throwing around words like 'phenomenological'—or even the other one, 'eschatological.' Look, I'm sorry, let's go back to Orwell and Emma, safe ground—same church."

"Oh, so?" I was furious at his facile, quick putdown, Wham-bam, I know your type, ma'am. "Look, I did not get my ideas about Emma Goldman from reading Orwell." I drew a deep breath. "I lived in Paris with a Spaniard. If you need your precise label, non-affiliated left will do. We met when he was nineteen and I was seventeen. He felt the Spanish underground needed to be reorganized. So he went back into Spain. He was successful in getting people out of prison via the underground. I went with him. I didn't know about Anarchists from books by Orwell. Among the people we tried to get out of Spain were"—I hesitated—"several Anarchist organizers. One of them was hiding in a cave outside Madrid. Then, later in Paris, many of the people I was close to those next five years came out of the Anarchist movement."

Clancy Sigal was quiet. He looked me up and down. Then, slowly, he said, "Mrs. Solomon—you make me feel like a *shlump*." He paused. "Okay, you had this adventure. I must say your working-class boyfriend sounds somewhat grandiose, but—"

"I didn't say working-class boyfriend; that is your projection of what you imagine an upper-class girl would do. He was, in point of fact, an upper-class intellectual."

"Okay, Barbara Solomon, you win, hands down. I admit, I did not dare to have such fancy dreams; by me, a stroll through the Communist Party and making it as a brash Hollywood agent was flashy dreaming enough. Clearly I was a late bloomer. But, love, don't feign disingenuousness. When we first started our little repartee umpteen peanut-butter sandwiches ago, and I said to you, straight out, that there was an intense political quality to everything you wrote, instead of playing guessing games, you could have said straight out that you lived with a Resistance leader of the non-Communist Spanish left."

"Why do you say 'win'? As though we are having a contest?"

"Oh, I do feel sorry for your husband—poor fellow, I'll bet he's a great admirer of Malraux."

"So?"

"Well, we all were. Surely you must be aware that the great moral *ur* memory of my generation—that probably includes your husband's time capsule—was Spain. Malraux, Hemingway, Bogart, Gary Cooper off with Ingrid; it's a great blend in our heads, the awe-inspiring fantasy. Then here you come, walking down carpeted staircases, with diamonds stuck in your ears, very la-di-da, with this 'who me? Oh, I don't care about anything' routine; 'I'm just a casual, non-political type'; then, wham, 'Oh, by the way, by the by, there I was in the caves with Gary, and Humphrey and Hem, and Orwell, and Malraux. Look, Ma, no hands.' You tell me that my occasional I-am-a-Jewish-boy-from-the-streets-of-Chicago can be used as a weapon—well, what about your fancy past? Can't that Malraux stuff also be a weapon?"

"You are inconsistent. First, you accuse me of being too reticent; then when you persist in dragging out of me past business, you accuse me of using it as a weapon." I paused; he did seem crestfallen. "Look, maybe it was easier for rich girls to get to those Malraux caves first—I didn't have to earn a living. But about the McCarthy era, I didn't mean to sound cold. It was just that having first had some experience in a country where the stakes were so high—in Spain you sneezed and got twenty years in prison—the American left seemed to me to run so scared; they caved in not over loss of life but over threatened loss of jobs. I've spent a lot of time wondering why the ante was so low."

"And what is your conclusion?"

I shrugged. "That most Communists wanted to be considered patriotic Americans. *They* weren't very political. Not used to living without the good esteem of their fellow countrymen. Well, it doesn't much matter now."

"Look, love—I really do feel in awe of you."

"In awe of *me?*"

"In spite of what you say about the rich-girl routine—calculated to make me feel good—that's a mighty potent myth you managed to live out. Why, everything about your life is so oddly perfect. The intelligent husband, the children, you write good, you dress good, you've never been divorced. Two point zero children and then, for good measure, the perfect Resistance hero lurking in the perfect past. I mean, you've managed to do it all—and you wonder why I feel like a *shlump?*"

"Me? Perfect?"

"A life oddly lacking in blemishes, love."

"Tell you what I'll do—if you stop calling me love—or *luv,* I won't mumble about phenomenology." Suddenly I look at Clancy Sigal and this wild thought occurs to me. Here we are, the two of us in Chicago. Why, we're Americans. Americans who have been exiles at different times and in different places, and we are ranting and raving at one another; he's annoyed I sound too European, and I'm at him for all that "luv" and "daft" business.

I noticed that Clancy was gazing out the window. Hidden in the bushes across Dorchester Avenue, crouching to see what the two of us are up to, was Daisy Schmulke, wearing her husband's storm coat. Clancy got up and closed the brown shutters.

I burst out in wild laughter. Poor Daisy Schmulke, her imagination's run amok, and here I am, a woman, who this week had wanted to kill herself. And here, next to me on the couch, is this handsome, quizzical-eyed, lonely, full-of-bravado man. I kept giggling.

"So, what's so funny?"

"Clancy, you are not English, and I am not a French-Spanish cocktail, we're American." Then I leaned closer to him and whispered, "Did you use the little blue book of Lenin in your AYD group?" I leaned over and, mocking, sang an old AYD song we had learned as kids:

> *If I eat too much jam,*
> *Mother, look how young I am—*
> *Father dear, please recall,*
> *that at one time you were small . . .*
> *Tweedledeedee.*
> *Tweedledeedee.*
> *We're the younger generation*
> *and . . .*
> the FUTURE OF THE NATION

which made Clancy laugh.

That winter—the winter before Kennedy was killed in Dallas—America was just starting to come out from the flush of mid-Victorian morality that flourished during the 1950s under McCarthyism, Freudianism, and the heavy commitment to the sanctity of married life; we staggered under the weight of the seriousness of such happy marriages. The insistence on perfect love marriages by the 1960s had climbed to nutty, exalted heights. Before our generation, who had heard of such business? The women died young in childbirth; the men worked seven-day weeks. Who had such leisure, to be in love all the time?

The following afternoon Clancy and I met in Jimmy's, a U. of Chicago bar located on Fifty-seventh Street, around the corner from a new row of town houses built for the university. Giddy from unaccustomed midday martinis (neither of us were big drinkers), we indulged in high-school necking, my nose squashed against the wet poplin of his British raincoat. I didn't want him to take undue responsibility for the affair into which we were rapidly drifting. "You are not the first," I murmured to him. "I've already had one infidelity."

He said nothing, but kept kissing me. "Adultery happens in the best of families."

"No—you don't understand, what I minded, in that affair, was that I wasn't in love. I always hoped I'd be unfaithful—for *something*."

He pushed me away from him. "God, you are greedy—you live on such an exalted plane, the Spanish Resistance, the great marriage, even the adulteries have to be so high class, so *virtuous*. No casual friendly fuck for Solomon, eh?— Haven't you ever just slipped on a banana peel and let your legs flop up on the pavement?"

Oh, how can I get him to stay on in Chicago? My face was pressed against the hollow of his neck; just then, two of Harold's law students walked into Jimmy's. The place was crowded but they instantly noticed us. We left. Later, necking on a park bench along Lakeshore Drive, Clancy again pushed me away. I smelled my breath, wondering, What's wrong? Suddenly he sprinted north across the park. Two teenagers were bicycling fast in his direction. After Clancy talked to them, he ran along beside them, keeping pace while they pedaled. Later he told me that several members of a street gang had been coming up behind them, attempting to grab their bikes. I looked across the park, I now saw that the boys were talking to a policeman. But that same cop was there before. People were in the park, mothers were pushing baby carriages, but nobody was clued in to the frightened teenagers. How did he spot danger so quickly? As though he had an extra pair of eyes peeled and open, always awake, in the back of his head.

We swapped notes in the Art Institute, looking for the parallel lines in our lives. He was the first person I had run into who had actually joined AYD, or even remembered what it was. Well, there we were, in Chicago in 1963, Roosevelt's orphans, gabbing away, checking out the map of what had happened in our generation. We found so many coincidences. During the same period that Clancy was attached to the U.S. Army of Occupation in Germany, I was living near Mainz, with Paco, who was teaching in the French Zone. I had managed to get a permit to join him in occupied Germany after surmounting innumerable difficulties.

"An American girl wandering through Munich in '48? God, what I would have given to have met you then—"

"I *hated* the Army of Occupation—I was so ashamed, so ashamed of being American—all chocolate bars, and fuck the fräuleins. The soldiers I met all looked like rednecks to me."

"Well, your old pal Clancy from the AYD was there, along with the rest of them. Look, *I* was no black marketeer, passing nylons and penicillin on to the local population."

"It would have been fun, to have met in Munich—"

"So, we've touched base, finally, in Chicago. Back in the old days," he pointed out, "I used to think it was real classy to bring a date to the museum. I'd always take my girls to the Impressionists first." Abruptly his mood changed. "God, how scared I was in London when they cleared my papers. Suddenly it meant nothing to have been a Communist. The passport people merely telephoned us and said, Okay now, you can pick up your papers. I was terrified—what was it going to be like? I dreaded coming to this town." Earlier that morning we had walked together through his old neighborhoods, and Clancy had found for me his high school of industrial skills.

We had lunch downstairs in the museum cafeteria. Beneath my raincoat I was wearing the second dress, the plum tweed. Will he stay on in the city four days for the four outfits? My grasp on life was tenuous; I perceived of the duration of our relation in small terms. I wanted him not to vanish.

Clancy wore the same navy pullover sweater beneath his jacket. His hair was medium length, his eyes intelligent, flecked hazel, his movements quick. He suggested that the next day we could meet at a hotel in the morning and have the whole day. "Look, I'm not a man for assignations in hotels," he said somewhat soberly, "but my friends' place, down on the South Side, is loaded with their kids, I'm parking on the living room couch, sooo, that's out. Your place—with that Daisy Schmulke policing the street—is clearly out; I mean, I would rather not run into irate husbands."

"So—it is wham-bam, thank you, ma'am?" I attacked him on grounds of easy come, easy go. My anger expanded, what started out as a minor attack, once I got going, turned into a full-scale assault. But when I heard the sound of my own explosion, my fury at the entire male race, I began to wonder what was happening to me. I had always been told, by men, that I was one of those women who had real feeling for men. There was none of that in my voice now. Even I could tell I was raving and ranting.

Clancy stammered, "You've got fre-freckles."

I'd gone too far. I stopped. A woman at the next table in the cafeteria had been listening to our conversation. She walked over to our booth. "Young man," she said firmly, "pay no attention to her. I think you seem fine."

Before I had time to regroup my thoughts, a camera crew walked into the cafeteria; they started clicking. A woman dressed in a business suit, wearing horn-rimmed glasses and carrying a notebook, pointed in our direction. "Snap *them*," she ordered. One of the men immediately clicked his camera. If you were to trace back through the February editions of the *Chicago Tribune*, 1963, under city news you would find an item reading: ART INSTITUTE REFURBISHES CAFETERIA, underneath a smudged photograph showing a man and a woman looking bug-eyed into the camera, their mouths open in surprise, as though they were each holding a small black egg inside their puckered lips. A smaller caption reads: *Art lovers enjoy lunch in relaxed atmosphere of newly appointed dinery.* Did Daisy Schmulke, with her retriever's nose, discover this mild clue pointing in the direction of our *flagrante delicto?* Oh, delicious year of 1963, when America was still asleep at the sexual switch; the last time in our lives when over so little—a few nights of breathy, straight passion, a natural extension of straight boy-meets-girl sex—could a woman be considered promiscuous! The period had its advantages; over mere trifles, men and women could convince themselves they were fast numbers, round heels, hot pants, Don Juans, Lotharios, easy come and easy go. If a woman had more affairs than could be counted on the fingers of one hand, she was marked as being in the nympho business for life.

The flash of white bulb in front of my face had the added effect of diverting my obsessive anger. Suddenly the ludicrous aspects of my behavior became apparent to me. Here I was, wanting to be dead, carried off as promptly as possible into a permanent oblivion, meanwhile complaining to Clancy that he showed no signs, if I bedded down with him, of being faithful. Prancing off to oblivion, so to speak, why should I have been so fussy? Here he was, this good-looking, intelligent, wacky guy. What could I lose? I convulsed into deep, wild laughter.

Clancy was unnerved. "Are you all right? My God, for a moment there, I thought you were going off into some sort of hallucination. Well, that's my own nuttiness—what's the joke?"

"We've gone to all this trouble to sneak away from Hyde Park, and now our pictures are going to be in the papers tomorrow. Which just proves you can't count on comin' up smelling like a rose in this heah life—"

"Look, I'll go to the Prado—the old hotel off the Lake Drive near Hyde Park, and I'll sleep there tonight. Then tomorrow morning, as soon as you can, you telephone there and ask for me. I'll give you the room number, then you grab a cab and come right over. We can have the whole day."

I looked at him. "I'll call you at nine."

In the morning, after the children left for Lab School and Harold to teach, I took a long steamy bath. I hesitated over black underwear. With your husband black could be a nice change, but put on, in the morning this way, it would take on some other, tacky, meaning. I settled on beige. Then I put on the third outfit, the green suit. My hairstyle seemed too schoolgirlish; I had the same side part and shoulder-length straight hair I'd been wearing since high school. Deftly I combed it all up. In other times I'd been a good sewer and fiddler, and once I started using them again, my fingers seemed to possess an independent intelligence. I smashed on my head a beaver beret.

I examined my getup in the mirror. Oddly lush, extravagant gear. Totally askew with the academic atmosphere of Hyde Park. Oh, it's not that those old-time, German-Jewish, Chicago Law School families didn't have dough, they had plenty, and there was a heavy solidity to their roast beef dinners, their apple kuchen, their parties in the big houses over on Kenwood and Woodlawn. But their style was affable, genteel. Rumpled substantial scholarly was what they aimed for; though frequently inherited wealth sweetened their academic life and paid for the extra perks of gracious living, their money never went into the service of the vulgar. Their wives never seemed to need beaver-trimmed walking suits. I used clothes in my covert rage against the puritanical, non-expansive messages sent out by the good universities across the country in the same way that angry students in the latter half of the sixties rebelled by wearing torn blue jeans, frizzed hair, beads, and caftans. Only my anger took a different form. I fished out of the bottom of my closet brown alligator shoes and an Italian leather bag, refusing any further attempt to look as if I belonged on a university campus.

Money. What was lying in the back of the closet came from the purchases of a former self, from the period when I had my own income. Harold and I were kids from moneyed families, but it symbolized very different things to each family. Mine was supposed to be the family with the real dough (you can never trust the rich). My old man was the flamboyant spender, made it quick in the early twenties, doubled it and trebled it during the 1930s by buying up heavy Protestant industries. The Depression was his salad days; he liked the challenge and was a born optimist. Then, when the war came, being in heavy industry meant you got A for war effort, and the millions skyrocketed. How could my introverted, intellectual brother have steered a fortune made by such a fast-moving, restless father? Mickey and he fought bitterly. Mickey thought my father belonged in the nineteenth century because he didn't understand the need for sophisticated management and always had to run his own ship. That was before my old man came down with Parkinson's and his tremendous energy floundered. After which he sat in a wheelchair, a vacant, fixed stare in his eyes, doped up from L-dopa. Occasionally there were some good weeks, and the juices momentarily returned; only now the companies he had owned and built were being sold low to stave off bankruptcy. The big place in Connecticut was up for sale. We Jews sure have assimilated into America; now we've been here long enough to have come down in the world.

When my own income ended, I stopped buying things for myself. Was my husband's earnings mine to spend? In a family nutty in other ways, but so free with money, how did I get to be so uptight? So timid? I forced myself to use Harold's charge plates for the Marshall Field clothes. I never had gotten into the habit of asking him for money. Used mine for me and for household bills. Lied to him about what it cost for four to live, with two kids in private schools. Gave him only some of the bills, paid the rest myself. I thought of what my income until the last years had been, and I measured it against the paltriness of what came in through my writing. I struggled with the confused economics of our lives, to make some sense of the chaos in which we lived. What was I entitled to? What was the right amount to spend? Should I find a more lucrative career? Defensively, as though all of the University of Chicago were lying in wait for me, outside on Dorchester, ready to criticize me for my getup, I snuck outside; a call cab waiting. For a moment I stood at the top of the stoop of the Dorchester 1910 house, twirling the long string of Polish amber beads around my neck; the beaver beret was tilted rakishly; I was wearing the diamond studs the color of winter sun; hand on hip, I felt like a high-yaller, fuck-you lady fast-stepping into life. I breathed the cold air; feeling wonderfully lighthearted, I jumped into the waiting taxi.

PRADO: that sign on top of the hotel whose front pointed to the windy lake could be seen clear over by the university. The big, old-fashioned lobby was run-down; there was a small cleaning establishment, a dusty beauty parlor, and a candy and newsstand off the main entrance. It was a sad, shabby building carved from ornate marble that evoked the Depression. Walking through Chicago streets, I fantasized, Was this the look of New .York at the tail end of those times? The whiff of wistful down-and-out splendor that Chicago had made me feel I was revisiting a lost city of my childhood. I sniffed at the air, almost expecting charcoaled potatoes baked in cans on street corners to materialize. New York is now a fashionable, dolled-up international paradise, but when I smell the chestnuts baking near

MOMA, I see, inside my head, old men roasting mickeys on the street.

I followed Clancy's instructions and took the elevator to his floor. I knocked on his door; he was waiting for me. We were both playing at this being very special. He told me nervously that he got the best room he could; did I notice the view—after all, we were on the highest floor. *He can't have much money with him, he traveled by Greyhound bus.* Suddenly ashamed, I put my hands over my ears to hide the diamonds. "No," he said, "don't do that. I go for it. All this for me, Christ, haven't you heard of revenge fucking?"

"Revenge fucking? So, what have I done to you?"

"Love, I'm from Chicago—those years, when I was a real meatball, *Clarence,* Clarence Darrow Sigal, I went to Industrial High School; oh, those Jewish broads, with their fancy mothers, not a chance, not even a peck in a hallway. Mil-dred, what are you doing there, in the dark, with *him,* Mil-dred, come inside," he mocked an ancient mother who had inflicted on him a remembered wrong. "A Jewish broad whose father didn't even like Roosevelt, hah, have I come up in the world."

He had his fantasies, I had my priorities.

"Look, Clance. I'm going to ask you to make me a promise." I sucked in a deep breath. "Sometimes writers get real ratty—face facts, we sure are a narcissistic bunch, there's the kind that would sell their grandmas to the Nazis, just so they could take notes and describe it afterward. But, Clance, that's true *shit.* I care for you, I care about us, and if things have meaning, well then, they remain private. I would never write about *you,* and I want you to promise me that we are both going to be ourselves, and you will never use any part of our relation as material."

His nostrils flared, his voice hardened, and he got this English accent. He was mad. "I will make no such nutty promise—and if I believed you would never use *me* as material, I'd be a certifiable masochist. A woman writer goes to bed with a man and doesn't record it for history, well, that will be the day. So what is this real versus unreal crap? You sound like McCarthy, making me sign in for a loyalty oath before we get in a little friendly screw. What is this? I left America in order not to testify; now I come home, and who's waiting for me?— this crazy broad, who is a secret heroine, whose father is a Republican Jew, and now I have to swear on a Bible I won't make like a writer! Your holier-than-thou act; oh, Clancy, who me? Oh, I will never write about you, trust me, because I am real and true, and truth is beauty and beauty is truth is shit. What is this with you? You can't write about me because our screw is *real,* you tell me you can't write about your experiences in Spain because your boyfriend was in the underground—okay, I sympathized with you for that one, and naturally you can't write about your husband, because he was a member of the CP, and you hint, when all is said and done, your true love. Lady, you've got yourself a list. So, why don't you change professions? I mean, you have stacked the cards against yourself. What are you going to do? Publish the laundry list?" By this time he was yelling at me. "What are we supposed to do? Use the Morse code? Now, listen, I've enough problems as a writer without taking on your crap on top of my own crap. And, pardon me—but the way you send people letters, well, they do read like the Jack Armstrong code. So, DON'T SLEEP WITH WRITERS if you need so much privacy. But for God's sake, if you are a writer, then in some clear tone that is your own voice you ought to be able to say, Look, fellers, this is the way it was, this is what I think happened to me and my friends in our time in our country. My friend Clancy had a birthmark on his shoulder, and I had a birthmark on my ass. And we made love in a Chicago hotel while my husband was off teaching law. So?"

"Clancy, you are a big gabber—but just because you can outtalk me, it doesn't make your point of view *right.*"

"Look, I want to make love"—he paused, stammering slightly—"but I c-can't promise you I won't be a rat and squeal five years from now, okay?"

I just kept staring at him.

"Don't forget—it *could* work out that you'll be the rat. So I'm letting us both off the hook. Christ, you seem to have taken so many vows to that husband of yours—who I have to feel guilty about because he was a fellow member of the Party, and Christ, that first boyfriend of yours off in the Spanish Resistance, I can't even begin to think about that one!"

We fell into bed. Clancy got me to leave the diamonds in my ears; we eased into a long, lazy, slow lovemaking, and when the rates for the room were up, at noon, Clancy decided to pay for an extra day. We had until five that afternoon, so we sent down for room service, ate sandwiches in bed, flopped on our stomachs, told each other our life stories, filling in the parts we hadn't already talked about, and then, each time, we went back to more lovemaking. Clancy whispered to me, in case I hadn't noticed his performance, "I'm showing off, you know. . . ."

He's taking the Greyhound to the West Coast: I have this terrible fear he will ask me to go with him. He says he is lonely, traveling solo, and I hear some inner music in his speech that convinces me he is looking not just for a lay but for a wife. And I am scared. Terrified I could just walk out the door and go roaming, like I did before I was married. Before the kids were born. "I can't go with you now," I said, "but when you come back to New York, in the summer, I'll be there."

He put his face in the pillow. Then he turned over, and we made love again. "Oh, man, oh, man," he cried at orgasm.

"Oh, *woman*," I corrected him. "You're not a bloody homosexual; Christ, you have me saying bloody."

Then, again, his face went into the pillow. "I'm leaving in the morning for Michigan." I flopped on my back, he kept reaching for me, I thought, Well he doesn't want to leave me. The most incredible new idea filtered across my consciousness, I saw myself as a child, perennially standing at some ship's pier, waving good-bye to my mother, to Marte, later to Mickey, overwhelmed and immobilized by my own grief. But it's not that way, I suddenly realized, *two* people take leave of each other. That day, in '63, I felt Clancy's pain at having to leave me, and the most wonderful thought formed in my head. *Two* people take leave of each other. Very calmly, I understood he was going to miss me. Hell, he was just going to Michigan. If I wanted to, I could take a plane and even meet him on the Coast. When the women of my family boarded those boats, I thought they had left me forever. Even if Clancy went back to England—seven hours on BOAC and there you are. No U-boats, no Hitler. Well, I mumbled to myself, I guess the war is over. I didn't think Clancy heard me. Maybe he never even realized that the first time I made love to him, I finally put it together, about there being two people in the essential transaction and the war being over.

After Clancy left for Michigan, I still had the fourth outfit. I put it on, just for myself, the red pullover and plaid skirt. *I could wear clothes like this every day and just walk around the house, looking cheerful.* I refused to be sad after he left. I kept reminding myself, He *liked* me; if I wanted to, I could join him on the Coast. He was just taking a puny side trip, he wasn't disappearing into a war. I kept reminding myself of the difference. *Going to Michigan is just a local foray.* When I was alone I took the pill jar out of my desk drawer in the study. Suddenly I realized that there were enough pills in that bottle to kill a bunch of humans. I took it, walked into the bathroom, and knelt down next to the toilet bowl. I was scared of what I was doing. The pills were my safety valve, what if the terrible pain returned? But what if I had written the same letter to another man, not Clancy, and the man, for whatever reason, had not answered? Or my letter lost? Did I really want to be playing Russian roulette, putting my well-being in the hands of such flimsy, happenstance fate? What if I had killed myself a week too soon and gypped myself out of some sensational lovemaking? But suppose the pain returned? Abruptly, firmly, I dumped the pills into the toilet and flushed. Some of the capsules, too light, bobbed up again. I flushed five times, until they were gone. I wanted to live, even if it meant existing beyond my husband's death. It was painful for me to admit that, come what might, I wanted my future.

I didn't connect with the analyst I had seen several times in Chicago. But I had the name with me of somebody good in New York. Clancy dazzled me, the way he reached into the unknown and fished out new relations with people he had never met before. He had read my stuff, liked it, and said to himself, Well, I'll try getting in touch with her. When I questioned him about how you contacted people, he got flip, "Remember Bogie and Bacall: Just pucker up your lips and whistle." *Okay, Dr. Frosch, I'm going to whistle.* I arranged with his service to have him telephone me the next morning. Then, because I didn't want to make my usual mistake of leaving out the essential, very carefully I wrote out what I planned to say to him: *Dr. Frosch, I am in Chicago this winter with my husband, who is a visiting law professor at the university here. He has had what they call a silent heart attack. I don't understand why he never went into the hospital, but I was told his condition is very serious; I would have felt better if there had been some ritual which defined him as sick. I do badly with this business-as-usual routine. I mean, if he is dying I would like to know, and not just feel it is in my imagination that he seems to be crumpling. His skin is yellow now. We fight. I am not sure we are good for each other anymore, but I love him and want to spend the rest of my life with him. Meanwhile, I have started an affair with a man who was passing through the city. By the way, I am a writer. I have two daughters. I don't want to sound dramatic, and now, it is all right, so I want you to understand I am not making a threat, but I think I have had a serious depression. For a long time I collected pills. But now I have flushed them down the toilet. I don't know what to do should my pain reoccur—so I thought if we were in touch, it would be helpful. There is something else. The man I had an affair with . . . is very nice. Harold is also very nice; it's not fair, he* deserves *his future. I want you to note down that is what I said—because sometimes, when I have been face to face with an analyst, and I recall some part of my life . . . or if time were to pass and I weren't to see my friend soon again, sometimes, I think, I have reported to analysts the opposite of what I mean. I think, in the past, I may have confused my analysts. I have figured out what I want to talk to you about. I think that there are two people involved in every transaction, in every leave-taking. I think, though, I need help.*

The next day I sat near the downstairs telephone, waiting for it to ring. Then it did and a deep resonant voice said: "I am Dr. Frosch." I had put on my horn-rimmed glasses (I am on the farsighted side), and I was ready to start reading. When I was finished, Frosch said, very casual, he had a free spot, a patient canceled for winter flu. "So, why don't you fly into New York for a couple of weeks?" I was relieved; he made it sound very simple.

I walked over to the bay window. Then I noticed. Frost on the panes, the temperature had dropped to four below. "Hulda"—I stormed into the kitchen—"what did the girls wear to school?"

She shrugged and mumbled that she couldn't be expected to do everything in the house.

"But," I yelled, "it's four degrees below!" I dashed to the downstairs hall closet and gathered up their mittens, some extra sweaters, and woolen caps. Then I opened the front door, went down the front steps, and in the wet snow I raced toward the Lab School.

8

That was in '63. We retain little memory of pain. Now Nuria has killed herself and it is difficult for me, in 1974, to recall the feel of that internal desperation, as Inezka and I mull things over in the Stanhope bar.

"But Nuria cared so for her kids—" Inez says, trying to fit together the pieces of an unshapely puzzle.

"When you are nutty, your steering mechanism goes off. Sometimes you get confused and mistake extinction for a warmer berth. It's a bad habit, trying to hold on too hard to being loved. I think Nuria was reaching for permanence," I comment flatly; it's all I remember now of my deep troubles during my previous state. I switch back to the problems of the living. "It's going to be hard on Juan. A father killed in the Civil War, his brother bumped off in mysterious circumstances, and now Nuria plunging from their garden window. While he is becoming, day by day, more famous as a novelist. It's going to be difficult for him, just because he *has* no problem. If a man becomes a widower, society rewards him. To be offered such goodies after your wife dies must make men feel awfully guilty."

Inez orders a fresh Campari-and-soda; she seems pensive. "Oh, Barbara," she suddenly says, "remember that old Madrid light? The skies were clear until the early 1960s."

Nuria was too fast; if she had waited an extra month she might possibly have been distracted by news of the *coup* in Portugal. I don't think Nuria, with her Republican orphan child's heart, would have killed herself if she had been listening to the TV news report on April 25— the morning a group of left-wing poetic young Portuguese officers seized Lisbon in a bloodless takeover. The political drama would have appealed to her. When I hear the news on my set, I am aware that just a month ago I could have shared the event with her. Juan Goytisolo is still in New York, and he immediately comes over; he is beginning to fill the void created by her death.

Ah, Nuria! She was so convinced that she was irreplaceable to needy types like her husband and me. "You and Juan [her Juan] depend on others," she was fond of telling me; "you say and do comical things, you both have a gift in knowing how to make your audience laugh— but, my, how you need those others." Poor Nuria miscalculated. She underestimated the agility with which certain types of dependent personalities can rapidly shift the object of their affections. When pushed to the wall, types like Juan Benet and myself show an amazing flair for striking out on our own. Nuria mistook her own need to be needed, and her own instinct for generosity, for genuine necessity on the part of those people near to her to whom she entrusted her fragile heart and uncertain future. Much later, when I would look back, I would realize that the two events, Nuria's death and the *coup* in Portugal, are intermeshed in my drafty storage-bin memory.

The week after that Nicolás and Graciela Sánchez-Albornoz invite me to dinner at their place in the Village; Nicolás teaches history at NYU. Our friendship dates back to 1948, the year Paco got me and Barbara Mailer to act as decoys while he rescued Nicolás and Manolo

Lamana from Cuelgamoros, a slave-labor camp near Madrid. They were part of a slave-labor team that was used to help build Franco's grotesque tomb, the Valley of the Fallen. Franco personally enjoyed having Nicolás help build his tomb because Nicolás's father, Claudio Sánchez-Albornoz, was President of the Spanish Republic-in-exile and one of the intellectual leaders of pre-Franco Spain. It must have given the dictator a special frisson of pleasure to have forced an intellectual "to his knees" by ordering his son to work as a slave in the construction of the crazy ornate tomb of the victor. Several Latin American diplomats tried to intercede in the case, but he was adamant. While Nicolás's father in Buenos Aires sank into despondency over his son's fate, in Paris Paco and his Sorbonne pals planned a do-it-yourself rescue, which had the bizarre luck of working out. According to the Madrid grapevine, when Franco was given the news, he went into a furious sulk and for days muttered, "Get them, get them." There I was, a teenager, and already I had provoked a dictator. How happy that made me feel!

Since the Portuguese *coup,* Nicolás has begun to realize that his father, living out his days as an exile in Buenos Aires, might just outlive Franco. While Graciela serves us red snapper, asparagus *al dente,* and Argentinian sweet-potato pie laced with guava, Nicolás, animated, talks about the possibilities that the Portuguese red flower revolution has created. He and Graciela have already canceled their summer trip to Italy. Now their plans include first Portugal, then a reunion in Paris with the old gang from our student days. My Spanish friends are beginning to make plans for the big return.

Graciela nervously pulls at her dark hair; the force of history seems to have taken her by surprise. Meanwhile, Nicolás has been in touch with his father. Excitedly, he talks of how good his father's health is; this summer will be a perfect time to be in Paris. *"Barbara,* you *have* to be in Europe. I want you to make me a promise. You took me out of Spain in '48—you must be in Madrid to welcome me home."

I stir my coffee. I feel I am the female equivalent of Dorian Gray. It dawns on me that Nicolás has been storing up this fantasy of returning to Spain since '48. Nicolás's relation to me never has had violent ups and downs; we've kept in close contact for a quarter of a century. Am I forever the good little girl who rescued him? Nicolás never perceives my defects, he has never truly *seen* me. Shit, I have no·choice but to go on being Angel Face.

———

The next morning Valerie telephones me. She and Ann-Jo want to history-watch in Spain in June after the CUNY semester is finished. They've already arranged for a cheapo flight and have started a chapter outline for their book on Spanish feminism under Franco.

So when Juan Goytisolo next comes to my house and offers me himself without history (he has momentarily deserted his wife for an Arab), his description of his cloudy sexual life seems, when compared to the fate of Spain, Nuria's suicide, and the Portuguese *coup*, like light times. Yes, I tell him, oh yes, I want to be in Paris with you.

III

///////////

Europe After the Rain

9

I meet Juan in Paris in the beginning of July, and soon after, I meet Ahmed. He is wearing a ten-gallon hat Juan has brought him from Texas, and he sips Coca-Cola with lemon rind. In the beginning I am very wary about being with Ahmed. With his gray hair, lanky stance, and knowledgeable stare, he has those cool good looks some men get after fifty.

You are invading his turf, taking Juan from him. Don't expect him to be grateful for having been done in. Now, what Juan wants clearly is not just one Arab male friend but an entire entourage. A re-creation of medieval Spain, where presumably Jews, Iberians, and Arabs gamboled together in Granada, happy times in the old days, never mind that the Jews were other Jews and the Arabs other Arabs.

In the beginning Ahmed is obsequious, flattering me outrageously. Juan explains to him that floweriness is not necessary for classy women. Sophisticated women, he points out, go for a drier style. "Why?" Ahmed asks. All his questions tend to be to the point. He is fascinated that my relation to Juan involves no exchange of money. Ahmed's favorite word is chic. He wants Juan and me to behave chic. Juan explains to him that for Juan I am free. "Ahmed, *ma parole,* chic women are gratis."

Ahmed and I, it turns out, are both fascinated by the precisions of money and society. That's what I mean about neither of us being very Third World, or what the left wing imagines the Third World to be. Juan breaks down the economics of our situation for Ahmed, who plies us with questions, a man in search of the concrete. Juan tells him that when he is in New York, he eats in my house, and when I am in Europe, he pays for my meals—"and cigarettes," he adds absentmindedly. Sometimes Juan forgets he is a *poète maudit,* and lapses into being a good son of the Barcelona upper bourgeoisie.

"Why encourage her to smoke?" Ahmed asks. "You want her to poison herself? She should stop—don't you pay for more than meals and tobacco?"

"*Ma parole,* Ahmed, classy women don't get paid."

"What I have to sweat for, you get for free?" Ahmed is incredulous. "Juan, she isn't classy—she's *idiote.*" He turns to me and gets my dossier. Daughter of rich family who lost their money. Juan comes from another wealthy crew—his grandfather had bribed the church; a swap, in return for absolution for three generations of Goytisolos, who could sin like rabbits and still get into paradise; the old man had foresight.

"That's why Juan is the way he is. All his life he's known he gets off scot-free," I explain. "Now, my husband died young, so in terms of cash I got somewhat left out." Ahmed is staring at me. "And afterward?" "Well, I have known some very nice men. I had one long affair with a rich publisher."

"What did he settle on you?"

"Ahmed, we *liked* each other. When it was over, well, it was over."

"This man *enjoyed* you and you gave him the best years of your life, and he settles *nothing*? He is a pig, Juan, this is *pas bon.*"

"As a matter of fact he got me after the best years of my life; I think my husband got that."

"*Idiote, plus qu'idiote.*"

"I am a female writer with good standing. Left-wing. Feminist. I can't go around conning men; American women don't do that."

"The women are *idiotes* and the men *la merde.* Barbara, *la vie est très simple. Pour les femmes, les hommes doivent payer,*" Ahmed turns and faces the sky, and sighs, "*Pas bon.* You are a woman no man took care of. A woman must have some sense. You are not here forever. When the man admires the woman, her thoughts must run to gold. You call what you do feminist. Woozy-woozy. Women who think woozy-woozy." He laughs. He talks to me of the days of Abraham. "Sarah was too old to bear children, but she had this beautiful serving girl." Ahmed tells me tales from the Koran, mixed with ancient biblical Judaic lore; his versions sound different. Occasionally I correct him with my more Jewish interpretation. Juan gazes at us, open-mouthed; he is glued to our dialogue. Suddenly he leans across the restaurant table and grasps our hands. "*Ma parole,*" Juan exclaims, and his voice shakes slightly. "You work hard all your life, you write books, you become known, and for what? You want, you want, and one day, life gives it to you, everything comes together—and you don't have to write books, because just living a hundred and fifty kilometers per hour is enough. Just to be happy, ah, Barbara, ah, Ahmed"—Juan's voice shakes—"use the strength of the three of us so that this day may never end." Juan trembles with emotion: then the Tunisian Jewish waiter comes to our table, and he slowly lets go of my hand.

Ahmed subsumes his jealousy of me by becoming my father figure. Later that night, while we walk through Paris, he drags Juan to one side and I hear what he is whispering. He wants Juan to take me on forever. I pretend not to be aware, but I am listening to Ahmed's reasoning. "She's a good woman, brought up her daughters, she writes on your country. I tell you, Juan, you've latched on to a princess."

Ahmed thinks I have a screw loose, and his protective spirit comes to the fore. He shakes his head, pauses on the corner near rue du Vieux Temple, and points at me. "That millionaire was not *bon. Pour une bonne femme, il faut payer.*" Ahmed has always *paid* for his sex. He tells me that he started out as "a poor black piece of ash," an orphaned Arab Berber growing up in the streets of Casablanca. His first step in upward mobility was marrying into his wife's cream-colored family. Ahmed slaved for fourteen years in Renault, always box lunches, no movies, whores rarely. The money went home, back to Zineb.

His big luck came when he collected a boodle after an industrial accident that shredded the bones of his right leg, giving him a permanent limp. With that money he became a member of the petty bourgeoisie, an upwardly mobile Moroccan. Now Ahmed has become a real-estate entrepreneur; after his travels with Juan and me he is going home to Casa to help his two sons become members of the managerial class. Because Ahmed is handsome and surrounded by French "niki-nikki," Zineb's family was sure he would defect. "I fooled them"—he slaps his thigh in enjoyment of a good joke—"this no good speck of dust has made Zineb richer than any of her sisters. What no Arab does, Ahmed did. I put the property in *her* name. When I get home, I'll improve her—send her to one of those feminist groups."

The next day I leave the Montalembert and move into Juan's *pied-à-terre* in the Jewish section. Ahmed is delighted I have been willing to join them.

Endlessly Ahmed and I discuss buying and cooking. Juan stares and listens; our conversation mesmerizes him. In his role as a left-wing Spaniard, he is expected to demonstrate a certain contempt for objects; yet his happiest days are spent watching Ahmed and me on our buying sprees. Our acquisitiveness is infectious. One afternoon Juan decides to shop with me near the Marais for groceries. He carries the food basket, and he grins with delight because the smocked Frenchwoman in the *épicerie* exclaims, *"Tiens, voilà le mari américain, comme il aide sa femme!"*

"For a paella," I point out, "we need Spanish macho rice, ballsy; the ordinary kind won't work."

"Macho rice?" Juan repeats my expressions, always taking notes. "Barbara, why did you say that you spent the morning doing a telofannade? What is a telofannade? Macho rice?" Juan watches and listens while Ahmed and I simply move through life. Ahmed has a strange fixation. He is hung up on Golda Meir, a rare beauty in his eyes; her sexual prowess has made Israel into a potent force.

"Ma parole, Ahmed, Golda Meir never had mysterious sexual adventures . . ." Juan disagrees.

"A temptress, she was *belle,* which is how she became queen. Not like Morocco. Kif—poison. Kif killed North Africa. Makes you talk woozy-woozy. *Pas bon."* Juan believes Ahmed will not be jealous of me as a rival for his sexual affections if I seduce Ahmed by making a great paella in the studio on rue au Maire. But when we carry back up the five flights of stairs the good food we have bought, Ahmed goes into a wild rage. He yowls at us in French and Arabic. "You said your friend is Jewish. Ahmed from Casa, who grew up with Jews, knows you are a Spanish poisonous liar. *Kasher, kasher,* a Jew buys a *kasher chicken;* the neck should be fresh-killed, clean. No Jewish woman puts pork in the paella, *les écrivains sont les grands menteurs,* Spanish pork eaters!"

After Juan convinces Ahmed that I am a strange breed of New York Jew, Ahmed slowly gains confidence in my cooking. He watches the way I chop and mix foods in order to report back to Zineb. When we eat in restaurants, Ahmed waits for me to order my meal. He has blind faith that a dollop of *kasher* custom has been retained in my Jewish genes; therefore, what I want he knows is not *trayf.*

That July the three of us take a trip in Juan's tan Citroën to Rotterdam to visit Zineb's relatives. Ahmed wants to show off his fancy writer friends to her family. As soon as Juan heads toward the north of

France Ahmed becomes picky. He worries about the Vuitton bag I carry. "It looks like plastic . . . hasn't she a leather one for Rotterdam? For the relatives? I am taking you to their house."

"*Ma parole,* Ahmed, the fashionable women in Paris are wearing Louis Vuitton."

"Ugly plastic crap."

We first take a small detour to Compiègne; in early July the forests there are soft; there is yellow-green grass and skies the color of smoke. We park the car and like good tourists examine the Armistice train, where on the eleventh of November 1918 Field Marshal Foch, and Erzberger for the Germans, and Oberndorf and Wemyss and Weygand signed the peace treaty. Juan, his arm around my neck, and I look through the slide lanterns. Juan finds the set of the American infantry at Saint-Malo, where my father was gassed. We call Ahmed, and he looks at the pictures, too. Juan says, "Ahmed, you were born in Casa, and I in Barcelona, and Barbara in New York, isn't that interesting?"

We are dawdling, in no hurry to get to Rotterdam. On the spur of the moment we decide, Why deprive ourselves of the French countryside, why not see the châteaux of the Loire, as well as go to Belgium and Holland? So we backtrack toward Paris and south to the Loire. Ahmed is very serious and insists we pay for the special tour of the châteaux; when the guide isn't watching, he likes to steal a feel of the white and gold china and inspect the porcelain marks on the underside of the plates. While Ahmed follows the guide, inspecting the castle bric-a-brac, I go back into the deserted royal bedchamber; I find Juan snoozing in the dauphin's bed. He looks like a wicked child, his head propped up against the red cut-velvet ornate round bolsters of the canopied royal couch. "Juan, get out of there!" But he pulls me down on the bed beside him; we are lying together that way when Ahmed comes back for us.

"The kings of France were short-legged," Juan says.

Ahmed puts on his gold-rimmed glasses. "*C'est pas chic.*"

"*Ca bouge,*" says Juan.

"What?"

"*Todo.*"

Then we go outside the château and walk over to the parking lot.

When we get in the car the heat of the afternoon is still thick. We circle north for a second time, and the next day we decide to spend the night in Cambrai.

The town has squares with rows of red poppies, and houses of a beautiful nineteenth-century French mercantile substance, and the July French light softens the beige granite of the buildings, turning the stone golden. Woolens are the main industry in this provincial city. When was I here? On the road toward Belgium? Seventeen? Eighteen? An American Sorbonne student traveling with Paco Benet, on our way to live in Germany, to Mainz, which was the only place a twenty-year-old Spanish exile could get a teaching job. I was entering Germany soon after the war, and I was scared to be living near Dachau, near the concentration camps.

In Cambrai, according to the legend at the local *confiserie*, a toffee-maker fouled up on his family's ritualistic fabrication of caramel. The man had left out the sugar or butter, and inadvertently invented a new kind of candy. *Les Bêtises de Cambrai.* We buy three canisters, give away the bonbons, sprawl on the wet lawn, with yellow-green grass smelling faintly of sun and poppies, and with a Magic Marker we scrawl our names, Barbara, New York City, Juan, Barcelona, Ahmed, Casablanca. ACHETEZ SEULEMENT DES BÊTISES DE CAMBRAI AFCHAIN. *Elles sont les seules vraies Bêtises de Cambrai.* Underneath the sentence describing the toffees as Cambrai's only *bêtise,* Juan writes: *il y en a d'autres. Moi. Juan.*

Ahmed puts his signed tin box in his knapsack with the other gifts for Zineb. We lie on the grass, the red flowers and fresh blades of viridian have made stains on my clothes, a crushed summer straw hat is half covering my head, Ahmed's Texas ten-gallon is on the lawn next to his Minolta. When I awaken from my short nap, Ahmed is firmly holding my finger; he has bought two wedding bands at the Monoprix across from the main square in Cambrai. "Marry him," he is whispering. "The two of you aren't getting any younger, I fixed it for you," he hisses in my ear, then he turns to Juan, "You are living with *her* now, no more woozy-woozy, the two of you, your future together—a king and queen!" "If you say so, Ahmed," Juan mumbles, and we both put on the rings; I think Ahmed wants us fixed up before he takes us into the home of his wife's family in Rotterdam.

If my grandfather had given our family money to the Church, so that I could get dibs on paradise, I too would be spending my life writing inflammatory novels against the clergy. Now, where would St. Germain des Près be (as advertisers say—thoughtwise) if Karl Marx's uncle hadn't stolen his nephew's future inheritance to help build Philips, the big European radio manufacturing conglomerate? Money is serious stuff, never mind all this minor confessional mode of when your parents caught you masturbating at the age of ten.

Ahmed has his doubts about Juan's novels. Painstakingly he has improved his reading French in order to understand them. "Caca? You write about caca? How it smells? How you do it? A man talks about his *besoins* in public? You make speeches in American University, you read from your books on shit? And the Americans pay you for discussing *besoin?* Juan, *c'est pas bon.* You are a clean man, you close the door when you do your *besoins. Les écrivains sont les grands menteurs, et les grands cons.*" Ahmed turns to me, "Barbara, in your books, you discuss *la merde?*"

"No, Ahmed, but what Juan does is a style."

"We do different things," Juan adds.

"Caca is a style? *Les grands cons.* Spanish pork poisoners and American Louis Vuitton plastic crap!"

Ahmed and I case Cambrai's shopping bunks. He fights for my rights in the supermarkets and open-air gadget pushcarts throughout France and Holland. He haggles, yells, and menaces until he obtains for me a desired object, a garlic press, a plastic tomato slicer, or a ceramic pepper mill for each of us. We buy bolts of Mediterranean blue and Venetian red cotton in splashy patterns for our homes; meanwhile, Juan pretends to buy refills for his Polaroid camera, but what he is really doing, hiding behind a pyramid of American breakfast cereals, is sneaking a little listen to Ahmed's and my conversation; we are back again on Abraham and Sarah. "I see you, Juan," I yell, "stop lurking behind those boxes of cornflakes—either join us or go away, but don't just *crouch.*"

In the morning we drive through the peat bogs, pyramids of black dust of northern France, then to Brussels. Ahmed finds for Zineb demitasse spoons with the figure of a Manneken Pis; I get my father good Cuban cigars. Then we drive on to Rotterdam.

In the lobby of our small Dutch hotel is a poster from the 1940s of Xavier Cugat and his band; the proprietor turns out to be a Catalan. Ahmed inspects my outfit; he wants me to wear an evening dress I had packed in the bottom of the suitcase—one of those things one wears once, to some special ballet benefit. As I sat in my New York bedroom, packing for Europe, at the last moment, one of my friends said, Take that fantastic evening dress, you never know what might come up in Europe. And here I am overdressed and shimmering, in a Rotterdam hotel, with no makeup, and smelling of Calandre. Juan is enthusiastic; he thinks this is the way I should look for dining with Ahmed's relatives.

Juan and I walk through the center of Rotterdam, Juan leads the way; in his free hand he carries our gift of Belgian chocolate. The brick Dutch walls are covered with international graffiti: LIBERTÉ POUR LA ETA. SAUVEZ LES BASQUES. VIVE LA POLITIQUE DE '68. The Chellah clan live on the third floor of a Rotterdam walk-up over a sex shop that features dildoes and oversized organs. Ahmed's family comes in assorted ages: women in caftans, children, and a group of men, the husbands of the clan. Ahmed and Juan and I are instructed by the women to join the men and sit in a semicircle while they bring us bowls of water and towels. One of the men is a ringer for Saul Bellow, and the bowls of water remind me of Passover. An Arab Passover in Rotterdam! I dry my hands, Ahmed introduces us, "My friend Juan, the great Spanish writer, and his American wife," Ahmed pauses, "she also writes." To please Ahmed I ostentatiously flash the wedding band he bought for me in Cambrai. We are served great mounds of Moroccan food. We start with a couscous with steaming baby carrots and pale shiny olives, and magenta aubergines. Then we move on to chicken *mqualli,* a *tagine* made with pickled lemons, ginger, onion, and garlic. The small room where we eat, seated in a semicircle by a round table, smells musky, of cumin and saffron and oil and steamed vegetables.

Juan notices my transfixed gaze; on the television are scenes from *Mrs. Miniver* dubbed in Dutch. "I know my defects," he hisses at me, poking me in the ribs, sniffing the odors of Calandre clinging to my skin, "but you can't complain that I haven't provided you an interesting life."

Zineb's sisters serve us cold carrot salad and oranges sliced in a syrup of cinnamon and sugar. We have had green mint tea before dinner, and now, again, at the end.

Her nieces motion me to come behind the second curtain, which separates the front rooms. The two girls, fourteen and sixteen, are giggling while painting their fingernails red. I have latched on to a few Arab words: *"Zouina, m'zin"*—with nice and sweet I can't go wrong. Then there is *trek. Zouina trek:* Paris to Rotterdam. My three-word vocabulary alters my thoughts. One of Ahmed's nieces is wearing pants, the other a short skirt. "Aren't you allowed to join the men?"

The girls giggle; we speak in French. "Uncle Ahmed has it wrong, he understands nothing." The older, Sheba, takes out a lipstick and a mirror compact and paints her lips red; she laughs. "We go out front when we want—but sometimes with the men it is dull—Uncle Ahmed, *il ne comprend rien.*" Zineb's nieces, clearly, have moved on. They ask me to try on a ceremonial caftan. *"Zouina surprise pour le mari."*

The girls open the curtains between the two rooms, and the three of us are revealed, laughing. Ahmed leans back against the couch. "Ah," he sighs, *"ca c'est bon."* He sips a deep draft of sugared tea made with crushed fresh mint; the Belgian chocolates Juan and I have brought are displayed on the dining table. Ahmed has put on the dog for Zineb's people; the relatives have to eat their mean words about his being a piece of black cinder from the streets of Casa. Ahmed is returning to Morocco as one of those rare cases, a worldly success.

Juan and I leave Ahmed with his relatives in Rotterdam, and we drive back to Paris. I have taken on writing assignments to help pay for the summer in Europe. Now I have to fly to Lisbon to write about the revolution in Portugal. It makes no sense, my overstaying my time with Juan; after all, he has a crazy situation. His wife, Ahmed, now me. The trouble is I have been happy with him. I don't know what to do.

"Call me from Lisbon," Juan urges, "When Ahmed comes back from Rotterdam, we could pick you up in Portugal and continue to Tangier—"

In the face of Juan's insistence, I am unsure how to proceed, I've had fun. But finally I say good-bye to him, and on the last day I am in Paris I move back to the Montalembert. I feel guilty. I've deserted my old friends. Specifically, Pepe Martínez. When I telephone him he sounds pissed, but says, So come over.

I walk along St. Germain over to Cluny. Pepe's small publishing house, Ruedo Ibérico, is on a street just in back of that part of the boulevard. We've known each other forever. Paco and I had been the first persons Pepe met after he arrived in Paris after being released from a French prison. He had been a member of the libertarian youth movement. And when he got to Paris he met our bunch. We were students then. I was the only American. The others were mostly children of Spanish exiles. Paco was one of the few who had come from Madrid. He had graduated first in Spain in philosophy and had won a fellowship to the Sorbonne. I have no technical connection with Ruedo. It's all just emotional. The idea of beating Franco with words had started with Paco. In the late 1940s, after rescuing Nicolás and Manolo, he had involved Pepe and myself in the creation of *Península,* the first clandestine magazine to have some intellectual substance. That was in '49 and '50. Paco, Pepe, and I worked hard on it.

I see myself in Paris then: seated on a stool, chin cupped in my hands, complaining to Paco that I was a failure. "At seventeen?" He laughed at me. "You don't know enough to be a failure. You've got to learn first—you're intuitive, but you've got to put it all together. You're going to be a writer." "How do you know?" "I just do—you and my kid brother." "What's he like?" "Juan? Smart. Wild. Timid. *Enfant terrible.* When you go to Spain I'm going to make you take him *Light in August.* He's in love with our cousin Nuria." Paco meant the world to me then, and, when he got a teaching job at the University of Mainz, I went with him to live in the French zone of occupied Germany. After Cuelgamoros, he was on the wanted list of the Spanish police and could no longer return home. Germany was rubble then. Scary. Lines of displaced people just waiting in railway stations. I look up, I am at rue de Latran. In front of Ruedo's bookstore. The weather has cleared.

Pepe is in his office. He is fiddling with his brown-rimmed eyeglasses, and he is wearing a nice Italian gray silk tie. He points his Roman profile up to the ceiling; despite the melancholy gaze, he must know he is very good-looking. I sense he is annoyed with me and Juan Goytisolo. He realizes something different is going on, but he isn't sure what.

"You come to Paris and don't look up your old friends?" Pepe flares his sharply defined nostrils, "Spain is in its crucial phase, and you go to Belgium? Why? Nothing is in Brussels."

"Pepe, I want to sightsee, be a *turista.* For years I've been coming to Europe and have had to interview this left-wing group or that band of prison protesters, maybe I just want to have a good time."

"Nicolás and Graciela are coming to the Massif Central in the beginning of August; you promise that you will be there? You will be back from Portugal by August 1?"

"Sure, Pepe." The four of us have planned a summer reunion.

He looks at me thoughtfully, then reaches into his desk drawer and takes out a copy of a new book. "This is going to be published in August. It will cause a sensation. It's the Basque account of their assassination of Premier Admiral Luis Carrero Blanco, Franco's number-two man. *Operation Ogro.* You can stay in my office and read it, but don't discuss it with anyone, and leave the book here."

After Pepe leaves and I am reading the book, out of a lifelong habit, I make notes in my ongoing political journal.

POLITICAL JOURNAL

Paris: July 1974

In Bayonne, France, on December 28, 1973, eight days after the assassination of Spain's prime minister, Admiral Luis Carrero Blanco, hooded members of the ETA (Esukadi Ta Askatasuna—Basque Nation and Freedom) gave their first news conference to the foreign press to explain why and how they blew up the prime minister's car in the middle of Madrid. Though there were some political roundups in Spain directly after the assassination, the police were not able to make any significant arrests. Despite the regime's angry demands for extradition of members of ETA living in France, Belgium, and other European countries, since the end of World War II no European country has handed back political exiles to Spain. Whether the police in Belgium and France could not find the members of ETA, or, as Spain suggested, did not choose to find them, has not been clarified.

Operation Ogro: A taped account of the four young men involved. The ETA define themselves as Basque freedom fighters with Marxist sympathies. As the Basque country has suffered severe political repression, in one form or another it has been at war with the Franco regime since the end of the Civil War.

Ogro is a spellbinder, but as Pepe has said not to mention it, I erase the book from my mind. When I get back to the Montalembert I telephone Clancy in London. He has some good addresses for me to see in Lisbon for the pieces I will be doing there. Then I telephone down to the desk clerk and ask him to pick up for me a TAP ticket for the next morning. I start to pack.

10

When I arrive in Lisbon in mid-July, the revolution has begun to sag, the dog days of summer have arrived, and the American Embassy appears to be in deep sleep. The man in charge has no clue how one gets to see key people. He seems to consider the press situation too snafued to be worth unraveling.

When one is in strange countries, sometimes the simplest methods work, like jumping into a taxi and saying, Take me to your leader, which is just what I do. A cabdriver takes me to the revolution. On the way to Palacio de Belém movie marquees feature films no longer censored: *The Great Dictator, Last Tango in Paris,* Luis Buñuel's *Belle de Jour.* Political graffiti cover the walls and bridges of Lisbon. THIS BRIDGE WAS TAKEN ON APRIL 25 BY THE ARMED FORCES MOVEMENT. WE WELCOME ÁLVARO CUNHAL AT THE AIRPORT. LONG LIVE THE FORÇAS ARMADAS.

Palacio de Belém, where part of the new government is now installed, resembles a nineteenth-century rococo palace commandeered into an army barracks. The building appears to be staffed by dreamy-faced, good-looking young men dressed in army maneuver khakis. Lisbon still feels like a liberated city, with all the confusions, fears, and euphorias that flourish after a long war has been declared over and won; red carnations are still blowing along the dusty patio in front of Belém. I'm in luck. A harassed Communist who is peddling his bill for legalization of divorce notices me arguing with the gate guard; instantly he spots a captive audience for his program. I am a woman writer with bona fide credentials from a North American magazine. In the confusions of revolution, any new face will do as a friend.

He rapidly fills me in on the problems of working-class women. Rape, infidelity, illegitimate children. "These women get deserted by their husbands; then they start sleeping with their bosses to make ends meet; when that doesn't work out, they find themselves jobless with a house full of children. They become prostitutes, the new children have no social or economic rights." The man pauses, anxious; he sizes me up: "Look, I have no bone to pick with the Catholic Church—"

I assure him I am aware that new-style Iberian Communists want no flak from the Church; the clergy and the Communists are in a period of détente.

The man arranges two appointments for me. The first, for that evening, is with Victor Alves, one of the captains of the MFA (the Portuguese Forças Armadas) who had staged the revolution—and the second, for the next day, is with Álvaro Cunhal, the head of the Portuguese Communist Party.

Take a taxi and you meet the world.

That evening, on the drive over to Palacio São Bento, I see more graffiti. THEORY OF HAPPINESS IS FREEDOM. My appointment with Major Victor Alves, Minister without Portfolio, is for eight in the evening. The floor where the young officers who are part of the junta are lodged has the classy look of an English gentlemen's club. The Portuguese are working around the clock. The country has no money, high inflation, unemployment, and troubles in Africa. A white-liveried waiter ambles along the palace corridor carrying a silver tray, balancing thin china cups, bottles of aged cognac, and gold-embossed snifters.

"Africa made me." Alves clearly is weary after another long day of the waning revolution. A summery dusk blankets Palacio São Bento. "After eleven years of senseless war, I kept asking myself, What am I doing in Africa? But I became in touch with the people there. We, the Portuguese Army, were doing the opposite of helping. We were—wrong, wrong, wrong." He pauses, refilling his pipe. "When you are a member of the military you don't feel *well* always going against your country. It doesn't feel good always to be against life."

Alves appears surprised, but pleased, when I ask him whether Africa had radicalized him. "You think I'm a radical? *Me?*" He gazes out at the Lisbon night. "I'm a career militarist who likes to read books. The *coup* came from the military; we were disgusted with the war in Africa and conditions at home."

"Why did you choose to have a junta of seven generals and admirals in addition to General Spínola?"

Laughter. "Haven't you always considered seven a luckier number than one? Now, de Gaulle was one. During March we wrote fifty scenarios of what we thought most likely to happen. The scenario we picked as most likely is what actually occurred." He pauses. "The *coup* was started during the early-morning hours. A disc jockey—he was collaborating with us—gave the signal. His instructions were if it was to be 'on,' if there had been no last-minute hitch, he was to play a popular song that had been banned by the regime. At dawn I heard the music, the *coup* had begun."

The following evening at a Lisbon dinner party, María Isabel, the wife of a Lisbon architect, tells me that when she first heard broadcasts on loudspeakers placed in strategic streets warning the inhabitants of Lisbon to stay indoors until further instructions from the army—nobody knew who the MFA was—she suddenly did a foolish thing. She grabbed her daughter and ran out into the street. "It's come, it's come," she screamed. Crowds were in the square. "We didn't know during the morning what group had moved in, but who could it have been? So we all yelled, 'It must be coming from the left!' "

A young group of independent leftists asks me to meet with them. I take the crowded second-class train that goes past Estoril and I get off at our rendezvous village. I can't find them so I go back to Lisbon. It seems they had fallen asleep on the beach in the sun. My friends feel very badly for me and invite me to a party. We listen, while standing on the balcony of a penthouse, to music coming from a nearby apartment: calypso. Blacks from Cape Verde. One of the women says she feels sad. "Before the revolution all of us were friends; now we have split. It is line A against line B." She looks out at the glittering light Lisbon night. "Portugal is surreal—poets running a country."

I live at the Tivoli in the center of Lisbon. While I am bathing the telephone rings. My mother, in New York, is on the line. With age she attempts a more conventional definition of motherhood. What, she asks, am I doing to my half-orphaned daughters? (That summer, Maria is studying Russian at Middlebury, Carla is at Yale.) Blood, she insists, is running down the streets of Lisbon, I must leave immediately. "Mother, what blood?" How can you have blood in the streets in a country where nobody other than one or two accidental deaths has been killed?

Time and *Newsweek* carry scare stories—the junta has replaced Spínola, anarchy has destroyed the revolution, Lisbon is in chaos. I am lucky—

The New Republic has no money for pointed, lengthy transatlantic queries, so I am left to make my own interpretations.

When I go downstairs the hotel manager, who has lent me a small hotel typewriter—a very old Royal portable—asks me if I shall be leaving for Madrid. "The press has gone," he says. "Moved on to Spain because Franco is dying." Later there is a phone call from Juan in Paris; he is almost gasping. "The dying has begun—I can't believe it." We agree to keep in touch.

The next day there is an uncomfortable pause during lunch after I remark I am beginning to understand some Portuguese. "We have been talking to you in Spanish," María Isabel says, unhappy. "Oh," I say. Then I lapse into silence, my cheeks redden. María Isabel and her friend María Teresa associate me with Madrid. Portugal and Spain have always lived in extreme isolation, one from the other. Now Portugal has done this fantastic thing, upset some imaginary political calendar in which the world had expected Franco to die and Portugal to remain in limbo. This summer there has been an unexpected influx of migrant Spanish leftists into the Portuguese capital. At an international reunion of libertarian Anarchists in Lisbon in July, Spanish students held newspapers in front of their faces.

María Isabel doesn't wish to insult me, but she says, rather mournfully, it might be better if the Spaniards stayed home. "They are too dramatic for us," María Teresa agrees. They want to talk about my meeting with Cunhal, the Portuguese Communist chief.

"Well," says María Teresa, "Alves and Cunhal are our two best lookers."

When I meet Cunhal I decide the women are right. He has the tight, austere features of a certain type of intelligent man. He is proud of his linguistic abilities and we talk in Spanish. He is cautious about Spain. A delicate diplomatic balance needs to be maintained; Portugal's Communist and Socialist parties are part of the new government, while in Spain similar parties are considered subversive.

The Portuguese Communists are conservative; the Spanish Carrillo wing, Euro-Communist. "Which wing of the Spanish Communists," I ask Cunhal, "do you consider the legitimate party?"

Cunhal phrases his reply with caution. "*When* and *if* Spain has a change, the Portuguese will recognize Carrillo's group." "During this interim period," I ask, "what could the Spanish opposition expect from the Portuguese?"

Cunhal is pensive. "Moral support. Perhaps an opening on a cultural level, but nothing more."

Suddenly Cunhal relaxes. He reminisces about Spain; he was there during the Civil War.

He goes on to observe that Washington is uneasy concerning changing events in Portugal. Cautiously he indicates, in his dry, correct voice, that he wants American business interests to remain. He sighs, "I feel besieged . . . I feel I have so many enemies . . . on the left, on the right," and reaches for comfort in an aloof, impersonal manner befitting a head of state. A busy man, his complaints are less directed at me, an unknown journalist, than at the walls, the desk, the hot history of the Palacio de Belém. When Cunhal realizes I am an essayist, and there will be no headlines the next morning, he seems relieved. My lack of professionalism soothes; perhaps my story will get lost.

Abruptly his voice fills with controlled emotion. "Why does the foreign press criticize us? Our prisons are filled now with thousands of Portuguese secret police—we haven't laid a hand on them, which was not the way they treated us."

The man who will escort me in the elevator, down to the main floor and past the entry guard, has come to get me. But I have lost my pass. In a hurry to find it, I spill the contents of my shoulder bag on the floor. My jumbled history rolls under Cunhal's desk—notes, photographs of my daughters, a cassette machine, unpaid New York City grocery bills, a wire brush. Cunhal gets down on the floor and crawls beneath his desk. On the floor, suddenly humanized, Cunhal recovers his sense of humor and retrieves my personal junk. He instructs his secretary to wait. "Calm, calm . . . If I could escape from the fortress of Peniche, I can get you, with or without a pass, out of Belém."

To live in short spurts in hotels (with *Le Monde,* the *International Herald Tribune,* croissants, and pots of hot coffee and boiled milk brought to one's bedside) is like getting quick whiffs of oxygen, but after two weeks I need familiar people back in my life. If I had to spend too much time in unknown cities interviewing the famous and the less famous, I would die of an unused heart. So when Juan telephones a second time from Paris because Franco has continued to die, I agree to meet him in Madrid. In the early-morning hours, as I speed in a taxi to the Lisbon airport, the sleepy pale summer light filtering through the trees along the broad *avenidas,* the quiet emptiness and whiteness of the city, and the faint smell of oil and sun remind me of Madrid, in 1948, when it was still a sleepy town; there were no big plans for it to become Western Europe's third-largest city. I was a Sorbonne student—seventeen? eighteen?

I board the TAP superjet; I mash on a straw hat decorated with red paper carnations, souvenirs of the flower revolution given to me by María Teresa and María Isabel.

The real reason I am going to Madrid isn't that Franco is dying, although Juan and I have agreed to meet at the Hotel Wellington, but that I don't want too much time to pass before I see Juan Benet and pay my dues for Nuria's death, and to the living.

11

Juan Benet, his eldest son, Ramón, and I sit in an outdoor Italian restaurant. Gloomy, we order supper. We struggle to put the conversation in order, but the trouble is that Juan and I have known each other too long, I must remind him of Nuria, and this night we are awkward with each other.

So Juan vents his fury on Franco. "Who cares whether the old man dies now? What difference could it possibly make to any of us? Should have croaked twenty years ago, should never have been born—" then he switches his anger to Juan Goytisolo. "He has so many brothers, a whole tribe!"

I say nothing. Juan Benet has no brothers now.

I feel smothered, mentally sandwiched in between two wacky Spanish writers—both Juans—in their own ways demanding, LOOK AT ME. Frequently I get their names so confused that even I think of them as Juan Goytisolo, or Juan Benet. I am supposed to be able to read between the lines, to understand that these writers, with their jazzy prose, their anger, their obliqueness, their stiletto, sadistic fantasies, their sophistication, and their Grand Guignol imagery, don't mean a word of it. Underneath all that stylish language of grown men, one is meant at all moments to remember the child. Juan Benet, with his father shot; Juan Goytisolo, with his mother killed by a German bombing of Barcelona.

When Juan is finished speaking, our eyes suddenly meet; a glance of affection is exchanged, like the old friends we are, and suddenly it dawns on me—Juan Benet will be furious when Paco's friends come back to Spain. A final reminder that his brother is dead.

Juan Goytisolo and Ahmed are waiting for me in the Wellington bar. Ahmed's long legs dangle from the barstool. He sips his usual Coca-Cola with lemon rind; his Texas ten-gallon hat is tilted forward over one side of his forehead.

He's brought bags of stuff for Zineb. He got blue jeans and polo shirts for his sons, an Osterizer, an electric beater, the Manneken Pis spoons. Wherever we travel, Ahmed loads up for his home; he is provisioning for the time he will leave Juan and me. Every two steps Ahmed makes us take his photograph, sometimes alone, sometimes with Juan or with me. Nothing arty. Ahmed goes in for stiff nineteenth-century group portraiture in front of a monument; the Tour Eiffel or a sumptuous château. Sometimes Ahmed poses like a bird in flight; he lifts up one leg behind him and thrusts his head horizontal to the ground, both arms outstretched in a flopping wing position.

Juan throws his arms around me; we are excited at being together in Madrid. It is the end of July and miserably hot in the city. We have arrived sixteen months too early for Franco's dying. Madrid is empty and baking. We walk the deserted streets, eat fish in seafood restaurants—*salmonetes, trucha a la Navarra,* nibble on the purplish-white summer asparagus from Toledo, drink Marqués de Riscal wine. The city is quiet and Franco does not die.

So we go about our own lives and have a good time. Juan hasn't been in Madrid since student days, and he sneaks about the city, taking peeks here and there. I won't go on to Tangier with them: I have given my word to meet Pepe, Graciela, and Nicolás on the first of August in the Massif summer house rented by Ruedo Ibérico. But I promise Juan that I will wait for him in Paris in September. A strange summer romance. As long as I am happy, it doesn't seem to matter about Ahmed or Juan's sometime wife. Where will it end? And Juan is as surprised as I when unexpectedly that September neither of us shows any signs of leaving.

By September 10 the tourists have vacated Paris. Fall and bad weather have set in abruptly. A darkness hangs over the city, and it is time for me to go back to America. When Ahmed returns from Casa, he is sad that I am leaving rue au Maire. Ahmed cajoles, threatens, and compliments me. I am a wonderful woman, a fantastic cook—look how happy I have made Juan. He warns if I don't return to Europe others will fill my place. Juan, such a fine writer, could have lines of women. In six weeks' time I will be replaced. No one wants to be alone, Ahmed insists. If not with you, well then, with another one. *"Ma parole,* Barbara. *Toi ou une autre."* Juan looks wistful. He tends to let Ahmed do the bargaining. My home has become the fifth-floor walk-up apartment in the crumbling building smelling of piss and stone on rue au Maire. Juan continues to play Judy Collins singing "Clouds." There it is, the television set, the makeshift kitchen, Ahmed's loot from our travels to Belgium and Holland, the Moroccan rug in the living room, the blond modern French cheapo furniture, Juan's mattress bed in the bedroom, the long sofa in the living room, the soapy smell of the Catalan Agua Brava in the bathroom. *Le Monde,* the *Herald Tribune,* the *Nouvel Observateur,* Moutik's Minolta camera, his aluminum couscous pots, the souvenir tin containers of *bêtises* from Cambrai. I will miss the small apartment on rue au Maire, smack in the middle of the old Jewish neighborhood, now populated by Algerians, Chinese, and Corsicans. Across the street, in the direction of Belleville, is a musty dancing palace, Le Tango. Ahmed never goes in, but Juan and I do. For coffee. He reads *Le Monde,* watches the dancers, while several times some formal, aging Frenchmen from one of the banlieues ask me if I will take a turn with them. I ask Juan if he really wants me to come back to Europe. "Well, as a matter of fact, yes."

When I want to hide my vulnerability from my married women friends who poke about too much, I lie. I try to sound in command, offhand, cynical. I have observed my friends invariably warn me (with intense interest) about certain types of men. They always explain to me how easily I could be destroyed, discarded, and how I am a woman much too sensitive to take such rejection. I always have been eager to find out more about these terrible rejections that these wrong sorts of men could give me. Why does no one ever warn about the dangers to the heart of becoming involved with a boring accountant? What about *that* fate? How awful it must be to be jilted by a very dull man. And some of the dullest think nothing of leaving you for some younger woman—*they* don't know they are not entitled. No, I prefer taking potluck with lively, unstable men, fully aware I am investing heavily in the ephemeral.

Now it is September. I have been happy. For a woman in her forties to be delighted with a man is a gratuitous gift; an intelligent female doesn't throw away such grace lightly. Juan's sense of urgency moves me, and when I get ready the next day to leave for America, I reassure him that I will try very hard to find a way back.

Which comes sooner than I would have guessed and due to unexpected circumstances.

12

POLITICAL JOURNAL

New York City: September 1974

We have just heard via the European press that on September 13, a bomb exploded in a Madrid cafeteria frequented by Madrid policemen. Twelve people were killed. Two members of ETA have been arrested, tortured, and charged with the crime. ETA, whose policy is always to claim credit for their acts of terrorism, is disclaiming involvement in the Café Rolando bombing.

September 16

Dr. Eva Forest, a psychiatrist and the wife of the Madrid playwright Alfonso Sastre, and seven other prominent intellectuals have been arrested. They have been charged with being a "link" between the Communist Party and ETA, and with having aided ETA in the cafeteria explosion.

According to police, the homes of these prominent Madrid and Barcelona intellectuals have been used as ETA hiding places, such as those mentioned in *Operation Ogro*. They accuse Eva Forest of having coauthored the book.

In a letter finally released in France and Sweden, Eva Forest reports being kicked and beaten on all parts of her body. The prisoners were held incommunicado the first twenty-six days. Dr. Forest was told she would be thrown out of a window, and the world would be informed of her suicide. After she had vomited, she was forced to swallow "the mess." According to reports in *Le Monde*, she and other prisoners have been repeatedly raped.

Her husband, Alfonso Sastre, has been released from jail. In order to help Eva he is remaining in Spain, and he writes to friends in Paris (who forward the letter to New York) that he feels as he walks along the Madrid avenues like a pariah. Several old friends, he says, have destroyed photographs in which they appear together with Eva and Alfonso. Suddenly this well-known Madrid couple has ceased to exist.

I am unexpectedly able to make an imaginative leap out of my Jewish skin. What made the Jews so vulnerable in World War II is that they were, precisely, outsiders and in trouble. I am startled just how quickly Europeans accommodate to helping *no one.*

Valerie calls me up and we arrange to meet at the Madison Avenue Deli—she is very worried about Eva Sastre. And with reason. She reminds me, while waiting for her pastrami sandwich, that she and Ann-Jo had spent all of August and part of September interviewing feminists in Barcelona and Madrid. Their last interview, she says, had been with Eva.

Finally, Valerie confesses that she and Ann-Jo traveled through Spain giving my name and Juan Goytisolo's as a reference. Now, with the arrests and torture of these women, she is scared. Could they have done anything wrong?

"Christ . . . Valerie!"

"We were just doing our book—how should we know we were landing in the middle of some wacky police net?"

"But, Valerie, Juan and I were in Madrid at the same time that you and Ann-Jo were interviewing Eva and company; we registered at the Wellington, the hotel clerk took our passports. All that stuff goes straight to Spanish Security."

Valerie stares at me, sobered by the news of torture.

"I'm sorry," she pauses. "A Spanish student who's just arrived in New York gave me a message from one of the feminists who had been questioned by the police. She wanted us to know that the police have inquired about Ann-Jo and me—"

"My God, Valerie, look at it from the point of view of the police. Juan Goytisolo—after a decade of not being in Madrid—suddenly shows up at the Wellington, accompanied by a left-wing journalist. We both have connections with Ruedo Ibérico, which one week later publishes *Operation Ogro.* Meanwhile you are hopping around the Spanish peninsula, meeting Eva, who then is found with a cache of *Operation Ogro.* If I were the police, *I* would be suspicious."

"But Ann-Jo and I had never heard of *Operation Ogro*—we're only American feminists."

"And Juan and I only intended to visit the Loire country," I add, suddenly tired. "Tell Ann-Jo to cool it."

I promise we will try to help Eva, but after Valerie leaves the Madison and I come back home, I get scared. The Franco regime is lurching to an end. There are, each month, more arrests, more possibilities of death sentences. My impulse is to telephone friends in Spain, but a crisis is precisely the wrong moment for that.

Instead, I telephone Pepe Martínez in Paris. He tells me that the Spanish government has persuaded the French to ban the sale of the Spanish edition of *Operation Ogro*. Meanwhile, Editions du Seuil has been allowed to bring out a French edition, and the Mexicans are publishing a pirated version.

I level with Pepe and tell him that Juan and I had both registered at the Wellington and that during the same month two American feminists, giving our names as introductions, had interviewed Eva and other feminists.

"You and Juan went to Madrid? Together?"

He makes it sound like the most unexpected occurrence in the world. "To the Wellington?"

"Just to see Franco die."

"Just to see Franco die," Pepe sighs. Then, not knowing what else to say, he hangs up.

13

The following week Roger Jellinek, at Quadrangle, telephones me about *Operation Ogro*. I am beginning to feel *Ogro*-haunted! They want to do an American adaptation. Am I interested?

I dislike boutique terrorism and cheapo political thrills, I loathe airplane hijackers, and I am not enamored of the Third World. I pace the apartment, gazing through the park window. The repression of the Basques by Franco and the Civil Guard had been brutal; there was a constant cycle of attack, resistance, torture, and murder. I don't believe in violence—yet suppose I had been a teenager in Nazi Germany and had had the chance to get rid of Hitler?

What Paco, his friends, and I did in the late forties fell more in the category of conventional resistance. We never had arms. But we treaded a fine line, even then. At that time we had known other young Anarchists who had engaged in more violent acts. We had talked, argued, and been considered *"constructivistas"* (another word for that pale category *reformers*). And yet I profoundly understood why, in the late forties, some of those marginal lost young Spaniards I met had resorted to more violent means. One terrorist had a crush on me. His name was Jesús, and he claimed to have killed known torturers. It was typical of me to have gotten an idealistic terrorist to moon about me, naïvely perceiving me as sweet and douce, while, briskly, I gave my real allegiance to the smartest intellectual on the block.

Paco believed in the force of the written word. But my pal Jesús didn't envision a future in which books were to give him a concrete place in the world. He was the only terrorist I have known. Paco remarked that an American could prove himself by becoming President, but a Spaniard was faced with a choice: To kill or not to kill Franco, and this act determined one's manhood. I remember the heated dialogues: were Paco and his friends cowards not to have made an attempt on Franco's life? That was a big theme back in Paris in the late forties. In the end, it seemed an impossible feat; even if Franco could have been killed, only chaos would come from it. But it plagued self-respecting Spanish males that so few attempts had been made.

My ambivalence toward the acts of extremism remains. I disapprove of terrorism, and yet I feel the book deserves a chance. More urgent, there was the personal business.

I had walked away from many of the world's well-publicized nightmares, but I was never quite able to unlatch myself from the Basque thing. Was it there but for the grace of God go I, or go Paco? Had we been caught smuggling people out of prison in '48, would we have been the terrorists tortured? Or was it that when the Franco police sought to arrest Paco Benet and his Basque mother sought help among the Basque nationalists, they had smuggled Paco out of San Sebastian, thrown him onto the floor of a fishing boat, and quickly motored him to France, while the police shot at the boat? In '48 I had been very grateful to the Basques. They had helped us.

We are bound by that hidden list of events we carry in our heads—the tropes that *didn't* happen more than the obvious visible events in our lives. When I was twenty-one years old, I aborted my first pregnancy at the end of the fourth month. Oh, Paco and I had had quite a list of all the things this future child would never suffer: no fathers killed in the Civil War, no parental broken marriages, no war, no cruelty, but perfect love, the perfect parents, total happiness, and security. We had both wanted so much, and we were so young, and so afraid of bringing more misery into the world, we agreed to abort that child. You can't breed babies and get signed guarantees warding off future pain.

But I didn't know that, until later, when I had my daughters.

(In Cambrai, at night, Juan said to me it was his fault his wife had had an abortion. "Takes two," I reply. "Maybe she, also, was afraid." And I tell him about mine. He looks at me. "Sometimes a man makes a mistake.")

I have never talked about that abortion to my Spanish friends before. Maybe I know unborn babies are not such ephemeral goods in a town like Madrid. But back in 1970—during the Burgos trials, which took up an entire fall and went on through Christmas, until the Pope asked for pardons of the death sentence as part of the New Year, I was struck by my own vulnerabilities. I couldn't look or hear about the stories of the tortures of those Basque students. Did I think then that one of those tortured students could have been born of my flesh? I was impelled—almost neurotically—to devote great amounts of time to petitions, pickets against the ghoulish trial.

A few days later I telephone Roger and tell him I will do the book, and he promises to help me help the feminists in their efforts to keep Eva Forest Sastre alive.

14

The next morning in my living room I start to sift through twenty-five years of newspaper clippings, private diaries, letters, and scraps of paper on Spain, and my ongoing political journal. Because of *Ogro* I am beginning to refocus on Spanish clandestine politics. The ETA claims, in their book, that the Communists tried to form a pact with them during the period of the Burgos trials. After the ETA refused to join with them, the Party began a publicity campaign against them, suggesting that Carrero's assassination had been a CIA operation. Their account tallies with some notes I made in the early 1970s.

POLITICAL JOURNAL

Madrid: October 1971
(ten months after Burgos trials)
Go with European journalist to Carabanchel (working-class district of Madrid) to visit female relatives of imprisoned trade unionists, the Workers Commissions. We meet in an apartment of Marcelino Comacho's wife or sister. (They don't indicate to whom the place belongs.) A third woman, María Sandóval, is helping Josefina Comacho organize leaflets to be distributed to women living in their district. They refer to their imprisoned men as the "Carabanchel 10." (Carabanchel is also the name of a Madrid prison.) When I ask María how come she is so open about mentioning her Communist affiliation, she says, as her husband, José Sandóval, has already been found guilty of being a Communist, she isn't giving us secret information.

María, good-looking, sharp, savvy, doesn't strike me as being working-class. When I ask her about her origins, she vaguely answers that her husband had done some journalism.

The more I listen to her and Josefina, the more I become convinced that the Workers Commissions are now being completely dominated by the Communist Party. (When they were originally formed, in the early 1960s, many of us had hoped that the formation of this new illegal trade union could eventually solve the traditional problems of Spanish trade unions, which have been split into huge warring factions.)

When Franco dies, if the PC has trouble surfacing, they could work through the Workers Commissions. The *Communist* label is a terrible problem for a party.

Crucial points:

Santiago Carrillo, its chief, has split PC in two. His anti-Soviet bloc is the more powerful wing. Says he wants no more Russian adventurers.

and:

Spanish Catholic Church has just made an official declaration separating themselves from the regime. They, too, want no further political embroilments such as the Civil War.

As the Communists and the Church are both saying *mea culpa* about the Civil War (and there exists a new Spanish middle class), Spain appears to be headed toward a peaceful transition. Should happen because it is in the majority interest: no one important needs a war.

But when I ask Josefina and María what they think of the split inside the PC, they become silent. Carrillo decides on such matters in Paris. Inside Spain, the Party bureaucrats are forced to operate in a vacuum. As I sense that they are unsure of what the new Party line is meant to be, and are embarrassed at being at odds with Russia, I change the subject.

The reason I am meeting with them is that they need international publicity on the stalled trials of the Carabanchel 10. The women have an askew, romantic view of the American public. They don't visualize the small space given to foreign countries in our press. Josefina proudly tells me about a visit they made to the American Embassy to claim solidarity with Angela Davis. (Spain's having an Angela love-in; slews of female babies are named after her.)

"Do you also consider yourself a feminist?" I ask María.

The Swiss journalist says it is awful for me to ask María feminist questions, her man's been so long in prison. But María brushes aside his protests. "No," she says, "I'll fight for our men while they are in prison, but when they get out, if necessary, I'll fight against them."

Josefina agrees. "We women are entitled to what's due us."

María stares pointedly at the Swiss journalist, by her gestures emphasizing her ripe womanhood. "José's been a long time in prison, and I've been faithful. Had the situation been reversed, I don't think our men would have stood by us to the degree we have them."

Considering how the Communists hate revolutionary movements, the women strike me as oddly pro-Basque; they keep referring to them as "our poor boys from the ETA."

"But you don't approve of revolutionary movements?"

"No."

"So?"

"The ETA is different, we are united—the same thing. Against Franco."

The women here are on unsure ground. I am skeptical of their mention of a "pact" with the ETA. During the 1960s the Communists always were mumbling about their Pact for Liberty, which was one of those numbers meant to include everyone. The problem of the Communists is that despite their efforts to expand their base, the Basques have been more effective in their resistance. Traditionally, before the growth of the ETA (during the 1960s), Basques belonged to the Basque Nationalist Party or were Socialists. The Basque provinces have been difficult for the Communists to penetrate.

María boasts to me of her contacts among well-placed Franco officials. One of her friends, the son of the aviation minister, has tried to get her husband released.

Madrid: October 1971
(one week later)
Being back in Madrid, interviewing the Opposition, gives me a chance to assess the extent that the December 1970 Burgos trials have been a true watershed for the Opposition. In a country lacking legal parties, trade unions, and elections, the tangible battleground for the Opposition has been the organizing and radicalizing of factory workers. Strikes and university protests are the two areas in which the modern Opposition can demonstrate its real existence. From the end of the Civil War through the mid-fifties, Spain had an underground. The next phase was clandestine opposition. Now the tip of the iceberg is showing, and the people I meet are operating within a semiclandestine mode.

Burgos was decisive. Although the courts presumably were trying fifteen members of ETA for their involvement in the murdering of a policeman in the Basque country, the real issue was the idea of ETA, and of open, strong opposition to the Franco regime.

For the first time in a Spanish political trial, the regime's tactics had backfired. The public image of young men and women, students and priests and workers, handcuffed, with plugs in their ears, at times blindfolded, obviously having been tortured, inflamed Europe. The international protest against the medieval "double death" sentences was enormous. The Burgos trials had the effect of uniting the Opposition. (The Spanish left has always been traumatized by internal clashes, which contributed to the defeat of the Spanish Republic during the Civil War.) Unexpectedly, the right has begun to show cracks in what was assumed to be a monolithic regime; the trial split them into doves and hawks. The young lawyers for the Opposition took advantage of the situation, and they were able to put the government on the defensive. The regime suddenly seemed uncertain of itself. The death sentences could not be carried out.

I stop reading my old diary and walk restlessly through the apartment. *You wrote the word "watershed" without realizing, yes, that's what it has been. You are witnessing an end of an era. The Portuguese coup was in April, the Greek dictatorship fell this summer. Perhaps that assassination of Franco's successor by those four young Basques will mean another end of things. His regime, the last of the Fascist dictatorships that dominated Europe during the 1930s, really was destabilized by Carrero's death. And, after all, Franco still is dying . . .*

Later in the week Juan telephones me from Paris. There is a mail strike in France which may turn into one of those general strikes that they have now and then. He is delighted to hear that I will have to do some more research in Europe for the American adaptation of *Ogro*. Which means Paris again. The threatened general strike, *Ogro*—our lives have acquired a sudden wonderful urgency. Even the badness of weather, when I finally do fly into Paris, in November, seems to us another sign or cause for our heightened happiness.

15

As soon as I get over jet lag, Juan, two Basques from Mugalde publishing house in Hendaye, and I meet in the office of the agent who acquired the book from Seuil and Mugalde for Quadrangle. The agent means to be jovial, and he offers Pedro and Javier instant coffee in waxed cups to make them feel at home. We have no real reason for the meeting. The man, to pass the time, makes an odd suggestion. He wants to telex Madrid officials that I might be going there to research *Ogro*.

Juan nervously taps the desk with his writing hand. "No, no. I wouldn't send such a message to Spain. ETA is *clandestine*."

Pedro's gaze is firmly sullen, an urban guerrilla publisher ill at ease with an American book-rights man. Later, while we walk over to the Café de la Paix, Pedro asks me if he is CIA. I say I don't think so, just a guy earning a living.

"I don't like him," Pedro persists; neither Juan nor I ask what he means. The thickness I felt in my chest on arriving has grown worse.

The sun doesn't come out during the entire time I am in France. I feel sick, but I go ahead with my plan to meet representatives of the ETA. And Juan comes with me.

While we are drinking soda pop at the café, Pedro and Javier attempt to act out parts of *Ogro* I need to visualize more clearly. I get no answers when I ask how Txabi, Jons, and Mikel (the heroes of *Ogro*) escaped from Spain. All they concede is that within twenty-four hours the entire group was in France. I have no indication whether Pedro or Javier had been part of the group; Juan and I speculate: are they the ones? I never learn their real names, but their ages are right. But I never find out for sure. A writer reporting on underground activity rarely does find out precise details. Which is a real problem. How much concrete proof does one need before writing on torture, clandestine political movements?

Javier wants me, in the next weeks, to visit the ETA headquarters in Hendaye and meet with more of their members. "Don't worry, we'll find you a French doctor, my cousin has asthma ..." Pedro urges.

He tells me he knows about asthma; a relative has obtained special medicine from England. Have I heard of the new English cure? Javier again mentions Baader Meinhof; he asks me why two groups so different in outlook are lumped together in the press. "Will getting *Ogro* in print in English help make things clear?"

"By adding new material, the book will be more your own," Pedro points out, handing over to me the tapes they have brought to the agent's office. "Writers like that."

"Did you finish university?" I ask, putting the tapes in my purse.

A woman with hair the color of shiny eggplant is listening to our conversation; she stares at the three men, hoping for a pickup; suggestively she caresses her rabbit-fur jacket.

"I'll finish my engineering degree when the political situation improves," Pedro answers flatly; then he quickly looks at Juan with a gaze of profound admiration. He seems relieved to locate a Spaniard who is identified as being on the left and isn't a failure.

Our plan is to go to Amsterdam for the weekend; then on Monday I will go to Hendaye, where the Basque publishing house Mugalde is based. But the dampness has gotten into my lungs, and my asthma gets worse.

I have scared Ahmed by getting that sick. I spend the next few days in the rue au Maire apartment mostly sleeping. Meanwhile, in the living room Juan alternates Judy Collins records with the boring, nasal wail of Om-Kalsoum, the great Egyptian Mama singer. In a deep-throated voice she chants her love song, "Robaiat Alkhayam"; Juan loves her greatness. Her passionate rhythms drown out the damp Paris walk-up in guttural sounds of romantic monotony. Probably poor Egyptians, overpaying for a package of Cleopatras in the bars of Cairo, find her powerful voice reassuring, familiar, and free. Mama's voice as the Egyptians lose their military battles and the country slips into deeper poverty; oh, mighty Om-Kalsoum!

The sicker I become, the more Ahmed begins to loathe me. "She is dying," Ahmed moans. "A Jewish woman dying in this apartment—*vite, vite,* get her out of here; *écoute Juan, tu es fou,* the police will say an Arab from Casa killed a Jewish woman. If she dies I spend the rest of my life in prison."

Juan warns me not to mention the word "asthma," only admit to flu. Ahmed has irrational superstitions. Once, according to Juan, Zineb became ill and Ahmed, convinced she had been invaded by bad spirits, took her to a farm where he boarded her until the evil spirit left her body. Ahmed understands concrete illnesses—an infected foot, the measles—but asthma is not on his list. It echoes for him Zineb's strange "warring spirits in the body."

The three of us, that evening, dine in a small Indochinese restaurant. My chest still feels in a vise. The weather hasn't improved, the intense humidity persists. When we are outside the rue au Maire apartment, Ahmed has a less claustrophobic reaction to my illness. He realizes if I die outdoors the French won't arrest him. It is hard for Juan to fully comprehend Ahmed's fears. Although he adores him, his passion never includes empathy.

In an attempt to make amends for his rotten behavior while I was sick, Ahmed offers to drive me next week to Hendaye.

"You'll be my Arab-Basque connection?" I laugh.

We plan to take a first-class train to Amsterdam. I am still tired, but after a weekend in Holland, I will be fit to visit the ETA. The next morning we drive in Ahmed's car to the Gare de Lyon in plenty of time for him to find a good parking space.

We pick up our tickets and walk along the outside track. The high domed turn-of-the-century station smells of kiosk, damp weather, dusty concrete, and cheap croissants. We act like children on a first Pullman trip, excited at the thought of eating in a fancy dining car, of having bought first-class tickets. Ahmed, tall, athletic, races ahead.

Juan and I walk more slowly; we talk about the canals of Amsterdam, the ETA stationed on the French border of Spain. Meanwhile, Ahmed has located our seats. Vaguely I notice him banging on the door of the train compartment. But I wait on the platform for Juan to finish describing a passage he has just written, part of a new novel. Suddenly all Ahmed's suppressed anger at me for having replaced him in Juan's affections explodes. He takes the easy way and explodes at me. *"Espèce de Juive,"* he screams. *"Sale Juive, sale Juive, sale espèce de Juive pourrie et malade. Tu es malade dans ta tête."* He is choleric with rage.

Stunned, I turn to Juan. Juan fails to react. I feel my face redden. Suddenly, overcome with ancient memory, Juan and Ahmed vanish from my consciousness. I don't get angry. Instead, both men, for me, cease to exist.

Forgetting his insults, Ahmed screams at me, "Hurry, the train is pulling out."

I point my luggage *shlepper* back in the direction of SORTIE and rapidly walk toward the exit, leaving Juan, paralyzed, standing alone on the train track. Ahmed yells, "Wait—wait for me." He jumps from the moving train, I hear the *clunk* of his suitcase falling on the cement platform.

Ahmed hollers that I have loused up his weekend; if Juan was smart he would throw away such a *femme malade.* I keep walking. Ahmed screams about his relatives in Rotterdam; he threatens to drive his car to Holland alone. "Like a normal man—what kind of a person are you," he screams. "Why don't you answer me? You are a deaf-mute, *une femme froide!"* I ignore him. "Who is this *princesse journaliste,* this rude bitch who makes no reply?" I turn on my heel. Outside on the curb I hail a taxi; I tell him the Hôtel Montalembert. Then Juan yells at me, "Stay right here until Ahmed drives back with the car." Ignoring him, I motion the driver to get moving. But Juan opens the door and jumps into the seat next to me; when Juan sees Ahmed drive by us, in his car, he asks my driver to stay abreast of him.

The rain pours down; meanwhile, Juan opens the window. "We are going to the Montalembert—meet me there," Juan yells at Ahmed.

The traffic is snarled at the Place de la Concorde. I can see through the window by the mottled color of his skin that Ahmed's rage at me has grown. The three of us had wanted to be on the train to Amsterdam; instead, we are driving in two separate cars through Paris in a heavy November rain. *"C'est ta faute,"* Ahmed screams at me. *"Tu es une mauvaise femme—Juan devient stupide depuis qu'il t'a connue . . .*

Pourquoi vous n'avez pas répondu?" he demands, in his frustration mixing *tu* and *vous; "Que je suis un sale Arabe? Alors, qu'est-ce que j'ai dit? Sale Juive, qu'est-ce que ça veut dire? Amchi falek!"*

Our French driver, disliking Juan's instructions to drive parallel to Ahmed, overhearing the yelling, mutters, *"Paris, pauvre Paris . . . des Arabes, des Israélites, alors ces gens là, ils achètent toute la France . . ."* The driver turns toward me; he thinks we are arguing about *"la guerre en Israël."* He growls that it is the fault of the United States, which needs to sell airplanes and war equipment to both sides: *"Pauvre France, entre deux géants—La Russie, L'Amérique."*

Juan tries to appease Ahmed. When we turn the corner to rue Montalembert, I ready myself and rapidly jump out of the taxi with my *shlepper* and suitcase. I yell back at Juan, *"Tu m'emmerdes!"*

Juan looks scared. I sense he is perversely drawn to whomever appears angrier, which means Ahmed. "I'll drive with him to Rotterdam—he'll calm down when he sees his family," Juan mutters hurriedly.

I stare at him. The doorman at the Montalembert reaches for my luggage. Juan misses the point. Angrily I repeat, *"Tu m'emmerdes!"*

Juan gazes helplessly at me. "I'll telephone you from Holland." I shrug and walk into the hotel.

It rains all of Thursday night. I am in a terrible funk and have a lonely meal, a piece of turbot which I fiddle with in the hotel dining room. I hate being alone in Paris. I am one of those easily intimidated people who, if forced to eat solo, evades embarrassment by intently devouring *Le Monde,* the *Herald Tribune* or the *Nouvel Observateur.* The waiter recognizes me; it is a hotel I have stayed in many times. He ceremoniously repeats my name, "Madame *Solomon.*"

When I pass by the desk, the desk clerk glances knowingly; the hotel is small, the comings and goings of customers are sharply observed. This is the first evening I am actually living in the hotel.

He notes the obvious. *"Madame Solomon, vous ne sortez pas ce soir?"*

"Non."

"Il pleut."

"Oui, il pleut."

I take the heavy metal key for my room from the desk clerk and I slam shut the metal door of the old-fashioned grillwork elevator. Upstairs, I dread the small room. I have no radio, no television set; there is nothing to do but to go to bed or resort my clothes or make notes on the Basque situation. I telephone Clancy and Margaret in London.

"So, what is it?" he says. "You sound disconnected—everything going all right with that new bloke—that Spaniard?"

"Oh yes, fine," I answer in a small voice.

"Which means terrible—where is he?"

"Oh, just off—for a few days." My voice trails. Without going into detail, I abruptly change the subject. "I think the French are anti-Semitic."

"Well, yes."

I tried to imagine how Clancy or Jakov Lind, Jewish men I have known, would have reacted at the Gare de Lyon. Hit Ahmed? I am dazed at Juan's failure to react. Juan has a Jewish wife; no, not an anti-Semite. I am diffuse, my anger at Ahmed chokes; something happened to me the moment I turned to Juan, and instead of reacting, he became paralyzed.

"It's raining in Paris, Clancy."

"Well, no one should be forced to be alone in Paris when the weather is bad. Christ, I remember how godawful being alone in that city was when I was young. If your plans get mixed up, do what you have to in Paris and clear out. Don't overstay, if the bloke doesn't shape up, visit us in London, or get on a plane and go home—don't try to juggle too many different things. You aren't on your home base—"

"Maybe I won't stay too much longer—it really is raining very hard in this city." Then I hang up. I walk into the bathroom, fill the tub with hot water, and soak. It is only ten at night. After toweling myself dry and making a ritual of brushing my teeth, my hair, I feel overwhelmed by the sadness of the hotel room. I deliberately force myself to dawdle over nonessential details in order to use the empty space of a long evening. I put on my bathrobe, crawl into bed, and write forty postcards home. My friends later remark I am a thoughtful traveler.

At eleven the next morning I go straight to Ruedo Ibérico. During the 1960s (balmy days for the left), Ruedo Ibérico had flourished. Pepe Martínez and his friend Marianne Bruëll were able to move the plant from the shabby old-fashioned headquarters on rue Aubriot, near the old Jewish section, right into the heart of the Latin Quarter. The new publishing house is light and modern. It has the affluent look that intelligent left-wing Europe got during the 1960s. Ruedo is, for Spanish Opposition, their Paris drop. Many Spanish-speaking students gather at the bookstore. In the sixties and early seventies I spent a lot of time at Ruedo. They had the most complete library and were the best source on political Spain. Also, they are my friends.

Marianne looks good. Oval-faced, regular-boned, she moves gracefully; her topaz ring catches the light she flutters her hand at Calvo Serer. The two of them are finishing a conversation when I walk into the bookstore.

Rafael Calvo Serer had been Prince Juan Carlos's tutor and an adviser to the prince's exiled father, El Conde de Barcelona, Don Juan. He is a member of the liberal left wing of the strange lay Catholic organization, the Opus Dei. He is an odd man who seems to dart like a bat into dark, unexplored political corridors. Calvo Serer likes to be thought of as an *éminence grise,* the man who with Carrillo in the summer of 1974 had created the Junta Democrático, the new umbrella organization of the Opposition. The Communist Party and Opus Dei— what a wacky combine! Because Calvo makes frequent transatlantic trips, visiting senators in Washington, holding hurried lunches at the University Club in Manhattan, he has become a mystery man "waiting in the wings." Several years later, just after Franco's death when Juan Carlos de Bourbón does become king, neither he nor the Communist Party would need Rafael Calvo.

On the other hand, nobody in 1974 considers Xavier Domingo to be a man waiting in the wings for a rendezvous with destiny. Xavier walks in, in his raunchy Fidel Castro fatigues, and Marianne instantly reacts like *Swiss Miss.* She rushes into Pepe's office, pulling me in with her. "Let's wait here until he leaves," she whispers.

Meanwhile, Xavier leafs through the new collection of books on the display table. When I walk out to greet him, the smell of Gauloises emanates from his clothes.

As Ruedo now has to ready itself for the big push back home (plans are already in the works for Ruedo's being brought to Spain as soon as the big event, Franco's death, takes place), the time is over for Marianne to behave like an elegant Swiss fräulein adrift in a sea of Spanish revolutionary rape artists. Still, Xavier encourages this view of himself. He always seems to me a shy man who *pretends* to be a bottom pincher—"Come up to my room and see the Seine." In the 1950s, when Xavier first arrived in Paris, he was interviewed by the French press as being an example of the "exiled Spanish writer." Had he escaped to France to avoid political persecution? "No," he replied, "I came to Paris for ze fucking of ze Frenchwo-men."

"Ola, Bárbarita," Xavier greets me.

"Gee, Xavier, I loved your wacky novels, *El Dinero del Opus Es Nuestro* and the *Viuda Andaluza.*"

He grins, his hands in the pockets of his fatigues. *"Es verdad?* Do you think in America they'll want to read them?"

No one—Xavier least of all—knew he is the Man Who Is Waiting in the Wings—but after Franco's death and his return, Xavier becomes a combination of Art Buchwald and Tom Wicker. In this metamorphosis he would blossom as top journalist for *Cambio 16* (a Spanish-type *Newsweek*).

After Xavier leaves Ruedo, I take a pile of *Cuadernos de Ruedo Ibérico* (the political journal published by the house), and sitting in Pepe Martínez's deserted office, I soberly read them. My hands feel clammy, the salt smell of anxiety rises from my body. Well, what about the Jewish thing? Most of us here have known one another over a quarter of a century. We date back to the late 1940s. Oh, those enduring, painful friendships of late adolescence, when love was equal to politics and to have soul was to have passed through the gates of paradise!

All these years I have accepted Ruedo's existence, I dutifully (and without conflict) worried about the fate of the Catalans, the Basques, the Socialists, Anarchists, and Communists. Weren't Jews and Spaniards, all of us, the victims of Hitler and Fascism? Now, in 1974, I wonder: What are my rights? Can I suddenly switch gear, complain to Franco's victims: So what about us? Do you understand our troubles? I am awkward at playing victim, but Ahmed's rage and Juan's acquiescence are too much. The French press is becoming outrageous. I bite my lip. I am a lousy pleader for my own cause. I leaf through various issues, finding only one pro-Arab piece, written by a Jew.

I get this awful flash into the future—me meekly saying to my friends, Remember old times, when I helped you, couldn't you *do* a little something for Israel; remember when Franco and Hitler—

But the left wants purity, not tit-for-tat. They would answer, *"Bárbarita,* you did what you did against Franco because you *believed* Franco was evil. How can you expect us to tolerate Israel when we *know* it is in the wrong?"

You reported the plight of the Spaniards in American periodicals; why, all those years, not one article on the Jewish plight in Ruedo? You were a child of the 1950s, the '60s, anti-Semitism assumed a thing of the past, a sin of the ultra-right. I try to see the situation clearly. Would Pepe—now, in 1974—print a piece sympathetic to Israel in *Ruedo?*

The French left-wing press reports: *Les Israélites sont des racistes.* We are Nazis, *racistes;* we harp on the six million, we count only the Jewish dead. Juan has a Jewish wife, but he doesn't react when Ahmed mouths insults. Ahmed I comprehend. Spit upon by the French, in his fury he repeats the garbage he has picked up in Casablanca street fights. No, I don't mind Ahmed. Don't even consider him anti-Semitic. But the words he used *in a European context* are unsayable. In the Gare de Lyon, in Paris, those words are not to be tolerated. It is Juan, with his intelligence, his moral stance, whom I mind, because he is the *European* who fails to react to the unsayable. Yet Juan urges *me* to understand, *me* to be tolerant of Ahmed's ignorant, inchoate rage.

I think back to 1971, Madrid. I had interviewed a lawyer for imprisoned Communists. He was, for me, used to the "old left," a new breed. Rich, Catholic, a former Fascist. He spoke of "losing faith" in Franco. He gave me leaflets. After I had read several of the articles, I remarked that I was surprised there was so much emphasis on the Palestinian plight, so little on Franco. The lawyer smiled, "It must be very difficult for you being Jewish," he said. "You must have a terrible conscience concerning the Arabs."

I rejoined, frosty, "Here I am in Spain, risking possible arrest to write on political prisoners—why should I have a bad conscience?"

But did you pay attention to that lawyer in 1971? You were arrogant. He's provincial, you thought to yourself; the left is getting a new bunch: Dummies. But those converts, ex-Fascists, are mouthing the language of Socialism, and are creating a debased left.

Arafat this week is king of New York, of the UN. Would Paco in the Gare de Lyon have remained silent, hearing those words *"sale Juive, sale Juive?"* He's dead, you'll never have that answer. And Pallach, your daddy figure on the left, POUM hero whom you and Paco worshipped?

When we lost Nicolás and Manolo in the Pyrénées, we followed Paco's instructions to find his friend Pallach. The Catalan Socialists in Perpignan sent us to Collioure. He was dancing sardanas with Teresa in the square. Summer. August. I saw them both, I saw the Mediterranean. "We've lost Nicolás and Manolo," I said. "I'll find them," he answered. Brittle blue sea, the smell of grass sweating in the sun. That was the summer (she told me later) he fell in love with Teresa.

They became your substitute parents in Paris. Could Pallach be among those who now call the Jews Hitler? The smells of my anxiety rise in my armpits, making odors in the underarms of my gray wool sweater.

Probably there are no Jews connected with Ruedo. Just you, giving sisterly affection. Why didn't you recognize, as Ruedo was being sent back into Spain to give informed news of the world, that Israel was part of the outside weather? You were dumb, you wrote about being Jewish for *Commentary* magazine, which didn't need to be informed of your stray thoughts, and with the Latin left, which you perceived as victims doing big time in the world's tragedies, you remained silent. Klutz, you should have shut up for *Commentary* and written for Ruedo. I argue with myself, But did you want to have the soul of a propagandist? A "me" against "them"?

"*Bárbara—qué haces aquí?*"

Pepe comes up behind me. I am startled, my face flushes; I am embarrassed, caught at my anxious detective work, reading years of *Cuadernos*, the shaky Jewish soul at work.

He walks in front of me, gray-haired, distinguished, the handsome Roman profile still steady. His expression beneath his heavy brown-rimmed glasses appears perplexed.

"*Ah—Pepe,*" I reply, absentminded, "*uh . . . comment vas-tu?*"

He curtly observes it is odd of me to reply in French.

"Oh, was I speaking French?" I repeat nervously. "Oh, well, in Paris it is easy to slip into French . . ." But after that I am careful to talk with Pepe exclusively in Spanish.

"*Qué te pasa, mujer?*" Pepe is intuitive about my moods, my silences. After a quarter of a century we are hostage to mutual memory.

"*Pues—nada.*" *Say something. Have coffee, or go with him to the Chinese restaurant on Sommerard, just the two of you and talk.* TALK.

"You are in Paris a week—you hardly call your friends . . ." Pepe stares at me. "Are you looking for the articles Juan Goytisolo has written for *Cuadernos?*"

I am startled. Pepe thinks I am so in love with Juan I am searching for his critical pieces!

(*Pepe has never read what you have written about your childhood, all your work is in English. Talk to him. Tell him how it was, your being Jewish.*) *In your family none of the nostalgia for Yiddishkeit, or easy access to the Jewish religion, food, mamas. Remind him, "Pepe, I am Jewish."*

All my daughters' relatives are mixed, both Harold's family and my own have gone in for eighty percent assimilation. Oh, the new left would have approved of my father! He loathed Zionism, thought Israel a mistake, had no use for religion. Some successful Jews of his generation tried to pass themselves off as Protestants. But that wasn't his style; he told us we were Jews. But not much on that subject. And, oh, yes, we had a sort of Passover ceremony. A small vestigial memory, a backward nod to the past. Mickey and I have never had a conversation about us being Jews; it just has never come up.

I never knew, as a child, about "we" and "they." My family never used words like "goy." How could I have felt *they?* Take Marte, who considers herself my daughters' grandmother and my mother. Lutheran German Marte; she scrubbed my hair with chamomile tea, and wept, when she got news from Germany after the war that her boyfriend in the SS had been reported missing. After that, all she had was Mickey and me. I was not so crazy as not to recognize the mama love Marte gave me. But when I returned to New York from Europe, after living in Germany with Paco, and I said to Marte and my parents, At seventeen I saw Dachau, I was there, I saw it all, three years after the crematoriums were shut, before the places got fixed over for the tourist trade, my mother, my father, made no reply. Oh, they were against six million dead. It was their distant relatives in Europe who got polished off; our family is a smaller number now, and made up of few Jews. Marte also made no reply. My father said we were a civilized family, and civilized people don't blame a nation of individuals for its maniacs. But all I wanted was that Marte would say something. Just, "I'm sorry" or, "It never should have happened." Marte said nothing, she just kept on loving me, I was her daughter. And because I was trained to be civilized, I gave her the sympathy she wanted for her dead boyfriend in the SS. But, Marte, who asked you to go back to Germany in the thirties and pick up an SS type? Why did I have to be burdened with such rotten, civilized understanding? Why couldn't I be like some vulgar Miami Beach lady, with too many diamonds on her fingers, who shrieks, Oy oy oy, they killed my family? Why did our relatives have to disappear, shot, burned up, turned into lampshades and soap bars, dumped, and afterward such silence? Why couldn't my anger be recognized, legitimized? Bunny, my father said, don't be a blamer.

So I became Jewish. My married name, Solomon, is very Jewish compared to the original Probst. Harold, after a week of feverish new love, coupling together in his East Ninth Street skylight walk-up, took me to Orchard Street. "You're savvy about existentialism," he said, "but your life's been lacking in a solid pickle." He bought a gallon jar from the Rumanian pickle works, and three months later we married. In my twenties, I read Bellow and New York urban Jewish writers, and my writing rhythms aped their slang. I learned words like *"shmuck," "shmatte,"* and *"gar nisht helfen."* I said my mother was my mother, and Marte the fräulein.

Buried was the formal, colorless Protestant language of my childhood. I learned Yiddish argot as I learned French and Spanish. And Marte stayed on, my fräulein. Until the night Harold died. We had come in for Christmas from California and were visiting my parents. We never went back. That New Year's Eve, the winter of '67, he was taken to Mount Sinai Hospital because of a heart attack. Fourteen days later, at four in the morning, the doctor telephoned. Bunny, my father called from his room (he knew), the doctor needs to talk to you. I guessed, too, I took the call in the guest room, and afterward stayed in there alone. I was very quiet. Then, after I had collected myself, I told my daughters the news. I told them in a way that would make them cry; I was conscious of that. Oh, I was cool that first day. I made the arrangements for the white chapel at Campbell's on Eighty-fifth Street; I ordered banks of flowers to be put on the casket. In my mind, I planned a funeral that would be right for young daughters. Somebody at the *Times* arranged a lengthy obit with a picture; Harvard classmates would do eulogies. Then Mickey, now Mark, spoke quietly to the rabbi and pointed out all that was needed was that Jewish prayer at the end, the man was to make no extra remarks. Harvard would do the talking.

I was silent and cool; the memory nodes inside my skull cracked. I combed my hair, and instantly forgot I had ever had a husband. *Tabula rasa.* Mark sent for Marte to come back to America. She had been vacationing with nieces and nephews in East Germany, Magdeburg; that's up in the north of Germany. She walked into the apartment vestibule, her suitcases deposited by the elevator man at her frail knees. She was bent over; she was wearing her dark-blue wool winter coat and her good gold lapel pin. "What happened? Harold, oh, my God!"

Then I stared at her; the inner controls broke. "Marte, Marte, Marte." I heard my voice rise in a terrible shriek. I kept screaming, and suddenly, with a terrible force, I threw myself toward her. No matter how hard I tried, coolly, intellectually, to arrange the allegiances of my heart, in crisis, I turned to Marte.

Speak to Pepe. As a Jew I am not as qualified as most, I am a stranger to Israel, I do not hate the Palestinians, but let me speak about Europe. I have this hunch that nothing will work out if Europe abandons Israel. It is Europe, not the Arab countries, that breaks the heart of Jews. I cannot give you Marxist information, I cannot write dialectic. When I became involved in matters Spanish, I never took a vow to speak as a Marxist, so, you see, I am not even an ex-Marxist. I was your friend, an observer of Spanish fate long after Orwell was dead. I can't give exact information about territorial rights, but let me tell you about Jews. In Europe, until the twentieth century, we were not permitted in many regions to own land. Forget our biblical claim to Palestine, I don't think like that. But until Israel, we owned no land, and we were not farmers. Just marginal. Europeans feel we have outworn our welcome as twentieth-century victims of tragedy; other countries are clamoring at the door. Jews of my generation were taught that we were too passive a people, we didn't do enough battle against the Nazis. Perhaps Israel does too much battle. Perhaps we remember Hitler too much—but is it normal, rational, or fair to expect people within a generation to obliterate from their hearts such genocide? Is that a normal expectation? Arafat is in New York; he wants Israel suspended from UNESCO. I only know that if Europe rejects Israel, it will break Jewish hearts. Jews have no inner protection against being despised by the left. Where are we to go? To the right? The left has taken away from us our identity, our place in the world. Jews have no answer when the left attacks them and names them Hitler. It is Europe that breaks the Jewish heart. Europe has the power, Europe did the damage. Poor Proust, he thought he was French, but he got crushed by the Dreyfus case. *Remembrance of Things Past* is not about sponge cake, but Proust's isolation from French society after he became a Dreyfusard. No Arabs fought in the Spanish Civil War to aid the Republican government. The Arabs, then, were Hitler's friends. But the International Brigades were filled with idealistic young Jewish men; Inez's uncle, from Warsaw, died at Teruel. If I were to bring that up now, the left would say: No tit-for-tat. Jews these days are the imperialists. In 1974, it turns out, the Spanish left inside Spain are Arab lovers and Israel haters. But I am not to notice that; I am not to name such things as anti-Semitism. *Talk, talk!*

Pepe stares at me; he runs his hand through his hair. We go to his favorite café, on the corner of St. Germain near Cluny, and sit down at a small table.

Pepe brings up the ETA. He is worried about my trip to Hendaye.
"The Basques have suffered huge raids from the police; I don't think
more than two hundred militants are left. The ETA is discouraged,
paranoid. And there have been killings among rival factions. The police take photographs of everyone who enters Mugalde publishing
house. Eva got caught that way."

"You want me to go home, then?"

Pepe looks at me. "Well, I don't want to interfere with your personal life . . ."

"No interference. About the ETA"—I try to make my voice neu-
tral—"do you think they are getting support from the PLO?"

The way his nostrils tighten, I know he realizes what is behind my
question. Suddenly I sense he feels awkward with me.

Pepe keeps talking about Mugalde publishing house. "The ultra-
right has bombed it because of *Ogro*."

"Is Ruedo safe?"

He shrugs. "We've lost our shirt on *Ogro*—the Spanish government
has leaned on the French to ban the sale of our edition in France. Anything can happen. We've taken Ruedo's archives on the Resistance
out of rue Latran. For safekeeping."

Pepe's jaw juts out. He's not been back in Spain since he was a kid.

I sense his tension about the next phase, and I am afraid for him.
"Will it be hard?" I ask somewhat foolishly, "to get Ruedo moved
into Spain? Will you install the plant in Madrid or Barcelona?"

Pepe taps his coffee cup and fills it with extra sugar cubes. "Hard?
All of it has been hard, *querida Bárbarita*. We are only a small publishing house. And a small group of independent intellectuals isn't a
vast political party. The Communists and Socialists already have their
guys in Spain. Slicing up the post-Franco pie. They are big business,
we are small-time entrepreneurs."

"Well," I say uncertainly, "everything will all work out."

"I think, Barcelona—"

"If it were up to me, I would pick Madrid—less cliquey."

"That's what Nicolás says."

We stare at each other; then some friends of Pepe's come over and I
say good-bye to him and slowly walk back to the Montalembert.

After several false starts and battles with international telephone oper-
ators, that evening in the Montalembert, I reach Teresa Pallach in

Barcelona. When I abruptly question her on what she and Pallach think of Arafat, Teresa, immediately understanding what I am driving at, says the Spaniards are off the wall in their extreme pro-Arab stance. Her opinion, strongly voiced, reassures me. Some part of my past holds up.

After finishing my conversation with Teresa, I keep going. I telephone Paco and Juan's mother, Doña Teresa, another solid mother figure from my complicated past. I confide my troubles about being Jewish to Doña Teresa. For Doña Teresa, Paco and Juan's friends are still "the boys," not grown men. She, like Teresa Pallach, is unambivalent. "Well, of course the boys aren't thinking clearly; you must explain to them. Write them a letter, and tell them that Israel is your *raza,* why should a woman go against her *raza?* It's not normal."

Next I telephone a friend of Graciela's, Odette Ginsberg, who is flying to America the next morning. I want to be out of France, and I am afraid of being in the airplane alone.

"Can I join you?"

"I am flying an odd route because of a special rate. First to London; then I am taking BA straight to Philadelphia."

"It doesn't matter—I can visit old friends in Jenkintown, let me come with you."

She agrees, but sounds puzzled. I feel relieved. Then I telephone Clancy. I am evasive on detail, but I tell him I am suffering from an overdose of anti-Israeli sentiment; I feel isolated, living in Paris, among the Latin left.

"Look, Barbara, London and the universities in England are thick with the stuff now. But, kid, let me tell you, the old bit about how we lost six million won't wash. We sound awful, like a bunch of punchdrunk klutzes, dragging behind us our suffering history and a gang of indignant rabbis. We've got to improve our act."

"Clancy, are you pro-Arafat?"

"Look, we need updating, more razzmatazz. We Jews have got to think up some other way of talking about ourselves."

"I can't bear it—I'm going home."

"Well, home is one thing, but you're not giving up on your Spanish friends?"

"I just don't know."

"You can't do that, Barb; hell, you were our New York connection, our New York conscience, all those years getting us to sign those endless fucking petitions for God-knows-whom. Now that Franco is dying, you can't cop out. Listen, Barbara, after they bury the old boy, you go back with the rest of your pals and announce your presence, and be who you are—I don't care if forty million Spaniards are pro-Arab. You go back there and be yourself, an independent American, a woman, and a New York mixed-up Jew. Let *them* deal with *you,* don't hand over the show to a bunch of smoothies and ex-Fascists. Christ, Barbara," Clancy insists, "you're our New York connection in Spain. Just take your head and your heart with you, and give us some modest reporting."

"Clancy, you make me sound like a sort of political runner . . . carrying the facts back and forth across the Atlantic."

"Well, aren't you? Aren't I?" he asks.

I am less panicked. I feel *defined* by Clancy, by Teresa Pallach, by Doña Teresa.

When I return to the Montalembert, the desk clerk, his mouth arranged in a smug smile of contentment at my obviously askew plans, hands me my jet reservation back to America via London. Nasal-breathed, he announces to me that a Monsieur Guy-te-seau-lo has been telephoning for me—he is on the way back to Paris from Rotterdam. But I have already geared myself for the return flight, Juan has ceased to exist; Juan and I both have a child's toughness and narcissistic expertise at making people appear and disappear at will. It is a trait neither of us will accept in the other.

POLITICAL JOURNAL

Paris: November 16, 1974

You are an observer, a woman who observes people, politics. What are you witnessing? The decline of Marxism? The growth of Euro-Communism? By the time a phenomenon becomes popular and is *named* in the daily press, it is already disintegrating. Paris, November: Rather than the growth of Euro-Communism, I am seeing the decline of Western European Communism, the death throes of Marxism. China, Russia, and Cuba have failed. There is no ideal country to fuel the dreams of the left. And America, instead of being lethal, is merely half bad. European intellectuals are experiencing a heightened new state of anxiety, their creativity may be slowed down, as Latin countries live by certainties.

POSSIBLE THEMES FOR NOVEL

1974 in Europe. Focus novel with historic backdrop, the end of Marxist ideology, the recognition by European intellectuals of the bankruptcy of their beliefs.
The end of the Franco and Salazar years.
The end of protection of Israel.
Arab world????
Question: If the left, in Europe, is deeply split on the Israel issue (and with some exceptions, those who are dovish toward Israel *tend* to be of Jewish descent, well then, do we have a new situation of the left dividing itself along religious grounds? Isn't this, for Europe, a throwback to the religious wars? Shall we be divided into Jewish Socialists and Christian Socialists? Potentially a dangerous and explosive situation. You have written notes on many "ends"— where are the beginnings?

Marianne and Pepe have twin apartments on the top floor of a turn-of-the-century apartment house on rue Sommerard. Marriage, for Marianne, carries the odor of Geneva, her aging German-speaking mother, *le chocolat blanc de la Suisse.* So Marianne retains her freedom by maintaining her own apartment. In Pepe's place are archives of Ruedo Ibérico and the Spanish Resistance, as well as several leather-bound volumes of photographs of his close friends. He has kept a visual record of all our lives in those books. The dinner parties take place in Marianne's quarters.

Tonight Marianne has prepared for Nicolás, Graciela, myself, and one of the Spaniards who help out at Ruedo, Alfonso Colodrón, a dinner of very pink leg of lamb, carrots, endive salad, cheeses, and fruit. While we busy ourselves setting up the Swedish dining room table, Pepe fusses with the plant growing near the window. Pepe endlessly inspects the beauty of things. In another incarnation, he could have been an architect or perhaps a designer. He always asks me to take off the semiprecious jewelry I am wearing; then he holds up the stones to the light and examines their color. *"Bella"* is one of his favorite words, when he is relaxed and not thinking of politics. I stare out of the window; the Sommerard apartment overlooks the Île St.-Louis, Notre Dame's ass.

Neither Nicolás nor Pepe knows Spain. My fear is, once back there, Ruedo will be seen merely as competition for pre-existing presses. The same Spaniards who court Pepe in Paris might ignore him in Spain.

"Qué estas pensando, Bárbarita?" Pepe asks.

"Nada—qué bella es París desde aquí."

Pepe wants us to look at his book of photographs. There are snaps of Carla, Maria, and Pepe's own daughter, also a Maria, taken in France in 1959.

Graciela laughs. "How lean and healthy Nicolás looked after leaving prison! If Franco had died during the past summer, Nicolás and I could have crossed over from Portugal on a donkey. Just wandered in like two *turistas*." Graciela sees herself as belonging to Bleecker Street, Greenwich Village. But Nicolás will have to make a very formal return to Spain with his father. I don't think she likes that idea.

Marianne serves us the lamb; the talk is different tonight. I get the sense the men are *waiting* for events to happen.

Nicolás turns to me and repeats the request he first made in New York. "Barbara, when I go back, will you be there to welcome me?"

I am silent, then I mutter, "Of course Nicolás." He so permanently connects me with his life—how can I be a shit and say I am pissed off, wounded, alienated at the short shrift the European left is giving Israel? *Franco is dying, and it is all very historic.* I suddenly look up. "I don't like Arafat."

"Arafat?" Marianne repeats.

There is silence. *"Ah, oui,"* she says, and cuts us some of the lamb. The pink, garlic-smelling juices are running. "Barbara, give me your plate."

Pepe gazes out of the window at the pre-winter Paris sky. "Have you heard from Juan?"

"Juan?" It seems centuries instead of a week since I went with Juan to meet with the two Basques.

"Goytisolo."

"No—why?"

"No reason." Pepe pauses. "I brought Max Aub's *Campo francés* for you to read on the plane back to New York." He hesitates. "It was hard on Aub—being an Anarchist during the Civil War and having a double identity. He considered himself Spanish, but his parents were German Jews who moved to Spain in the 1920s."

Pepe and I stare across at each other. I say nothing, then Marianne serves the endive salad.

You have no fantasies about going back to Spain. You've gone regularly to Spain since 1948; how can you feel what Nicolás and Pepe do? The power of their exiled dreams? They can't let go of you. Because you are part of their homecoming scenario. How can they hear you, when in the middle of their frozen dream you suddenly insist on walking around in your own space, in plotzing Jewish trouble on their Spanish return?

As though reading my thoughts, Nicolás says, "Think of it, we were together when we came out of Spain, and now, twenty years later, we will go back together. Extraordinary."

I peel a chilled pear taken from the bowl Marianne has placed on the table. "We aren't *all* going back—in that car were Barbara, who is in New York, Manolo, who is in Argentina, and"—I pause—"Paco, who got himself killed, or whatever."

"I mean—*symbolically* we are together. We have remained friends . . ." *Don't be a bitch, don't make him feel awkward.*

"Well," Pepe adds, "we will all die one day. That just happens."

We talk until after midnight. In the morning I will be flying home. When I say good-bye to Pepe and Marianne, waiting at the door for Nicolás and Graciela, Pepe comes up behind me. "You forgot your book, Barbara," he says, "you forgot Max Aub." Then, in the semi-darkness of a badly lit Parisian hall, we kiss good-bye. I wait, with Graciela and Nicolás, for the creaking iron grillwork elevator to reach the top floor.

Odette must think me an odd nut, going with her to London, just to have company. On the short trip across the Channel, my chest tightens; by the time the plane descends in London, I am obviously ill. The stewardess suggests that I be put on a cart and wheeled to the BA gate for the jet to Philadelphia. I feel like a stupid sick pasha, being carted through the cavernous Heathrow airport. I've no longer a desire to be the traveler. My mind now is on reaching Philadelphia. I get put on the waiting BA jet, which is only half full. I am able to stretch out and spend most of the flight dozing and dreaming. When we reach the Philadelphia airport, I telephone my friends in Jenkintown, who tell me to take a taxi to their house. Odette puts me and my valises into a taxi. When I get to Jenkintown my old friend Miriam is preparing for a dinner party. Relieved to be back, at first I entertain her guests with hot political news right off the European griddle. Then I collapse. Miriam puts me in the guest room. I am grateful, and I slip in between the cool, starch-smelling sheets. I sleep and I sleep. The next morning Miriam calls in a doctor. Later she tells me, "You're going to be all right, but he told us that you have walking pneumonia." I get better, and later that week Miriam and Joseph locate a special taxi service, so that I am able to get back to New York City without taking the train.

IV

/////////.

Dreams

16

My doctor in New York loads me with antibiotics, a humidifier is installed in my bedroom, and I doze through the winter days. During that first week back in the city, as I am sleeping heavily, I dream deeply. In the first dream I am with a British architect who is explaining to me the modern university he has helped design. He makes me walk with him through the buildings. But I feel confined. I tell him I want to leave this modern schoolroom; I want the old amphitheater back. I describe the great Roman amphitheater with musty, stone-smelling benches, the semicircular curve in which "we" all sat, the nearby grove of plane trees, the moist smell of the earth in spring, the green leaves spreading from the boughs of the plane trees, the smell of the Gauloise I no longer smoke. Staring out the window of the modern schoolroom, I see Paco outside, rushing by, his tall frame stooped over; he is carrying many books, while he walks through the amphitheater that I have just described to the architect. "Paco"—I beat my fists against the window—"I am here, wait for me." He turns and recognizes me, but also sees the British architect. "Who is he?" "Don't pay any attention," I plead. "He is only a modern British architect—just an ordinary man—I am not having an affair with him, I've always only wanted you." I keep beating my fists on the window. Then, after I explain that the man means nothing to me, suddenly I find a door. I open it, and I am standing in dazzling sunlight, so white I squint, and in front of me is Paco. Behind him is the great amphitheater with the curved benches made of ancient Roman stone. He stands straight, his blond hair falling in slants across his forehead, just the way I remember him last. "Barbara," he says, "I spent my life looking for you—and here you are, the original one, the girl with shoulder-length straight brown hair, wearing a pleated plaid skirt and a rust-colored suede jacket. I spent my life looking for that girl in that jacket and that pleated skirt," he repeats; "only the first is the real one." I want to go to him, but he makes me stand still. He takes out a Kodak camera and snaps my picture; I want to go to him, but he asks me to pose against the steps, so first I do that. "Paco, Paco, didn't you understand I spent my whole life looking for you—I wanted to *talk* to you, you knew so much, I wanted you to teach me everything about the whole world." He smiles at me; I stop posing and get up to move toward him; the sun behind him blazes white, so white there is no more color in the dream. Then he disappears and I wake up.

It is a dream of youth (dreams never lie). The truest evocation of what we were, of what we had wanted from one another. My eyes fill with tears, and I am overcome with unconsolable sorrow. My daughters are the age I was when I wore that jacket, that pleated plaid skirt, and some young man is looking at them, engraving them in his heart in that special way; every moment, future memories are being created, and some other woman, a quarter of a century later in time, will have another such dream of unfulfillable longing, while now, in another part of the city, my own father, bedridden, past eighty, lies crippled with Parkinson's disease. When I visit him, I hear him call the names of men in his regiment from the First World War. Most times, he insists on a stance of optimism. In the trenches he was nicknamed Gypsy. I am not as strong as he was. I do not visit him often enough. Maria and Carla spend long afternoons talking with him. I've given him, in place of myself, my own daughters. I cannot bear to see him die. Jack, Gypsy. J. Anthony, Tony, J.A. The sunlight in the dream came down across Paco's head like musty shafts of happy light. The telephone rings. It is Juan from Paris. "Barbara," he says. *"Bárbarita?"*

He tells me he fought with the *antipático* desk clerk at the Montalembert, a man, Juan says, who lied and told Juan that I had gone to England, then Philadelphia, a story which Juan knew was crazy, so he threatened to punch the hotel clerk. Juan tells me that Ahmed is contrite, he brought me gifts from Rotterdam, no one thought I would disappear so fast from France. "Barbara, are you there?" "Yes, yes I am here—it's all right." I put out of my mind the vision of bright sunlight, of Paco smiling, of his wanting to find me still wearing that plaid skirt and suede jacket, with my hair parted on the side and falling straight to my shoulders. "Juan," I say, "Juan." I repeat his name and tell him what has happened to me, and he tells me what has taken place with him. We attempt to straighten out our misunderstandings, our quarrels, our differences, as each of us struggles to fall in love with the ongoing present.

The next week, when Juan telephones again, he tells me *his* dream. He was staying in an extraordinarily lush hotel in Andalusia, which originally was named Al Andalus; sitting near a bright-blue swimming pool, he smells the heavy perfume of the roses, the sun on the orange trees, and the oily odor of nearby olive groves, and there is the scent of blood oranges, clementines, from North Africa. A waiter tells him that Juan Carlos is King of Spain. He sees me swimming toward him. He jumps in after me. He is told that I have married Juan Carlos. He swims deep into the pool toward me, but he loses me. You are gone, he cries out. A voice tells him, No, that is not true. You can wake up now, you are only having a dream, and strange things happen to writers while they sleep; you have been writing too much, so you think she has abandoned you—it is something that has to do with being a novelist.

Juan tells me all this over the transatlantic telephone. "I've been working too hard," he says anxiously.

"It was only a dream," I say; then I laugh. "Did I really marry Juan Carlos?"

Several days later
About the dream—who was the British architect? What do you mean by reassuring Paco that the British architect is just an ordinary man? Why do you tell him that all your life you have remained faithful to him? When in your early thirties you fell deeply in love with Clancy, who has had a profound effect on your adult-woman life— Is he the British architect? Why are you justifying yourself to Paco? Why have you schematized it so Paco stands invulnerable as your great love? You refer to Harold as "your real husband," the first marriage as the real marriage. But there are no real and unreal marriages. If you had a new husband, wouldn't that union be equally real? Are you appeasing Paco by making Juan less? Do you make him less in order to keep Paco "untouchable"? Why? You don't like it when men do that to you. When you slept with Daniel Heltzer after his wife died, you wanted to leave him because after he made love to you on his boat, you heard him through the ceiling pipes (while he was in

the can) murmuring, "Sylvia, Sylvia." You thought: Daniel, I am here.
And alive. Daniel never appears in a dream. Ze bad man left you, off
with his head. Oh, unforgivable act of desertion!

Dr. Max Schur, your favorite analyst, was getting to the heart of the
matter before he died in the early seventies. He could talk to you in the
necessary two languages. German and English. He could anticipate the
world you had lived in without your describing it to him. Schur said that
Germany in 1948 was a landscape of death, and Spain not much differ-
ent. Overexposure to death. Which needed to be overcome. But then he died,
before he could cure you. You were afraid to complete Arriving Where
We Started. *You said to him, "Here I am a writer, profiting by the spec-*
tacular deaths of all my friends. I get chummy with misery, then I earn
from it."

Schur said that it had taken him over twenty years to write his book
on Freud. "I was his last doctor." Freud ordered Schur to help him die,
and Schur gave him a small dose of morphine. "Well, you do have a
problem," Schur said. "But look at it another way, it is better to be
recorded than not, if you leave what you know unwritten, a blank,
whom have you helped? You needn't worry about taking money,
writers don't earn that much."

When *Harper's* magazine published a part of *Arriving Where*
We Started, the woman in charge of graphics visited me. She wanted
a selection of old photos to go with the piece. I was aloof; I didn't
relinquish the pictures. Dr. Schur pointed out that I was furious.
"You want to tell so much of your life and no more. You also do
that here, in this office." Dr. Schur asked if I would show him the
photos, which I did. "The woman was right to want to publish
them; they are very appealing photographs, full of life. The fragment
of your book would have been enhanced by their inclusion." Schur
looked at me. "Clearly you weren't *ashamed* of these photographs?"
Not all secrets are repressed sexuality or thoughts of shame.
"It is the *happy days* you hide from view, isn't it?" he said. I was
amazed at his imaginative leap into my soul. "You don't want me
to use the language of therapy, of Freud, to destroy, to corrode
the language of the heart as you remember it." I nodded. "You
don't want the men you have cared for *reduced,* the *experience*
minimized by analysis. So we leave some mystery." He was momentarily thoughtful. I sat watching for him to say something.

Schur said I was always testing him, to see if he would stumble on the right thought. Then he made a suggestion. "Very well, let's do it your way. You don't have to tell me everything. Leave some part of your life for yourself. So just don't give me more than you can."

"And we can still go on?" I asked anxiously— Did this mean he was giving me some cut-rate bargain-basement analysis?

"Yes, Mrs. Solomon." Dr. Schur was in his seventies when I became one of his last patients in the late 1960s. He always called me Mrs. Solomon. We sat facing one another in the office of his Central Park West apartment, where he lived with his wife, Dr. Helen Schur, whom he often mentioned. She also had her office there. Neither of them attempted to create an antiseptic atmosphere; this was their home, they made no effort to conceal the quality and style of their life. "You do not have to tell me everything, but next time, if an editor asks you for photographs to go with a piece of your work, you could give him one or two, make the selection yourself, just don't mention there are more pictures."

Sometimes Schur talked about his own interests. Lithium was then a landmark discovery; if he were now a young man starting out, he would study chemistry. Freud didn't like people who didn't know the names of flowers; he had no patience with the stupid, and had an obsessive need to be told the truth. "I know you were Freud's doctor," I said, "but tell me less about Freud. I wanna know about *me*." Dr. Schur would gaze at me, frequently saying nothing. Other times he discussed the problems the New York Psychoanalytic Institute had in choosing candidates. Some of the most imaginative ones were too neurotic to become analysts; but he didn't like the uninspired, mechanistic approach of many of the medical school graduates. "They completely misunderstood Freud; he never insisted on total silence." He asked me if I had read Noam Chomsky's books on linguistics. "He was doing original work," Schur insisted. "Too bad he got waylaid by his political adventure. He is destroying a great, innovative career..."

When he found out that I intended to go to Paris and do an article on the writers of *Tel Quel*, he got out his pencil and pad and drew for me Lacan's mathematical interpretation of Freud's theory of Fantasy: ($\cancel{S} \diamond a$) and tried to explain it to me. I don't think Schur agreed with Lacan, but he found him *interesting*. He read whatever he wrote.

"A woman friend suggested, as I have many problems in dealing with older women, that I should sort it out with a female analyst. What do you think?"

"I despise people who make stupid suggestions, it is an *uninformed* opinion by someone who hasn't a clue to what you are about; you call such interference 'friendship'? Now, Mrs. Solomon, you and I are going to step back and investigate your way of being. On the one hand you had an intelligent, strong father who overindulged you. He had a little upper-class Jewish anti-Semitism typical of Jews of his time and his background, but that we can deal with, and taking that in its proper context, you can forgive him; he never abandoned you, never betrayed your trust. On the other hand, we have your mother, whose main problem was that she was not there. How can that be analyzed? You go to a woman analyst—all that dormant masochism you have toward women will be reawakened, thank God, you have that in only small doses toward men. She will search to reach you, and God knows what regression will occur, and what for? So that at the end of thirty more years you understand the processes of your life? But that isn't practical, you haven't got thirty years to go off on such adventures of maybe yes, maybe no. No, you and I will work this out—your father gave you just that much extra, he managed to throw you a lifeline, so we begin with what we have, we build a bridge from what he gave you. Mrs. Solomon, please stop asking me, 'Why haven't I remarried?' and step back, as though you were writing of another person, let us try to look at the total picture, and soon you will phrase the question differently.

"You were a child of a permanent trio which, to this day, has never ended. Your father perceived your motherlessness, and feeling guilty, he denied you nothing. And the family constellation took place on two continents, and in two languages and two religions. A dreamy mother given to severe postpartum depressions, who had trouble with physical contact, who needed to be away from her family, and a melancholy North German nurse who chose to go back to Germany and fall in love with an SS officer and, in the midst of all this, World War II. Mrs. Solomon, as you and your brother spent considerable time alone, or in the presence of this or that domestic, did you wonder where your father was nights? Did you wonder about the young companion he installed in your summer home? Did you wonder about your mother's need to be on another continent? Did you wonder *what* your parents were doing? The women went running off to Europe, but your father came back from his forays into the world. So on that piece we will build. He did two good things for you. He gave you permission to use your intelligence and remain his feminine, beloved female child, and he was dependable. That's enough, with that, we have just enough."

"What about the women?"

"No—we leave the vulnerable, sensitive mother and the German nurse to one side for the moment; we aren't going to deal with them directly, or you'll get caught in a trap, whichever of the two women you discover to have loved, the other woman will need appeasing, no, we leave them and their problems alone. Now, Mrs. Solomon, we deal with you. Suppose, Mrs. Solomon, I was to tell you such a story, about such a child, such a young woman—and then I added: By the way, she grew up, went to Westchester County, married in the suburbs, had several children, and lived happily ever after—would you believe such a tale?"

"No."

"What is wrong with it?"

"The end doesn't match the beginning."

"Good. So why do you chastise yourself, why do you ask me, 'When will I remarry? Why did my marriage have problems?' When you pose such questions, you are accommodating the women in your past, you are accepting your mother's version of your history—that you were just an ordinary little girl who grew up in a nice place with no askew sexuality on the part of the grownups. In that version, well then, yes, the route your adult life took must seem very odd. But turn the story around; accept your guilty father's version, that he had to protect his little daughter who suffered from great losses with insufficient parental love, then you will see you have not done so badly. The miracle was that you *did* marry, your biological needs to produce children *were* gratified; that later the marriage contained problems, and your husband died; the first element was to have been expected, the second element was the happenstance of life."

"Happenstance of life? But my daughters have no father. You call that a *happenstance?*"

"No, for them it is an enduring tragedy. But you can't enter into their pain; they will grow up and tell *their* therapists many, many times about the death of *their* father, and he will enter in their pain and work that out. All you can do is to remain their mother. But in your anxiety over them, do you recognize that although your daughters lost one parent, they also *have* one parent. Aren't you confusing what would have happened to you, if your father had died, with them? No, you cannot enter in their pain, you can merely do what you are doing. Send them to school, listen to their needs, discipline them, provide a home."

"So, now back to you, Mrs. Solomon—we know now that the ordinary daughter of a well-protected upper-class home never existed, so we don't have to ask why you are not securely married in Westchester County."

"My father criticized my mother for not knowing what school I had attended (it was Dalton). I remember him saying to my mother, 'I had to be both mother and father to her, I had to go to the school to get her reports.' "

"So your father threw you a piece of reality, he did not pretend you were leading a normal life, good, we have those pieces of reality he threw your way to work with, so you know you existed, and you know the first part of your life had major gaps, major losses . . ." Dr. Schur paused, he was a tall man, with somewhat bony features. In age, he was a man whose face seemed to have become more severely sculpted, and I have no knowledge of what he looked like younger. Then he continued. "So—off to one center of your life, now we are seeing you as an adult, are these repeated profound relations with a series of men. What quality does each of them have in common with the other?"

"They are wanderers and smart."

"Smart?"

"Well, talented."

"Talented?"

"Very talented."

"Good—we are making progress. What type of analysts have you consulted?"

I smiled. "The best—top of the heap."

Schur smiled. He was gleeful. "We are getting somewhere. And I'm no slouch either! Suppose we take that version of yourself as ordinary child, uneventful upbringing, your mother's version of your childhood; is it likely that child would grow into a woman who would have such repeated relations with men of talent?"

"No."

"This woman, who at times you have sought to maintain, was just on her way to Westchester County, which she never reached, while hidden off to one side are the talented males. Is that a believable story?"

I smile. "No."

At four, in Westbrook, Connecticut, you had your first great love. The Italian neighbor's son, Poochie Sinatra. His father was a bandleader, and they summered in the next house. The two of you huddled in a moored rowboat; Poochie swore he'd get you to China, the sea would be quicker than digging through the sand. The local pharmacist immortalized you both in a sepia-tinted postcard he snapped: VIEW OF LITTLE STANDARD BEACH; *published by Neidlinger's drugstore. You wore a white piqué bow in your side-parted hair, and Poochie's Uncle Frank hadn't yet got started.*

"Why does it happen that way, then?"

"Collusion. Between the men and me."

Dr. Schur gazed at me thoughtfully, he shook a bony finger at me. "As an analyst, Max Schur is one of the best—no false modesty permitted in this office—no obscene sentimentality." He paused, reflective. "So, now we pushed these smart males to center stage. It is very hard to maintain steady relations with such men, but there they are, now let us take the two halves to see if they fit. The daughter of a trio, a young girl who possessed an intelligent and adventurous father who indulged that child and permitted her to experiment with her own intelligence; the deprived child of two moody women, one who ran off with an SS officer, the other an involuted beauty with artistic talent who suffered from phobias and dependency relations—all this enacted on two continents in two languages. Now we take the second half, the bright unstable men in Europe, your career involving two continents, a multitude of languages; do you think our 'child' could have evolved into our 'woman'? Do the halves fit? Can we forget about a mythical Westchester County and why you are not remarried? Do you see how such a child could have become such a woman, and would have *drawn* to her a certain type of male, enmeshed them?"

"Enmeshed?" I wailed, "Dr. Schur, what of me, didn't they involve me?"

He looked at me sternly. "*You* are the doer. Now—listen. You are eight years old, or one or two years old; the women in the family disappear into Europe. Oh, it is so sad, you cannot reach them, you must stand still, later it is even more frightening, there is a war going on, in the place where these two women go. You are Barbara. You sit still, like a good sad little girl, and you wait." He shook his finger again at me. "Now we leap to the present—you are a woman in her late thirties, you are *free*, you pick up the telephone and call TWA, you give them your American Express card number, and in a day you, the doer, have arranged to be in Europe, you are the prime mover . . . So, first we locate you in the playground in which you are prime actor . . . we make sure we have the right playground, Europe, and the smart males."

"What of me?" I complained, "what about my life?"

"First we build the bridge together, then you walk across it . . ." He looked up at me. "You trust me?"

I nodded.

He said soberly, "Eventually you will make the choices. You cease repeating—and you will choose your appropriate geography."

"When I go back into myself, examine the miserable sludge pile," I warned him, "I suffer from anxiety attacks that lead into asthma. Dr. Schur, you don't want me to choke to death?"

"Telephone me when you feel an anxiety attack coming on."

"Telephone you? I call too many people as it is. Listen, you have a reputation to maintain. As a vigorous, stern, Viennese Freudian. The real McCoy, the *echt ur* analysis. How can I tell my friends that the great Dr. Schur says, 'So what, so keep in touch?' You should be *curing* me of my neurotic tendency to contact friends. It can be a very annoying intrusion to people bent on doing real work."

"Real work?" Dr. Schur shrugged. "What is real work? Freud had no use for those who didn't know the proper names of flowers. We are interested here in result, not Junker discipline. What do I care what your friends think? I am a young old man, I can do what I think best, trust me, Mrs. Solomon"—he leaned toward me, whispering his words of seasoned wisdom—"a little overindulgence is better than under, we will build a bridge."

Dr. Max Schur is dead.

Several days after dreaming about the British architect and Paco, I think about him and become more speculative about my dream. Could Clancy Sigal have been the British architect who led me into the modern room? Clancy, who saved my life in Chicago and pulled me into the present? But in the dream I am restless, I feel claustrophobic, I do not want to stay in the modern schoolroom with the British architect (Clancy), I pull away, until I find the door that opens onto the semicircular Roman stone amphitheater where Paco is standing among the eucalyptus trees. Roman—ro-mance man standing in my semicircle, waiting to be devoured in my romance? Novel? (How could I have married Clancy, if I was always searching for exits? In real life I went back to Harold when Clancy asked me to go to England with him. Is this why I can maintain this friendship with Clancy now that he is married to Margaret? My ego wasn't hurt. Margaret came long after me; we didn't collide with each other.)

Did Harold prevent me from staying with Clancy? Or did Paco stand in the way? Who was I appeasing? Rule of thumb: The woman who has many affairs is secretly faithful to some past memory—father, first lover, maybe both. The morning after the dream I weep; it seemed at first a dream of youth, of nostalgia. But look more closely. What is happening between you and Paco? You are restless, yet you acquiesce; he snaps your picture. (You stand still for Paco, yet not for the British architect, Clancy.) Dream of sexual submission? The grove of eucalyptus trees? A bargain, a conscious trade-off. When Paco says he has spent his whole life looking for your younger self, you answer you want him to *tell* you about the world. He was your first lover; well, yes, you did "stand still" for him. In return (you bargain) he will give you his intelligence, his Spain. Clancy told you to be a thief, steal all you can, he urged, become better at filching, he handed you permission to steal from the best of men. But that was the literary language that existed between you and him at a much later stage. When you knew Paco, neither of you used a vocabulary that contained phrases like "permission to steal." Now it is 1974, Franco has begun to die, and images from the past are being re-created. You and Paco are taking on a new form, you are beginning to emerge as creatures of the Spanish Resistance. Perhaps the dream is a reminder to you, its insistence that what he wanted was the girl in the plaid skirt and suede jacket, that such emphasis on your political past does not correspond with your own memories. Both of you yearned to have been old enough to have participated in the Resistance, but you were born too late for such adventure. You worshipped Pallach, who had been in the POUM, and Paco tried to emulate him. But it never occurred to either of you that in a future period you would be considered to have been *part* of the Resistance. Schur would say, If you now emerge as militants of the Resistance, for that metamorphosis to take place you would have to give your cooperation. Collusion. Do it,

Schur would say, if it suits your needs, but be aware you are making such a change occur; do not pretend you were on your way to Westchester County and events in Europe "overtook" you. Be aware of your active role in reshaping your destiny. Do you have Paco's permission for such latter-day tamperings with the past? What you actually remember now was his coming to America, as an anthropology student, and laughing when he saw his first movie here, *The Moon Is Blue*. He said the young woman in the film reminded him of you— If that was his image of you, which fits with his asking you to stand still, that goes with his saying what he wanted was the young woman in the plaid skirt and the suede jacket. So you said, Okay, but let's trade. Swap me your intelligence, and I will pose as female youth. You both made that deal. My Roman man, my roamin', ro-man, romance man. I run into the Roman amphitheater, the Roman language, Spanish versus the Anglo-Saxon schoolroom, the modern schoolroom, filled with objective knowledge, the theater, against the objective modern world; am I struggling in the novel, fact against theater, the door opens, fact onto theater. *Mein Mann, mein Roman Mann*. Row man, row! Row, row, row your boat gently down the stream, merrily, merrily, merrily, merrily, life is but a dream. But in the dream you leave the modern schoolroom to find Paco in the Roman amphitheater, but you can't stay there, you are no longer frozen into his image, no longer the young woman in the plaid skirt; you are a woman in your forties, now, with

Juan

We make up, we find each other again. We travel through the United States and to Fez, Rabat, and Marrakech, and unperturbed at the symbiotic nature of our relation, in the early mornings, heavy with sleep, we recount to each other our dreams. What occurs in part of mine is finished in his; characters wander from dream to dream, we are able to find explanations in parts of mine for missing pieces of Juan's. One night, the spring after Franco's death, in his house in the Casbah, in Marrakech, I wake up screaming—my mother has died, and it was she I loved, my mother has died. No, he says, your mother is alive, it is the anniversary of my mother's death today, it is she who died, a German bombardment of Barcelona, today is the day, go back to sleep. It is early morning, and I can smell in the outer garden the odor of the clementines, the blood oranges that appeared in Juan's reverie of the lush hotel in Al Andalus in which he lost me as I disappeared into the pool, the dream he reported to me, which he had at the same time as mine of Paco and the British architect, and now, finally, I am in that house, and I inhale, through the open window, the scent of the lemons and the blood oranges in the garden of his house in Marrakech. I go back to sleep, happy days.

V

Seduction and Spanish History

17

During my restless adolescence, my female friends and I, giggling, consciously experimented by dabbing wads of cotton soaked in imported perfume on our wrists, behind our ears, and in those old-fashioned, décolleté days, we stuffed the scented wads down between our budding breasts to smell good, to entice. Such behavior now seems antiquated. Does analysis, with its emphasis on the conquering of neurosis, the notion that the healthy woman will have a better chance at achieving fulfillment, inadvertently trivialize *seduction?* The therapist may say to a patient, "You are being seductive to this or that man," but he rarely stresses, "You should *learn to be seductive.*" Analysts value good relations—no emphasis on mystery. Feminists pooh-pooh the prejudice against seduction in both feminist and analytic thought. These two groups have had major influence over women. In some future time, when this period is re-examined, collusion might appear more obvious—neither group stresses seduction as a desired goal, analysis-health, feminism, self-fulfillment. Both optimistic? Puritanical?

The men I have been drawn to were awestruck by sex, faithful to the idea of sex, though not necessarily to me.

I mean not to be writing a book of "thoughts on a rainy spring afternoon after HE left *me,* Madame Wonderful." But that doesn't signify that many "HEs" didn't leave me, or that I didn't have plenty of grim thoughts, on many rainy spring afternoons. Only that I am bored with that particular literary cliché, so, deliberately, I underplay that aspect of my life.

The aftereffects of fever leave me worn out. I spend much of the day in bed; books, pads, and newspapers piled on top of the white eyelet spread; the plastic humidifier near my bed makes a whirring noise. Although I haven't yet enough energy to work on *Ogro*, I publish an Op Ed piece on Eva Sastre in the *Times*. Ann-Jo and Valerie, through the feminist movement, supply me with additional information about Eva.

A few years later, after I meet Alfonso in Madrid, in 1976, he tells me the afternoon Eva's lawyer, Juan María Bandrés, handed him the piece, he realized that the worst was over; Eva was no longer anonymous, her case existed in the United States. Which made the Spanish government nervous.

Arafat has abandoned New York: American intellectuals take a full-page *New York Times* ad, joining the protest of European intellectuals (Ionesco, Sartre, Simone de Beauvoir) against the vote to exclude Israel from UNESCO. I finally send the letter about Israel which Doña Teresa had urged me to write. But my message falls in the sea, like a gaffe committed by me, a letter never written, never spoken, the problem doesn't exist.

My father raised me never to insist on agreement with my friends. Don't be a blamer, Bunny, there's *this* point of view and *that* point of view. But I am depressed by it. I notice the thinness of the European signatures. Sartre, Simone de Beauvoir had come of age before World War II. Creatures of their historic time, they draw the line: the state of Israel must continue. The Spanish and Latin American intellectuals are missing. Mexico jeers at Israel. Franco's children get their information mainly from PLO propaganda. One day, while Valerie is visiting me, the two of us cease talking of Spain and unexpectedly a new topic comes up. We are Jewish women, are we helping revolutionaries who would have us pushed out to sea?

Valerie, running her hand through her mass of red hair, reports to me the bad experience of American feminists who had gone to an International Congress in Mexico thinking they could discuss matters in the free way we do here. The women were taken off guard by the political nature of the meetings. The Arab delegates, under instructions from their husbands, walked out when it was the Israeli women's turn to speak.

"So the Congress was rigged?"

Valerie answers with a sigh, "Since when have Arab women been the free ones?"

Following my doctor's advice, I spend mornings in bed. Feverishly I indulge in my new obsession: the history of the Jews in Spain. I reread Américo Castro's *España en Su Historia: Cristianos, Moras y Judíos.* His is supposedly the liberal interpretation. His main point is that Al Andalus (as much of Spain and North Africa was called) can be understood only by combining Spanish, Arabic, and Jewish history; and he makes some nice literary speculations about the picaresque novel, with its quirky, alienated hero surviving on the hoof and lam, having its origins in the life of the underground Spanish Jew. (As Gerald Brenan puts it: Spanish literature, until well into the sixteenth century, has a Jewish tone to it.)

But then he makes a wild leap of the imagination, and all Spanish history is traced to Jewish influence. Finally, almost without consciously realizing it, he evolves an idea in which the Jewish-Christian symbiosis becomes the cause of the Inquisition. He insists that the Jews were the inventors of *limpieza de sangre* (purity of blood), one of the basic obsessions of the Inquisition. He gets his information by rummaging through and misinterpreting Jewish scholars like A. A. Neuman. In his book *The Jews in Spain*, there is a description of a rabbi's letter written in the fourteenth century, in which he verifies that two brothers are worthy of marrying into the most honorable families of Israel, as on neither side is there impure blood. The real reason for the letter was that the rabbi was denouncing an informer who had wrongly accused the brothers of having been parented by a slave, which would have made them illegitimate.

Sounds almost comic. The rabbis fuming about a whisper campaign concerning low life, adultery, slaves begetting bastards, and so forth. Yet from this *single* document, which at worst was family snobbishness, a hush-hush of medieval *scandale,* Américo Castro derives an explosive theory that proves the Jews are the original racists and originators of the Inquisition. Ignoring all documentation (which dates back to 612) concerning Christian punishment in regard to intermarriage and Christian concern with the religion of the offspring, he observes: "We have therefore the oldest text of a proof of *limpieza de sangre* in Spain ... a text without parallel in the Christian documents of that time." (He takes a leap from starchy family law to genocide without barely pausing for breath.) "In the sixteenth and seventeenth centuries in Spain the *limpieza de sangre* converted into a main preoccupation of the nobility and ecclesiastics ... as a result of these preoccupations which had been injected in them by converted Jews."

His other example of Jewish racism (also taken out of context from Neuman's book) is a tale of illicit love. In 1319 a Jewish doctor visiting Segovia discovered that a Jewish widow there had recently given birth to twins sired out of wedlock by a Christian. One twin died, the other was baptized by the Christians. The event was the source of juicy gossip. The mortified doctor in Segovia asked a local rabbi, "How are we to prevent our Torah from looking ridiculous in the eyes of these people . . . the whole town is talking about that woman, and our religion looks like nothing after this. If I could, considering the talk this case has aroused, I'd cut off her nose, disfigure the face her lover was so taken with."

Américo Castro sails right past the essential point: the Jewish religion is based on family law, not fanatical "observances of the blood." Both these cases concern adultery, bastardy, in other words, threats to family well-being. How can he equate family law with the maniacal Inquisition, which wrecked Spain in a period that lasted four centuries? He turns reality on its head by involving Jews in several basic aspects of the Inquisition: purity of blood, which was drummed up by Spanish zealots; the use of Jewish tribunals as a model of the Inquisitional trial (it came out of Roman law and became popular in southern Europe during the thirteenth century); and persecution of the Jews by converted Jews, which is the only thing to have some historic validity. His Jews, therefore, are omnipotent. Good things (poetry, literature) as well as odious things (the Inquisition, the expulsion of the Jews from Spain) are all to be traced to their Jewish root. He also is neurotically hung up on the beauty of Jewish women. He fantasizes a tribe of Rebeccas guarded by stern Jewish males who want these glorious females for themselves instead of sharing them with their Christian neighbors. Although Américo Castro keeps quoting obvious evidence of Christian intermarriage with Jews as examples of their openness, he neglects to point out that one of the main reasons the Goth nobles enforced such punitive laws against Jewish and Arab males who married Christian women is that the Arabs and Jews had been assimilating at a dangerously high rate.

I continue my reading. The nineteenth-century New Englander, author of the *Conquest of Mexico*, William Prescott, has a much steadier and less dangerously romantic approach in his nice, solid, three-volume *Ferdinand and Isabella*.

He points out that the Inquisition flourished in the thirteenth century in the South of France as a method for the growing Church to gain absolute territorial control, and was brought into Spain through the Dominicans and Cluniac monks. A rising middle class in Spain rebelled and engaged in mob violence against the Jews, who were perceived as wealthy and who lived under the protection of the kings and nobles. For Prescott, fanaticism and financial opportunity were at the heart of the matter.

> Under the Visigothic empire the Jews multiplied exceedingly in the country, and were permitted to acquire considerable power and wealth. But no sooner had their Arian masters embraced the orthodox faith than they began to testify their zeal by pouring on the Jews the most pitiless storm of persecution. One of their laws alone condemned the whole race to slavery; and Montesquieu remarks, without much exaggeration, that to the Gothic code may be traced all the maxims of the modern Inquisition, the monks of the fifteenth century only copying, in reference to the Israelites, the bishops of the seventh.

Prescott has both the respect and the mild social prejudices toward the Jews common to a well-educated New Englander of the nineteenth century. Although he admires the diligence of the Jews (a good puritan virtue), he finds them *flashy*.

> But all this royal patronage proved incompetent to protect the Jews when their flourishing fortunes had risen to a sufficient height to excite popular envy, augmented as it was by that profuse ostentation of equipage and apparel for which this singular people, notwithstanding their avarice, have usually shown a predilection ... they were prohibited from mingling freely with the Christians, and from exercising the professions for which they were best qualified, their residence was restricted within certain prescribed limits of the cities which they inhabited; and they were not only debarred from their usual luxury of ornament in dress, but were held up to public scorn, as it were, by some peculiar badge or emblem embroidered on their garments.

Despite Prescott's admirable steadiness and sound historic vision of events, he disapproves of Jewish glitz. Were they really such a sporty, flashy, Miami Beach crowd, getting into trouble for their *nouveau riche*, overjeweled, overfurred garb, as they cavorted among the Arab caliphs in Seville and Granada? Just how did the Moors and Spanish nobles dress? Was the Christian-Arab gang breaking into British tweed while indulgent Jews sported Maxmillian minks? Prescott exhibits the fair-play New England mind, as well as the social prejudice toward Jews of his own time. Yet the Anglo-Saxon social snobberies vis-à-vis the Jews (do we really want them flaunting their furs in our good old leather-chair clubs) is less inflammatory than Américo Castro's view, because it does not involve placing onto the Jews a status of omnipotence. Prescott has some mild social prejudice; Américo Castro's Jews are grandiose and mythic.

In 1918 another North American Spanish historian, William Chapman, published a workmanlike history of Spain; really an English-language condensation of Rafael Altamira's big *Historia.* According to Chapman and Altamira, the opposite was true—all of Spain were fancy dressers during the fifteenth century. It now appears that the *Christian* court was on a materialistic splurge.

> All that can be said of Castile as regards the immorality, luxury, dress, superstition, and chivalric pursuits of the aristocracy and middle class applies generally, not only to Catalonia, but also to Aragon and Valencia. The nobles endeavored to emulate the King in extravagances, with the result that many were ruined, and their attempts to avoid paying their debts to the Jews were one cause of the massacres of the latter. The luxury in dress brought in its train the development of tailoring to such an extent that the Catalan modes were well known even in foreign countries.... In fine, the customs of the period were made up of a curious mixture of passing medievalism and coming modernity.

But after the Spaniards rid themselves of Jews and Arabs, they didn't have sufficient skills to rule the country; many Arabic and Jewish accomplishments—medicine, science, astrology, mathematics, finance, and agriculture—fell into disuse. The Jewish emphasis on family was devalued, and too many Spanish sons were lost to clergy, army, and territorial adventure. Spain overexpanded, couldn't manage her foreign empires, while at home nobody was trained to run the store.

Spain is like a man who has dumped his wife, only to find his house is in chaos and the new mistress is a shrew. Soon he forgets he sent the first one packing; he longs for her return and begins to believe their separation was her fault. Loss of greatness always foments brooding; the Arabs and the Jews, ah, how wonderful was our first bride, what poetry, what nights, what paradise then! Américo Castro was a well-intended man—his shaky thought process seems to have stemmed from a combination of adulation and unconscious resentment at the Jews and Arabs who had escaped, leaving Spanish Christians and *conversos* to crawl out of the Inquisition four hundred years later as best they could. Also, he was not a historian but a philologist.

Question: What are the Spaniards really mad at, in their love-hate relation with the Jews? Why always so much more cordial to Jewish women than to Jewish men, from whom they remain more aloof? Consider the custom of *barraganería* (concubines among the Spanish nobles) and the frequent literary allusion to the "beautiful Jewess," (Américo Castro harps on their pulchritude). What, actually, was the state of Jewish and Arabic women under the early caliphs, as compared to the women of the more primitive Goth nobles? The Arab and Jewish then were the high cultures. Were Jewish women, therefore, specifically coveted? Did beauty here stand for economic wealth, general culture, or, perhaps, inaccessibility? Numerically, were there enough Jewish women to permit extensive intermarriage, especially as Jewish males were forbidden to take Christian wives? Was fear on the part of Spanish males concerning the wrath of Jewish males behind all this fantasizing? Check into actual status of Jewish women, and their real appearance and education as compared to high-born Spanish Christian women of that time. Results perhaps interesting.

My fever, the remains of the pneumonia, reoccurs intermittently during the next month. Later I remember the period, after Arafat storms New York and I am in bed, surrounded with so many history books, as my "Jewish time." After I finish arguing in my head with the Christian historians, I begin to ask questions of the Jewish ones. If Américo Castro is odd, the attitude of Jewish scholars vis-à-vis Spain also strikes me as strange. The Golden Age of Jews was there—yet the Jews tiptoe around that period; except for the experts like Baer and Neuman, the Jews sidestep it. Aren't they proud of Maimonides? Do they have trouble with the Spanish Jews being such a bunch of sexy sports—high-stepping, full of erotic poetry and dash?

The Jews were victimized some of the time in Spain, but during certain periods they lived high, hobnobbing with kings and nobility; does our Jewish mind like to think of us only as victims? (True, we've been that much of the time.) But shouldn't we examine our history during periods in which we have been less victimized? I don't think that the annals of the Inquisition or details about massacres are enormously useful; torture is what occurs at the end of the line; horrors have a boring sameness of horrendous detail. I am more interested in learning about the *just before*.

I invent a play, *Tortosa*. I visualize parts, the pageantry, the extraordinary clothes of the period. What I have in mind (aided by a slight and varying fever) is the great panorama of the disputation of Tortosa, which took place in 1414. The papacy brought the Pope and his councils to the seaport of Tortosa, south of Barcelona, to meet with the rabbis to argue matters of faith. We Jews—when assaulted by pogroms, ovens, and so forth—always ask the same question, Why? And always the business of "Christ killer" comes to the forefront of our minds. We argue that the Romans killed Christ and it is all very unfair, but this line of thinking doesn't help us very much because that was never the main issue. At the time of Tortosa the medieval Church was transforming itself into the powerful modern Church. It wanted *legitimization* from the Jews. As we conceive of ourselves as powerless, frequently we don't understand what has been wanted from us. By the fifteenth century, the church had great arguers; it beat us Jews hands down in the polemics. It poked around in the Jewish Haggadah, and in peripheral Jewish sources, and used Jewish thought to come up with the conclusion that the Christians, not the Jews, were the legitimate heirs to the Jewish religion. They felt it represented modern advancement and universal truth.

While I am sick in bed, I read more about the period: the Jewish rabbis complained to the papacy that the Jews were inconvenienced; they couldn't think of proper answers, as they'd not been allowed to bring along their wives. I shake with laughter at the idea of the Jews complaining to the Pope that they are being deprived of their women! The Pope thundered at them, *"Sensualistas!* Can you not think without fornication!"* Hmmm. I think about what the Church was up to at Tortosa; it had to clean up its own act (prior to Tortosa the Spanish ecclesiastics kept very flashy and well-turned-out concubines); was that crack about *"sensualistas"* in that Star Chamber performance for the populace meant to demonstrate that the Church had reformed and gone monkish? When the Jews, tiredly, asked the papacy why it was always picking on them, why couldn't the Church do some business among the Turks or Saracens, how about the Church converting that crowd, the papacy replied, No, it wasn't interested in Saracens, the Jews were nearer to it, the Jews meant more. Here's where we get to the root of our trouble: we mean too much. Clearly some of the remarks about missing their wives and families was a Jewish stall. I visualize them in the corridors at Tortosa (this was a generation after the mini-holocausts at Seville and Barcelona, the Jewish position in Spain was already disintegrating). They were probably whispering among the rebs, "Let's cool it, stall, waffle, edge our way out of this trap." Maybe that's why they brought in the business about their wives. As an excuse. Or were they afraid that prolonged absence from their homes would leave their families and property unprotected against further raids? I get the feeling that the Jews *muttered* their way through the proceedings; they made pointed remarks: if the Christians were to be put on trial in Arab territory, even the most devout Christian could be proven wrong. All this sounded very *sotto voce*. Meanwhile, the Catholics were using complicated casuistry. There is a nice bit when they ask the Jews if they really believe that their Messiah could be alive, standing in readiness for two thousand years, and the Jews, still muttering, replied that the Catholics have some acts of faith (referring to Virgin birth) which try Jewish credulity. Great throwaway lines, but the Catholics won the debate.

The issue, of course, is legitimization. The papacy, using Jewish material, was battling against the Jewish Messiah. Now, the Messiah was a late Jewish idea and the least interesting part of Judaism. But during the Middle Ages, a superstitious time when many groups believed this or that Messiah was coming down the pike, we Jews increased our vulnerability by showing up, unprotected, with a real big-time one in our hip pocket. Which made us a powerful threat. *It is a bad idea to have Messiahs without an army.* Two big Jewish problems: no proselytizing and the possession of a threatening Messiah. True, we frequently have been prevented from proselytizing, and perhaps we were never in a position to claim territory, to *have* had an army. Which is why it is interesting to study Jewish behavior at times when we have had some power. In the previous centuries, when Granada and Seville were considered virtually Jewish cities, could the Jews have more pragmatically defended their land? Did their idea of a Messiah who was to lead them back to the earthly paradise interfere with a development of natural aggressive drives? What was the rate of non-forced conversion? Another fact we Jews do not dwell on is that throughout history there have been two types of conversion to Christianity: those who were forced to do so and those ordinary people who simply converted because it made life easier and they didn't wish to become martyrs. These *ordinary Jews* who vanished into Christendom, don't they represent certain mundane habits of life? Do we Jews get a distorted idea of ourselves because we study our more noble traits? Tortosa was a disaster; many delegates returned to their Jewish communities as *conversos;* several of the leading Jewish poets also became Christians. The Jews had major losses almost eighty years before the actual Inquisition.

What interests me about Tortosa is that, unlike former papal disputations, which proceeded like genuine disputations, the one at Tortosa seems to be an early forerunner of the European Star Chamber. The technique of using the language of the Opposition to obtain admissions of guilt and, therefore, gain your own legitimacy has continued to be used in European battles until the present. The Church won the psychological battle before the physical fight had even begun. Putting together a theory, an army, and an aggression is typical of modern Europe; we Americans flounder in such endeavors because we aren't used to placing such high values on dialectics—Manhattan was bought for twenty-four dollars. We never *theorized* or proselytized among the Indians—we merely advanced, willy-nilly, fighting them for the territory. I keep a notebook on Tortosa, reminding myself why I always lose all battles with European Marxists. Their dialectic—a Jesuitical quickness—leaves me scratching my head in defeat. I am dumb that way. We didn't win America through no theory. And we forget the *realness* of the verbal to Europeans.

Once the masses of Jewish conversions got underway, due to the techniques used at Tortosa, which weren't torture but were psychological and power-based, Christianity suddenly seemed fancier, dressier, more new, less trouble, more likely to succeed, and, among certain poets, more avant-garde. These conversions, coupled with the later defeat of the Arabs at Granada, meant the way was open for the Inquisition. The Arabs were pushed out of Spain, and the Jews were no longer needed to help out with the wars of the Reconquest.

We also have underestimated how powerful, how legitimate our religious claims have seemed to Christians. We are like a powerful, bookish old brother who prevents a younger, feisty brother from taking over the family business. The bookish brother says, I won't fight, I'll be good, I'll go on reading my books, *and* I'll keep the factories because they are mine. Then, wham-o! the younger brother, better armed for battle, grabs the factory and is forced to try continually to displace his bookish older brother.

We Jews conceive of ourselves as eternal victims, but Christians at various periods nevertheless have seen us as powerful. Because we are the mother religion we need a handle on both points of view.

Freud and Marx instinctively recognized that Jewish thought could not stand still. We had to think our way around and away from our hip-pocket Messiah. We needed to throw an intellectual curve ball, away from Jewish religion, onto new theories that have a little something in them for everyone.

Several nights later I dream about Tortosa. In color. A great magenta plush curtain divides the parts into Acts I, II, and III. Juan, his blue eyes sharp, is dressed in the Pope's robes; he argues with me in Latin. Two Jewish men are walking inside a glass-domed corridor. Tortosa is a jagged castle set on a mountain plateau overlooking a shimmering stream. I am seated inside a carriage, which spins up the hill road; the palace has no walls, the pageantry of the disputations unfolds before me. Speeding up to the castle in a white car is my father; he is the poet, the Jewish bard who converts his own people to Christianity, Anthony, Tony, J.A., reading scrolls of verse, leaning with one foot on the flashy running board of his old-time Packard convertible. I wake up; the musty sun filters into my room. All I remember, at first, is that my father was the poet. No, he was the lawyer, the tycoon. *I* am the family writer, pleasing him. Half awake, I remember the first editions of Christina Rossetti he gave my daughters, the endless recitations, the Milton, the Shakespeare, Keats, Wilde, *Dover Beach.* I stretch lazily in bed; I see myself as a child opening my mother's top dresser drawer, finding sheets of penciled, slanting script; poems to my mother signed "Gypsy" or "your Tony." When I showed them my mother smiled. "Those are the love poems your father wrote me. Imagine scrawling those things in the middle of the night." I blink, and I wonder, What was in those poems? Well, he loved her, my father loved my mother. I've come of age in a different time. I have lived with many real writers, and none has written poetry to me; my fever is down to normal.

VI

/////////////.

Short
Flights

18

During the winter of 1975 I write the American version of *Operation Ogro*. In January Juan Goytisolo comes back; we make up and travel through America. While we are cruising through the New England night on the Greyhound bus, I notice his fatigue, the black growth of stubble appearing on his face; in his sleep, his hand automatically reaches for me: I feel his vulnerability; sense the shy, self-absorbed child hiding behind the adult novelist. I also recognize his selfishness, as that night, inside the Greyhound, I fall in love with him, calmly and realistically aware of the pitfalls. Despite the star treatment given him by the Spanish departments, Juan neither speaks to nor is reached by America. He yearns to be shocking and daring, but he is a *poète maudit* in the European style. He comes to his lectures with formally prepared texts, blasphemes against the Roman Catholic Church and authoritarian repression of sexual freedom. But his modern European invective is too abstract for American taste. Here, college audiences have become accustomed to poets who unzip their flies and pee on the podium. Within a year, according to Lucy Lippard's anthology, *From the Center*, Carolee Schneemann, in a mixed-media performance, will appear nude on the stage and read to the audience from a long scroll which she removes from her vagina. Middle America has forgotten the meaning of blasphemy. Juan aims for high, condensed audacity, while we gringos are letting it all hang out. *Deep Throat* is playing at the Eighty-fifth Street Trans-Lux; we are bursting at the seams with our own sex shops and vibrators; we snooze, asleep at the switch in the face of such European imports. When Juan goes back to France and Morocco in May, I don't join him. I am needed in New York—my father is dying.

———

Clancy is in from England, and he spends that summer in my apartment writing about California. We are lucky, July is clear and cool. The three of us—Clancy, Maria, and I—lazily talk about driving to the country for weekends, which we never do. In the beginning of August Clancy and I see Maria and a friend of hers off to Europe for their junior year abroad. At the airport, Clancy whispers to me not to be one of those mothers, "Do a quick good-bye"; he shoves me in the direction of the exit. I turn back for a moment and watch her. Exhilarated in anticipation of a year in France, she and Jennie, khaki packs strapped on their backs, run into the terminal tunnel; they don't turn back.

When we reach the muggy city, Clancy says, "Let's go to the Eighty-sixth Street Loew's and the Madison Deli." The East Side looks deserted; it's a summer Sunday.

The next day I go with Clancy to visit my folks. My father is in a wheelchair, his eyes have a vacant stare caused by L-dopa, the drug for Parkinson's, and his hands, now floury white with liver spots, tremble. He gives Clancy an essay: "Solution to New York City Traffic Plan." Clancy, on the spot, reads it. The three of us sit in my father's bedroom; he's always used it as a study. "What do you think of it?" My father's voice has an unaccustomed quaver.

"Sir, it's wonderful—very Paul Goodman, a *visionary* view of the city."

"Would the *Times* want it? They should care about what's happening to the city."

"Why not try?"

I stare at my father; *he's never before asked for praise.*

My father looks thoughtfully at Clancy. "Would you like a glass of Scotch?"

"Yes, sir."

"Bunny, get your friend some Scotch."

Then he motions me, when I get up for the drinks, to take the essay from Clancy and bring it back to him; he has rolled his wheelchair next to the desk. Marte always keeps the wood-grain surface and the brass knobs heavily polished; he bought it years ago, in New Orleans, after a fishing trip in the Gulf.

Because Clancy is still living in my apartment in late August, I am not thrown off base by a moody letter from Juan Goytisolo. We had been happy that spring while Juan was in America. Now he writes that he is convinced he can't live with anyone. Ahmed has a horrible temper and is interested only in his family; Juan is in despair and probably won't return to America. At first I am alarmed. But, on rereading it, while Clancy is in the kitchen making us both iced tea, calmly I decide I don't believe a word. Juan is very professional. Cool in career. Whatever emotional crisis is gripping him, by September 15 I figure he'll be teaching his first class in Pittsburgh. Juan will be paid a nice sum for the fall term, he won't default. Ahmed is Ahmed—a temperamental Berber who has always put his family first; so? Ahmed and Juan were bored with each other's company long before I came into the picture; how else could I have made such inroads? No, the trouble is with neither Ahmed nor me. Translation: Juan is unable to truly leave his wife and doesn't know what explanation to make. Not the sort of man who can say, Stick around, but I'm not ditching anybody for you. Most men have difficulty coming right out with it. I'll just wait, see what happens next. When I was younger, I didn't know how to do that.

When September rolls around, just after Clancy has left on a trip with Margaret, who has come over from London to join him, I hear via Ann-Jo that Juan has been a week in New York. I move fast. I stuff Juan's leftover belongings, a snow jacket the wrong shade of green, a pair of bedroom slippers, papers, and books, as well as half-used medicines, into a large grocery bag with THE BIG APPLE scrawled on it; then I grab a taxi for the Village and leave it with the doorman of Nicolás's apartment building, one of the New York University highrises at LaGuardia Place, with instructions to leave it in the Romance Language Department for Juan.

The next night Juan telephones me. *"Tu m'énerves,"* he says, furious. "You've the worst temper of any woman I've known."

"Good." I hang up.

Later that week Juan telephones me from Pittsburgh—could we discuss things on the weekend, in New York, with calm? When Juan arrives at my place that Saturday morning, he has the wistful, nesting look, as he sniffs at the familiar surroundings, of a man who has been expelled from Eden. Only *he* can be allowed to do the leaving. Now he has to come back so that we can begin the process again. This time he tries another tack. How can he be expected to give all this up? Plus compliments. I have lots of vitality, a wild sense of humor, and I am a good cook . . .

"So—who asked you to give me up? *You* ran away."

Juan stares at me, gathering his powers of argument. "That was yesterday," he says firmly. "Now we are on today." He pauses and becomes victim. "They gave me my things in a paper bag. *Dumped* on the floor of the Romance Language Department—"

"Never been thrown out? About time. You are pro-experience, chalk it up to new happenings ..."

"My wife is a far more reasonable person," he snaps.

"Clearly."

"You are spoiled and demanding—"

"Good."

Juan isn't bothering to throw any more compliments my way, but he is surprised at my holding my own in the fight; his blue eyes glow in anticipation of what I will say next. He has begun to enjoy himself. He plants one foot firmly on a horsehair hassock near the baby grand, and he leans over, resting an arm on the piano surface. He is confident he is regaining lost territory. Soon he will be finding me a reason to make him coffee with milk. "Less mature than she."

"My immaturity," I breathe, "has been the making of you. When I met you, your act was boyish diffidence. Now, after living with me (and with Ahmed), you've been forced to take control. You can't overcount on me, why, Juan, my being 'spoiled and demanding' has done wonders for you. Who is interested in a coddled man? No, now that you've entered the world of two-way uncertainty implicit in all affairs, you are much more of a catch; why, I ought to get a reward!"

He's getting interested again. Sock it to him.

"So—you've gone back to your wife. That is, if indeed you ever left her?"

Juan pauses, chooses his words with care. "We have an arrangement ... we plan, each year, to spend some time together." Hastily he adds, "Like you and Clancy."

"No." I am emphatic. "Clancy is in love with Margaret. *Both* are my friends. Don't mix apples and pears—you mean to tell me you could, freely, bring me to your house and say to your wife, Oh, by the way, this is Barbara ..."

"No."

"Your situation bears no resemblance to my friendship with *ex-*lovers. You make yourself sound like a freelancer; then wham-o, you change the script. A Parisian-Catalan bourgeois in revolutionary disguise, merely on an exploratory trip to America." I pause, then seize on an example from one of Juan's books. "You criticize your materialistic forebears for having gone to Cuba, in the middle of the last century, making dough off the sugar plantations, ransacking the people—*fucking* the natives, then with the mint returning to ye olde Catalonia to live high. Exploiters, colonialists, you named your ancestors—so how is this different from us?"

"Us?"

"Yes, us. I am that Cuban native woman, used and screwed, while, meanwhile, you are exporting the money from my country right back to Barcelona or Paris, just like your great-granddaddy." I pause, fascinated with my comparison. Amazing what you can do with words. Just a twist here, a tug there, and I come out the poor native and Juan the colonializing imperialist.

In my last attack, it is clear to both of us I have touched Juan.

He gazes at me with authentic admiration. "Ahhhh," he murmurs appreciatively, the white light of joy in his eyes; the drama has begun.

"Now I don't mind dealing with a rigged deck, but I do mind being made to feel sorry for you, just because you have chosen to hang it with your wife. Why can't you be more open, why can't you just tell me what you want?"

I've overshot my luck.

Juan's blue eyes widen; shyly he taps the black ebony piano surface. He seems to be trembling, his free hand shakes slightly. Overcome with the confusions of timidity, daring, assault, and expectation, he breathes in slowly. "Men, women, marriage, no marriage, countries, languages, fame, privacy, adoration—" He pauses, and meekly pleads, "*Todo.*"

Ask a dumb question, you get a dumb answer.

The last anti-Franco protest I make is a telegram mailed on September 25, 1975, which is the day my father dies. Eleven students had been given the death sentence, Franco's final throes. WE JOIN THE GOVERN-MENTS OF THE WESTERN EUROPEAN COUNTRIES, THE VATICAN, SPANISH BISHOPS, AND CONCERNED INTELLECTUALS THROUGHOUT THE WORLD IN PROTESTING THE BARBARITY OF USING THE GARROTE ON ELEVEN YOUNG SPANISH MEN AND WOMEN. IN THE NAME OF COMMON HUMAN-ITY WE URGE THE COMMUTATION OF THEIR DEATH SENTENCES. The usual well-known Americans signed it—Bellow, Mailer, Roth, Hellman, Galbraith, Clancy, as well as Juan, Nicolás, and me. Five students were executed. During the days prior to the execution I spend some of the time on a vigil in front of the UN Plaza—our demonstration gets mixed up with a Ukrainian anti-Soviet group, and the Spanish secret police, by error, photograph marching Ukrainians instead of Spanish students; both the demonstrations are covered on the New York TV roundup news. When Juan asks me how can two meetings that are ideologically *opuestas* mix that way, and march so happily together in a blended circle in front of the UN Plaza, I say, "Well, things are different, politically, in New York from Paris." But most of the time these days I spend in Mount Sinai Hospital watching my father die.

Daily I show up at Mount Sinai, but I avert my eyes from the humiliation of his worn, aged flesh wired with tubes. I want him to die; I curse him because his mind lasts to the end. He jokes with my mother about needing *The New York Times* and the St. Anthony medal (given to him by an Irish judge) always at his bedside. His white, plucked-chicken, loose folds of skin have been shot through with purple streaks from the tubes. Frightened, small-boy eyes stuck in the middle of an old man's face. Startled. Jacob Anthony Probst. Must have invented the Anthony, as he invented himself. Child of a lech father—a bottom pincher who went on wanting until he was in his nineties; half-blind then, he grabbed for whoever was at hand. The old Probst ran up debts, gambled, never worked. His three sons hated him. My father was the eldest; he brought up his two younger brothers.

In Mount Sinai, I watch my father's struggle toward breath, his lungs filled with liquid, his terror. *Let him die.* Why couldn't my life be more resolved when he died? *I have remarried, you don't have to worry about the girls and me, we are all right.* I couldn't make such a report. Instead, I hand him the just-published copy of *Ogro.* He looks at it. "Fine, Bunny, it looks just fine." Then, because I can't invent a husband or a stable income with which to reassure him, I tell him I had been on the *MacNeil/Lehrer Report.* About the Spanish political situation. "I argued with generals, Daddy."

"Oh, Bunny, why that's fine—you're in politics." He respects that; he kept company with Carlyle and Hazlitt's *History of the Republic of Venice.*

"I stuck up for my point of view."

My mother muses (we have long, meandering conversations in the hospital) about the feminists: "Why are they so busy wondering what happened in *A Doll's House* after Nora slammed the door? I'll tell you what happened to her—she was *my* mother-in-law." She giggles. "Ended up on Central Park West set up by three sons, who gave her a view of the park, a full-time nurse, and a springer spaniel—and her second husband was as no good as the first." My mother goes off into gales of laughter. "Which makes *you* Nora's granddaughter."

Still in his teens, my father brashly talked himself into becoming Woodrow Wilson's youngest aide; by the time he came back to America after the First World War—trenches, gas, and three years in a French hospital—he had invented himself. "Your Tony, your gypsy," he wrote to my mother. Married her, in the early 1920s, sent his younger brother to Dartmouth, took a deep breath, wham, he dived into Manhattan and came up a tycoon lawyer with drive and dash. Sidney Cohn, who married John Garfield's widow, had often pointed out to me that younger Jewish lawyers in New York had emulated his manner. "He gave us a style—a way of behaving in a Protestant world when all that was still new to us."

He has always controlled his own universe; dying, he attempts to prop himself up, his lip trembles, he needs Marte's help. "I'm going," he says abruptly. I don't answer. He knows he's dying. Marte and my mother are on either side of him; the three of them have spent almost a half century askew-wedded to one another. He takes the hand of each and gives a kiss. Then he blows me one—wants to show he is still in charge. "Bunny, tell me more about that Channel 13 show."

Later, in the waiting room, the doctor, my mother, and I agree—no extraordinary measures. That means we are going to let him die. "We don't want more pain."

"No," my mother agrees, uncertain, "we don't want him suffering—" She turns to me questioningly. "No extraordinary measures; do they always die, the men, after you say that?"

"No, Mother, just if they are already dying . . ."

I want him to go. I shut my eyes. I want the last eight years not to have been, the staring look in the eye from L-dopa, the shuffling walk, the wheelchair. I see him running across the lawn in Great Marsh, winning. I was the favored child. Conned me into thinking I had good character. When I was thirty-five years old, I observed myself relishing a ratty, bitchy act. Who, me? I had never questioned his appraisal of me! Was startled when people complained to me about my faults. Didn't they know? I had the *wonderful character*. Daddy, I want you to die. Please die, please go away. Don't stare at me with your child's blue scared eyes.

"I really argued with the generals."

"Come closer, Bunny."

I freeze in terror. He's going to make me come near him; then I'll smell his old-man fear. *Daddy, say something like "It's time enough, I've lived enough." But it's a lousy lie. He wants to go home with Marte and Mother, he wants to keep on living, he wants your girls, he wants to go back to his study, even in the wheelchair. No extraordinary measures. Does he realize what we've done? He would have had faith; if it had been you, he'd have breathed life into you until the last. He'd have called in a whole new team of doctors, he wouldn't have given up on you. But you are giving up on him.*

I go home. Later the doctor calls me to get back to the hospital; I know he's going. When I get there, the wife of a patient in the adjoining room is talking rapidly to my mother. She is taking her address and promises to send her a scarf from a clothing line she merchandises. I walk down the hospital hall; it is quiet in my father's room. He's dead, I think. I look at my mother, she is staring at me like a small child; she and Marte are waiting for the doctor to come, the women are unsure of what the quiet means. But we know. The hospital is short-staffed. It takes fifteen minutes for an intern to arrive and pronounce him a corpse. He closes the curtains; then they wheel him out. My mother looks up at me—Mark has come, we are her future now.

When we get downstairs it is pouring on Madison. Not a taxi in sight. We walk the two women in the pouring rain down to Ninety-sixth Street. Mark tells us to go get some tea in the Rambles while he looks for a cab.

"It's awful out," my mother says.

Marte says nothing; her life is over, she shatters, her shoulders stoop; hours after my father's death Marte becomes an old woman. My mother is different; her aloneness gives her courage to take a belated walk through the world.

Over tea my mother muses, "When you think of it ... I grew up here, on Ninety-eighth and Madison. After the First World War my brother took me up to the Alhambra—Harlem wasn't Harlem then; I mean, it was vaudeville ..." She sighs. "I kept staring out of the window of his room, thinking I grew up here on this street, and now he is here ... dying ... and where I grew up there are highrises now, that's what I thought." Mark comes back in a taxi, and we take the women home. We sit aimlessly in the kitchen. We'll make a small ceremony, have him cremated. We decide to throw the ashes in the Sound, the pier off Great Marsh, our summer home.

Marte weeps. "I don't want the mister cremated—it's not right, why can't you use the plot in Westchester near *die Schwiegermutter?*"

My mother shakes her head. "I don't want him buried near *die Schwiegermutter.* He's my husband, more than he's *her* son. I don't want a plot—I'm giving my pieces to Mount Sinai; it's all pledged, so they'll never bury me, I'll be just cut up and dumped in the eye bank."

Marte weeps. "I don't want the mister burned up."

My mother answers firmly, "He made me promise, don't let the rabbis bury me . . . so we'll send him to Great Marsh."

In part of Maria's letter to my mother, from Paris, she writes:

> . . . Just as Mommy called, Jennifer and I were about to go to a concert of Vivaldi's *Gloria.* It's one of my absolute favorite pieces and I've been looking forward to it for several weeks. It was in a church and was very moving. In a way it made Grandpa's death particularly appropriate and dignified, as I felt that I was having my own memorial service for him in my own way—with my own choice of music. I think he'd be pleased to know that in addition to all the other reminders of him is now also one of the most beautiful choral pieces I can think of. So I enclosed the program for you so you can share the feeling. I'm also enclosing the poem *Dover Beach* by Matthew Arnold. I took it out of a book *Immortal Poems* that Grandpa once gave me. I remember it was one of his favorite poems and that once he had Carla, Liz, Nick, and me in his room and he asked one of us to read it aloud. I had often had the idea to copy it out nicely and frame it for him as a Father's Day present or something—but never got around to it. So by giving it to you, I imagine myself going into his room, giving him also a hug and kiss and saying, "Here, Grandpa, Happy Father's Day." . . .

Then Carla, down from Yale, spoke for the grandchildren at the small memorial service. My daughters' lives have been backward; their father had died, their grandfather had lived. "In trying to decide how my grandfather was most meaningful in my life, I also keep returning

to recollections of Great Marsh . . . In doing this I'm also speaking for
Maria, Lizzie, and Nick, as well as all the Fresh Air Fund children with
whom we shared the Big House. First of all, there was the loveliness
. . . I have never seen the effect of early-morning sun hitting the water
quite as beautiful as I remember it there. Just being there gave us a
sensitivity to certain days and weathers that we will always be able to
draw on as adults . . ."

Carla looks up, her straight black hair and pointed chin, white,
small face, give her a pensive look; she seems solemn and young. Then
she continues.

"But that was the beauty of the place . . . it was the emotional atmosphere that was most important. Children always have a hard time dis-
tinguishing the real from the possible, the wish from the deed. Our
summers gave us the sense that absolutely anything could and did
happen in life. I remember, once, seeing an eel by the dock in a pail
and being told I couldn't keep it as a pet. Being accustomed to getting
most things I wanted, I naturally cried. But my grandfather assured
me that he would get something better, and the next time he came
out from the city, along with him came the most elaborate fish tank
I'd ever seen, filled with beautiful tropical fish.

"The freedom we were all given to act on what our imaginations
cooked up, with the assurance that the gap between the real and the
possible was negligible, led to endless productions of plays and bal-
lets." She pauses.

"As my grandparents' financial situation became tighter, we decided
that the four of us could easily raise enough money to build the
swimming pool we wanted, simply by writing and producing a musical and charging twenty-five cents' admission . . ." Suddenly Carla hesitates. In the end it hadn't been a question of swimming pools; the
place was lost. ". . . an atmosphere where creativity and sensory respon-
siveness were allowed to grow at a time when it's most important that
they do grow . . . and that if you wished for something badly enough,
the wish could come true. I've been an adult long enough to know
that life is not quite so simple, but I would rather have learned that
lesson well and have some disappointment result than the gray wisdom that the world is essentially opposed to our deepest desires, and
that satisfactions can only be the result of our constant struggles with
it." Suddenly I see Carla look my way, then abruptly she sits down.

———

The week after the funeral I explain to my mother that Juan will drive up to Connecticut with me to dispose of the ashes. "Juan? Juan Benet?" she asks, as though one Juan is a cloning of the other.

"No, another Juan—well, they know each other." I lie, not knowing what childish habit makes me do it. "This Juan will be driving up to Saugatuck with me; he has some Puerto Rican students who have a car."

"Oh, fine. Daddy would have liked being buried by Puerto Ricans—I mean, all things that are a sign of *change* are good, I say, if the blacks take the next round, well, long overdue. Eleanor Roosevelt liked the blacks."

"Puerto Rican, not black."

"Well, it's a change, that's what's important—look at our family. My cousins were in an uproar when I married your father. Barbara, should we have agreed to no extraordinary measures?"

"You don't want him to have gone through this Franco routine? Organ by organ?"

"Well," she continues, "my cousins said, So Frances is marrying one of these Christmas-tree Jews—but now all their grandchildren have names like MacPherson, McNulty, and Corning. Well, I can't change history, but we had *respect,* even though we went our separate ways, and no one could call us narrow-minded. I don't think back about the place; when my friends ask me, Well, what about Great Marsh, I say, Well, that was then."

Several weeks later my nephew Nick, Juan, and his Puerto Rican students drive with me to Saugatuck. Nick holds the box of ashes. I suck in my breath when I see the place. The large stone gates have been knocked down, the brass address plate is missing. The place has an awful name and has become a fancy suburban development. We drive toward the barn, which used to be painted red. Now it is stylish puce. The man guarding the gate to the new yacht club stops the car. "I'm Mr. Probst's daughter," I say, leaning my head out of the car window. He nods and waves us on.

We get out of the car, Nick has the urn; the two of us walk down to the beach, at the end of the walk used now for the boat moorings. The leaves are yellow and rust, the weather brisk—a good fall day. The sun is reflected at angles off the water.

"Shall I do it now, Aunt Barb?" Nick asks.

"Please."

I turn my back. I don't want to see the ashes. "Is it almost gone?" I ask Juan, who is staring at the water.

"Yes—I've never seen ashes."

When I turn, small white pieces of confetti roll along the currents across the sound, toward Long Island. I put my arm around Nick, and the two of us walk toward the Big House. The trees are flourishing, but on the site of the gardens and the old sundial is a new modern house. I lean down to pick up a broken toy off the road; then I let it drop. Cleaning debris off the walks is no longer my business. I turn back and give a last look. Out of lack of energy, or a frightened heart, I haven't the strength to evoke the whole past, the voices, the generations, the families, the picnics, the English croquet tournaments; neither Nick nor I say, Remember this, or Remember that; silently, we just let Juan buy us all lunch in the Italian roadhouse near the railway station.

I stare at Juan, wanting to share with him the experience of my past. But it is hard to describe, because we just lived here, in our own way, inventing our own traditions. I could talk to him about the McCarthy era. He can comprehend something very definite, visual, like La Marqueta in the barrio, which is like an Arab bazaar, but what eludes him, what I can't share with him, are the summers of my American childhood: the bicycles, the heat, the sun on goldenrod fields, the salt marshes, the scorched grass, the dopey fairs, our yellow Sunfish, swimming out to the red buoys, the waxed paper cups of oversweet mixed juices, and the charcoaled meats and summer fish. In an illuminating flash, I realize that my own daughters confuse their growing up at Great Marsh with my youth.

During my early childhood we were always packed off. From the time I was four until the time I was eight, I was shipped off with Mickey to summer camp. That was me, ze youngest camper. Have suitcase, can travel. We became more of a family after I was almost grown up, in time for my children to get it on the next round.

"Well," I say to Juan, waving my hand toward the Saugatuck station, "that was it." Afterward we drive back to the city, down the West Side highway, turning in at Ninety-sixth Street.

That night I get tired fast and I crawl into bed. Juan comes into the room, he sits on the edge of the bed; I am half asleep. He flicks on the TV for news of Franco. "He drank the blood of those students he murdered," Juan remarks. "Their blood is keeping him alive . . ."

"What does Channel 4 have on him?" I ask sleepily.

"Sounds as if he's going to live forever, just my luck, he won't die on a weekend when I'm here but during the week when I'm in Pittsburgh."

"We'll have a party and invite everyone, we'll plan it for next Friday night, he's got to be gone by then."

"Are you all right?"

"Yes, I'm fine. Parents just die, I'm fine." I close my eyes, marveling at how controlled I am. I feel nothing. I, his favorite, never am sad for my father. Days after his death, the Spanish part of my life takes over. *Ogro* is just published, and I am on many TV shows as a political expert. I am being my old man's daughter, smart and savvy on high-think politics. Why couldn't he have held out just the few more weeks? But Juan is with me, so I don't mourn my eighty-two-year-old father, and I am grateful that my mother, after his death, has it in her to become a late bloomer. The feminist movement buoys her up. Several years later, one evening at the Actors Studio, I would watch Harold Clurman put on a show. His irreverent, cultivated style, typical of certain types of New York men from his generation, would pierce me. I would notice his polished black leather shoes, so near I could practically smell the shine; my father was also a sporty gent, and if he had his way, he would have wanted to live on, even in a wheelchair, just to have remained with the action. *No extraordinary measures.* And I would cup my face in the two palms of my hands and weep unconsolable tears.

Late at night I get a phone call from Pepe in Paris. "Nobody's hurt—but Ruedo's been bombed. An ultra-right group has claimed credit."

"Pepe!"

"We're all right; they didn't get the archives."

"You've been bombed?" Dazed, I repeat what he said.

I am alone that night. I walk through my apartment, repeating to myself, Ruedo is gone. My father, now Ruedo. All that intelligence and work destroyed by a goon squad. A parting shot, just before Franco dies.

Juan flies into New York the following weekend, and Sunday night we walk over to Times Square, to watch the news teletype; we are waiting for Franco's organs to be pronounced moribund so Juan won't be alone in Pittsburgh when he hears the news. But nothing that weekend is final. Reluctantly he goes back to teach on Monday morning.

It isn't until Thursday, while Nicolás, Graciela, and I are eating dinner in a Basque restaurant in the West Village, that we get the news. The waiter comes over. "Say, Franco is dead—it's on the TV news." We are silent. Anita, one of the students on a year's fellowship, yowls hysterically, "The postage stamps—I never will have to see his face on the stamps!" Nicolás comes over and hugs me; then he orders champagne, and after we drink toasts to the future, the past, and so forth, we line up at two public telephones. Nicolás reaches his father in Buenos Aires, I locate Juan in Pittsburgh. Later that night a party in Nicolás's house just grows and at the end of the week, when Juan comes back from Pittsburgh, the two of us have a big celebration in my place.

Juan and I make plans to be together in Europe, but he goes back first. Then, in late December, I get a threat through the mails, which slows down my plans for several months. Because of the Letelier murder, and the Maryland postmark, the FBI is called in. A very jazzy young woman and her male partner show up at my apartment. I am surprised at how stylish they are. Over several Scotches they discuss the situation with me; clearly this is the work of the ultra-right, someone has picked up on my anti-Franco TV performances, or perhaps it is due to the American publication of *Operation Ogro*. The envelope also contains a clipping of the Rosenbergs' execution, and in the letter are several incoherent sentences attacking what they call my "flea of Israel."

The FBI offers me police protection. About my trip to Spain—why not cool it for a few months? But there is nothing they can do. Meanwhile, I arrange for a series of articles that will help pay for the trip. Juan writes that Barcelona is splendid, to hurry up, and Nicolás sends me letters and telegrams from Buenos Aires, to make sure I will be in Madrid to welcome him when he returns with his father. I realize that the return of the Sánchez-Albornoz family to Spain is going to be a major event. Pepe writes that the Spanish and European press latched on to the homecoming as signifying the *legitimization* of the new regime. By the middle of April I am ready to leave for Spain.

On the TWA flight over, I remind myself, my father is dead. I tap my nails against the cold window. You paid more attention to Franco's death, who meant nothing to you, than his. What has the death of an aging dictator to do with your life? Your father taught the girls *Dover Beach*. Behind Lincoln Center there is a small building. Louis Brandeis School. *Bunny, do you know who built America? Robber barons, now don't form the habit of believing it was some make-believe Rooseveltian dream.*

In the early-April Madrid morning, when I deplane at Barajas, I am still confused. What am I doing here? Journalist? Writer? Nicolás's friend? Through the glass customs door at Barajas, I see Marisol, Paco and Juan Benet's sister, waiting for me. I remember my father's odd phrase, *The big money is always in the imagination.* Relaxing, I forgive myself a little for my strained evasions in the face of his love, my cool watching him die; the air is brisk, and I run toward Marisol.

19

She smiles conspiratorially, communicating to me her awareness that our reunion is connected with the political theater that is taking place in Madrid. We are part of the new panorama.

She hugs me, and after we collect my bags and her car, she drives me over to Juan Benet's house in the Viso, the old residential part of the city. She takes me upstairs and shows me my room. Marisol is a calm woman with an innate gift for personal happiness; feather-cut blond-beige hair softens her slender aquiline profile. She has none of the Benet temperament. Juan is in China on an engineering junket. Both of us are relieved that he isn't in Madrid. Welcoming back his dead brother's long-lost friend isn't Juan's sort of thing.

On the terrace of Marisol's cool apartment at Fernández de la Hoz, near the center of Madrid, we have coffee. Her husband, Luis Cavanna, asks me if I am able to stave off jet lag; he needs to go to Carabanchel and Yeserías prisons and wants me to come with him. Luis's father had been one of Franco's generals, but Luis "married Republican" and had decided it was more fun on the left. He had been one of the lawyers for the five students sentenced to death in the fall. Being with the families of those men, Luis says, was the awful part.

Luis drives us straight to Carabanchel. The wife of one of the executed students has recently given birth to a child in the female prison in Madrid, Yeserías. Her husband's friends in Carabanchel have gotten permission from the authorities for the baby to be brought from Ye-seriás to there for a prison visit. Luis needs a written confirmation of this before he will be allowed to remove the baby from Yeserías. If all goes well, he plans to have me hold the infant while he drives the car. After he parks his Renault in the lot, we walk over to the inner court-yard. One gaunt young woman sits on the curb; she seems supported, as though life at any moment could vanish from her limp body, by friends surrounding her. The circles beneath her eyes are the color of pale-green moons; her skin sallow. She is a pretty woman, but her breath has a faint sick odor. On her lap are Xeroxes of prison poetry. Her husband was executed in September. She finds a poem dedicated to her dead lover. "You must do this one," she says, her voice more firm. She introduces me to a young man, Miguel Morrant Melis.

He fishes out of his pocket a picture of his fiancée. "She got the death sentence in September, but that has been commuted to thirty-five years. Would you publish her picture? She's pretty," he adds.

"Did they give you permission for the wedding?" a friend asks him.

"Next week."

"Say, Miguel, after the wedding ceremony will they allow you your night with her?"

"The authorities haven't told us yet."

I join Luis, who is talking to a middle-aged couple, one of his fami-lies. The woman points to a hyperactive five-year-old boy running up and down the far end of the courtyard. She sighs; her son and daughter-in-law both are serving prison sentences. The grandparents, meanwhile, have Alejandro. "When we don't bring him with us to visit his parents, he feels abandoned, but the days we take him inside with us he gets frightened. He is all mixed up. Last night he yelled at me, Grandma, you are my prisoner, and I will hit you and hit you and hit you, the way they hit my parents. The child's not normal—"

Luis promises them he will find a child therapist. He has been given the necessary pass, so we leave for Yeserías. Just as we are getting into his car, a young woman runs up to us. She seems to know everyone and clearly is acting as a liaison between the prisoners and the lawyers. After we are introduced, she asks me, "How do you like our Madrid Hilton; crowded, isn't it?" Then she informs Luis, "Ramón Tamámes is getting out tomorrow, with several other Communists; the place will be loaded with press . . ." But her real reason for finding Luis is to warn him that in Yeserías a two-year-old child is being kept in solitary. A young woman, in prison for petty larceny, has been placed in an isolation cell. The woman hadn't been able to discipline her child, who had been overly rambunctious, and an angry official has tossed both mother and child, as an example to other too-lenient mothers, into solitary.

Even Luis, used to prison life, is taken aback. He promises to notify London Amnesty and the new Madrid press.

When we arrive at Yeseriás we learn that the women inmates have made a protest against the director for keeping the child in solitary. The women that we visited inside the prison complain that the conditions for their children at Yeseriás are terrible. Lousy diet, no facilities, and a constant intimidation of the mothers if their children are overactive; the women complain that this creates enormous tensions between them and their children. Meanwhile, the prison official informs Luis that the baby we want to drive to Carabanchel has contracted a heavy cough. They are afraid of the pulmonary risks if such a young infant were moved from prison to prison in Madrid. The official and Luis finally agree that the following week the baby would be granted a two-day pass. When we leave Yeseriás Luis seems tired, and I am suffering from jet lag.

I ask Luis to drive me back to Juan Benet's house in the Viso. Rosario, the housekeeper, lets me in. Then, barely nodding to the Benet children, I stagger up the two flights of stairs and collapse on the bed. Fully dressed, shoes kicked off, on top of the quilt, I fall into deep sleep, not awakening until the following day.

The next morning Rosario wakens me. Juan Goytisolo is on the telephone from Casablanca. I am glad to hear his voice, and we make plans that I will fly there as soon as possible.

I get dressed and go down to the ground-floor level, where Rosario serves me breakfast. Juan Benet has designed a modern kitchen with an open bar through which food can be passed into the dining room. There is a long, modern, marble dining table near the passway, and at the other end of the tiled floor are potted plants, a low-slung sofa, and a large television set; the Benet children use the place as a general family room. The kids have gone off to school, and Juan is still in China. I have breakfast alone. Cornflakes, orange juice, toast, and Cooper vintage marmalade are on the table. Juan's modern red mugs are identical to mine in New York, and I drink coffee served from the same Melior Pyrex coffeepot; the world has shrunk.

Rosario hands me the morning newspaper and recent editions of

Cambio 16, Cuadernos, and *Triunfo.* In Spain this spring Spaniards are reliving forty decades at one throw. I feel I have walked into a history bazaar. In one booth, the actors from 1936 are performing, down the street it is 1945; on another *via,* the supersophisticates of 1976 are hawking their show.

There is no need for me to request my old habit of holding semi-secret meetings with Madrid journalists in order to get the real news. Most of what is happening I can find out by reading the daily press. Just as I am wondering what to do next, Gloria, a literature professor, telephones me and invites me to a meeting of FLM that afternoon, a new feminist organization formed in January. Feeling lonely, I immediately say yes and take down her address.

As soon as I realize how easily I can inform myself about current politics, I sink into a state of disorientation, panic, and mild depression. Since I have been eighteen years old, I have been an observer of *clandestine* Spain. Suddenly the habits I have formed are of no use. I need to come to terms with the fact that I am prisoner of those habits. I have always written of Spain as though the psychological effects of dictatorship happened to *they, them.* But if you get sucked in, as an observer, for a long period of time (merely my whole adult life), then *you* become part of the *they.* Now I am able to write everyone's telephone number down in a neatly organized telephone book. I could keep, if I want, a day-by-day diary, using the real names of people. I could telephone whomever I wish; Luis Cavanna was able to immediately contact London Amnesty about the Yeserías baby.

Suddenly what previously had taken enormous daring, time, and energy, in a new light appears to be just operational maneuvers, which can be dealt with in a matter of minutes. I have come to Madrid, as I always had done in the past, with many journalist assignments.

POLITICAL JOURNAL

Madrid: April 21, 1976

My ways of doing things no longer make sense. I grab a sweater, go outside and hail a taxi. I tell him to take me to Generalísimo, the *Cambio 16* building. I ask for Juan Oneto. When he comes out I tell him about the child in solitary. "We'll send a reporter right over to Yeserías," Oneto assures me. "This is our first tip on the situation." Now the Spanish journalists can handle their own stories of prison abuse. There is no need for me to send the story of Yeserías back to New York. All I have to do is pick up *Cambio 16*, decide on a topic, and write it. Now I can get facts from reading. No more street-corner meetings, no endless solitary guesswork journalism, no sense that it is me who is reporting otherwise unrecorded history. No peripheral anxieties about which political groups can be mentioned in the press. And no feeling that if I didn't publish a specific piece, about this Star Chamber trial, or that torture, the world would end. This new way of doing things leaves me unable to function.

Back outside in the daylight, I walk along Generalísimo, thinking unpleasant thoughts about myself. Now that I merely have to paraphrase the new Spanish press, I have no idea where to begin, or what's worse—*why* it is necessary. I feel it is irrelevant as to whether or not one more piece about Spain is published in the United States. What matters now—I try to assess my situation—isn't what Americans report—that phase is over—but that journalists here can now get the news in print. Spaniards writing for the *madre patria!* Well, well! Franco's death has done me out of a calling. I leaf through the daily newspapers; I blank, can't think of anything to write. Feel lost. My Spanish pieces had been written in an anonymous voice; I had no existence, purposely, in those articles. Now I am no longer sure from which viewpoint I should be writing. Do I continue using that cool, detached style? Do I then add, P.S., and by-the-by, I am part of what I am recording? Dangerous, negative abyss. The more I question my motives, the more unappetizing the truth seems. Had I expended too much energy reporting on the underground? What yesterday had seemed *urgent* in retrospect strikes me as primitive.

The American side of you is still intact. What I have written about it, precisely because it wasn't muddied with imperative, that this or that piece will keep a political prisoner alive, seems now to me to be more intelligent. Ruefully I recognize that other qualities, the secrecy, anonymity, guesswork, and danger, had been involved in the Spanish stuff. Clearly I would have made a first-rate spy, Nancy Drew, girl detective. Keep up with this self-doubt, you'll end up in a mental wheelchair!

Well, there is nothing I can do (I've probably made a mess and fucked up my life) but *keep* going. I return to Pisuerga, and go back upstairs to my bedroom. On the top landing I pause and look down from the window into the garden where Nuria had plunged to her death. *Don't think about it,* another era. I still feel no urgency to file articles; I need to relocate my own center.

I think back to past meetings with feminists; how different the circumstances had been. In 1971, after incredible maneuvering, I had been taken to a secret meeting of radical feminists. We knew it was neither legal nor safe for more than eight of us to meet in a Madrid public place. Although our group was small, the atmosphere in the restaurant was volatile with female sexual urgency. One of the women had complained that her husband didn't know how to arouse her; another replied, in an overly loud voice, "Tell him to masturbate you." The waiters and other customers had stared at us. Then one of them whispered, "Amalia, you are crazy, we shall land in prison." We spent an hour conferring: would it be productive if I wrote about the existence of feminists in Madrid, or would I be spotlighting the movement for the police? We vetoed the idea of a piece, but the women wanted me *sotto voce* to tell American feminists of their existence.

Now, 1976, an elegant young woman approaches me at a cocktail party in the Velázquez Hotel. "Barbara?" I don't recognize her. "Pilar—the 1971 radical feminists." She laughs. "I've had a nose job. *Mutatis mutandis.*"

What kind of telegrammatic sentences did I believe I was taking back to America? To whom, from whom, and why? I can no longer remember the *raison d'être* of 1971. To whom did oppressed Spaniards constantly imagine they were sending messages? What, precisely, was that free world receiving their information? During that trip I stayed at the Wellington and had a casual affair with a European journalist based in Spain. "I'll swap you twenty Communists for one feminist," Paul bargained; he wanted to do an article on the incipient radical underground feminist movement. I argued with him, the feminists didn't want publicity; the Communists, however, needed it. Two different situations. It was Paul who took me to visit Marcelino Comacho's sister and wife, at their home in Carabanchel. There were four women in the room of Josefina Comacho's apartment; they scrawled the names of their incarcerated male relatives on scraps of paper. Everything, then, was done on the backs of matchboxes. Josefina said, "Tell the people of America

...." Just who is America? Amnesty International, a short column in the *New York Review*, *The Nation*, or the *Times*? What those women had in mind was *Meet John Doe*. Gary Cooper grabs the mike in Washington, eluding a powerful, evil Edward Arnold, while a tearful, repentant on-the-make Barbara Stanwyck at the last possible moment throws her support to the good guy—Gary Cooper. *But the little fella is going to keep on fighting ... because I know ... We Americans aren't going to let the big guys take our democracy.* Barbara Stanwyck weeps, as Edward Arnold's goons cut the cords of the mike, while Cooper, undaunted, bravely carries on. I had loathed the political naïveté of the generation before me who relied on such easy sentiment—so, how had I gotten in such a fix?

In America, I write cool, intelligent prose. Here, in Spain, I keep uncool, uncomplex sentences in bits of hidden notebooks. To be a writer, you must dominate the raw material, subject it to your own form. I do that at home. But not here. Twenty-five years of raw data, prison names, dates, tortures kept on the same pieces of paper that were given to me. *Sacred material not to be dominated by a writer. Exist only in raw state. And locked in the memory lobes of my cranium. 1951, Tomás Centeno, member executive committee, Socialist Party, Madrid,* tortured to death in cell of Madrid Dirección de Seguridad. Police claim suicide. *Medical evidence of cadaver indicates torture including use of botte malaise, instrument that crushes bones.*

The sentences sit, unfixed, in the forefront of my brain; what am I meant to do? Make a novel out of them? *The archives of prison names, dates, and tortures no longer belong to you. Get them out of your head. It's over now, give the files to some other authority. Later others will use those files and make a new truth out of them.*

You have a nice afternoon meeting with feminists at Gloria's house. No complicated maneuverings. Your new existence in Madrid is much freer. All you have to do is let go. *Relinquish the files in the cranium lobes behind your eyes.* Let go, and just be.

When I arrive at Gloria's house late that afternoon, the five university professor women and myself are served whiskey and black olives by her children. I am wrong in thinking the most urgent problem to be discussed is the two-year-old in solitary.

After I settle into Gloria's comfortable living room in a sprawling house on the outskirts of Madrid, I tell my story. But the women stare blankly at me. *Where is their shock? Too passive.*

"It's not good for children." I search for a threshold of communication.

"No, no, Barbara, *es terrible, pero* . . ." One of them hesitates. "Is it a UPM situation?"

"UPM?"

"Unión Popular de Mujeres—they are connected with FRAP, the student organization that had five of its students executed by Franco just before he died. If this is *their* protest, there isn't any point in us getting into it. We're FLM. Frente de Liberación de Mujeres. We've just organized ourselves in January—our ties are with the Socialists."

"The mother isn't a political prisoner, she's in for petty larceny. Her child is neither UPM, FLM, or MDM. *You* can do something about that child right now, Franco is dead. You already have power to make yourselves heard . . ." I hesitate. *Don't deliver a broadside. Your personal friends in Spain have been a small, self-motivated group of elite intellectuals totally divorced from the mainstream of Spanish life. You knew them, you knew their domestic help, you knew, as a writer, students and political activists who chose to live on the barricades—what do you know, though, of ordinary Spanish life? Would you expect an average American to be concerned about what goes on in an American prison?*

Gloria senses I have retreated into a confused politeness; she wants to draw me back into the conversation. "Do you think we are going about it wrong?"

This time I am more cautious. "Look, Franco's been dead six months. I don't believe in asking people to commit dangerous acts, but, I guarantee, you already possess certain powers. If a group of you, just as women, not as FLM, visited the prison director—"

Ana, who teaches a ceramic course in a private studio near Calle Mayor, points out that the only group of women to perceive of their situation as separate from political movements are the Colectivos, who are considered superrevolutionary because they don't attach themselves to a male political organization.

In America you didn't like the feminist movement because it lacked a broad political orientation, too middle class and narrow in focus; yet here in Madrid feminist movements tightly dominated by political parties also seem inadequate.

Gloria is the only one of the group aware that Spain was one of the first countries to have a strong feminist movement. Later in the evening we talk of the extraordinary role Spanish women have played in politics. Dolores Ibarruri was head of the Communist Party, Federica

Montseny of the Anarchist movement, and Victoria Kent was one of the chief Socialist deputies during the Republic. In the thirties there were incredible women, Margarita Nelcken, Constancia de la Mora ... Mercedes points out that these women need to be tracked down, rediscovered. "In Spain, in politics, we have good female role models; it's odd, but it isn't as true in creative fields. Here, this has always been male."

Evening falls apart when I mention Eva Sastre still in prison. Women silent. Ana confesses Eva was her best friend. Says when Eva arrested she tore up photograph of herself with Eva. Avoided any connection. I want to ask, But why did you do nothing? You could have put a letter in the mail to Amnesty, formed a group. Why nothing? When I remind Ana that her friend Eva is still in prison, Ana is silent. Mercedes says, "An anonymous woman published a letter in Cuadernos *last week, demanding an end to the conspiracy of silence on Eva Sastre. Some women in Barcelona have formed a group for her." This is the week that political parties (excepting Communist) are legalized. Eva is a thorn in the side of both Socialists and Communists, a victim of political transition.*

Ana avoids my gaze. "*Es verdad, que hemos hecho muy poco por Eva?*" I stare at her. But what's preventing her from action now? The women suddenly announce, almost in chorus, "We'll do something now, *es verdad.*"

Then Gloria offers to drive me home. On the way back to the Viso, she turns to me. "Because of the child in solitary and our lack of action for Eva, you fail to take us ... seriously?"

"No, Gloria," I say slowly, "it's just the opposite; the point is that I take all of you too seriously."

We stand on the stoop steps of Juan's house. Gloria looks pale; her face has that intelligent, weary look women in their mid-thirties sometimes get when they have children, careers, and no husbands. Now Gloria is living with a new man, who is showing signs of leaving her. She runs her hand, tiredly, across her forehead. "Barbara, what do you think is going to happen here next?"

"Juan Carlos seems not bad. Maybe, if everyone tried very hard, some small reasonable changes could be accomplished—" My voice drifts off; suddenly I am sleepy. "What Spain needs now is forty years of boring, defective, mundane democracy."

Gloria gives a small, breathy sigh; then the two of us, European-style, kiss good night and part.

———

Spring asparagus weather; the next morning the air is mild and humid. I have the day marked off in my journal. April 23, 1976. After I dress, I go downstairs for breakfast. Juan and Nuria's daughter, Juana, is dawdling over her food.

While I butter my toast, she purses her lips and stares at me.

"Grandma says Uncle Paco was in the Resistance, which is why you and Aunt Marisol have to go to the airport today ... Did he do all those things she told us?"

"Yes, but we thought of ourselves as just keeping busy."

"My mother helped in those plans?"

"Yes, yes, she did." I pause. "Which made me part of it."

Then Marisol walks into the family room, her high heels make a great clatter on the cool tiled floor. Her manner is light; she interprets the day as a festive occasion and has gotten herself well turned out. She shows Juana and me the morning paper; the Sánchez-Albornoz arrival is the lead story. Graciela, Nicolás's third wife, is described as the mother of his children: no divorces are mentioned. They write that Nicolás left Spain in the late 1940s. Nothing is said about his having been in a concentration camp or his escape.

Luis drives Marisol and me to the airport. On the car radio we hear the latest news. "The Sánchez-Albornoz plane is now directly over Lisbon. They are thirty-five minutes from Barajas airport."

Startled, I turn around and look at Marisol.

But Marisol seems to be thinking of something to do with the past. "Barbara, what do you think really happened to Paco?"

In the late 1960s you spent hours in Dr. Max Schur's office puzzling out what had taken place. Among New York anthropologists rumors circulated: jeep accident in the desert, suicide, or foul play. You were very disturbed. A man you once had loved very much had vanished. No clear report of death ever was given. But after several years had passed, your life changed, and eventually you forgot about the past.

For a long time I don't answer. Then I say I believe there really was a jeep accident in the desert.

We arrive at Barajas. While Luis is parking the Renault, Marisol and I walk over to the entrance to International Arrivals. Spanish officials recognize Marisol and rush us into the special room the Spanish government, this spring, set aside for the re-entry onto Spanish soil of "special political arrivals." New rules for the new Madrid, daily, are being made. The place is packed with foreign and Spanish journalists. For the European press the return of key figures representing the Spanish Republic signifies the beginnings of legitimization of the new regime. As the United States doesn't regard the Franco regime as illegitimate, these symbolic acts of return have less significance for us. A friend of Marisol's whispers that Prime Minister Adolfo Suárez has sent his father to the airport. He points to a nervous-looking elderly man who fiddles with his tie. "He and old Sánchez-Albornoz as young men were pals—they both came from Ávila."

Marisol suddenly pushes me toward a group of women. When she informs them that I am Barbara, the room resounds with loud female shrieks. It takes me a few moments to realize that the women are wailing at *me*.

"Oh, my God, how terrible it was! The police rushed into our house in Ávila, demanding Nicolás. We were stunned, we had no idea what they wanted. They said, You always visit Nicolás on Sunday— why not this past Sunday? Nicolás had told us, Don't come to the prison this weekend. The officers kept yelling at us, that we *knew*. Why did you do such a thing? We thought he was dead."

I stare at them. *But all that happened long ago. A conversation that never took place in '48 now is being finished in '76.* The more the women moan at me, the more I back off. Luis Cavanna then comes and takes me to one side. "See that man talking to the French journalist? He is the official government greeter; the regime wants a good press on the returnees." Our quarters are being set up for the journalists and TV teams. Suddenly a man comes running into the press room. "The President's plane is coming down, the President's plane has landed," he yells. We follow the crowd to the macadam runway. An Iberia official orders us to stand back as the plane rolls to a halt. As soon as the ladder starts to descend, even before it hits the ground, the journalists and cameramen jump up onto the moving ramp. I lean against the outer wall of the Air Terminal building and watch what is happening. Graciela (months ago she was padding barefoot, blue-jeaned, in their Bleecker Street apartment) is demurely standing at the top of the ramp. She is carrying a fur coat and with her other free arm she protectively encircles Nicolás's Evelina, warding off the press stampede. Then I see Nicolás. *In 1948, when we got Nicolás and Monolo out of Cuelgamoros, Nicolás asked Paco if we could drive through Madrid. Paco said no, and ordered me to keep driving in the direction of Barcelona. Before Nicolás and I knew each other's names, I saw him turn back and wave at*

Madrid through the rearview window. When he comes off the ramp he runs toward us. Nicolás and his father have been weeping. Graciela, right behind him, says that as soon as the plane flew over Lisbon, she had to keep passing the Kleenex to father and son.

"Your flight over Portugal was on the radio," Marisol says.

"Really?" Graciela is astonished.

Nicolás says to me, "Well, well. You took me out of Spain, come on now, take me back in." So the two of us cross the threshold into the jammed press room. I remember to tell Nicolás that his friend, the economist Ramón Tamámes, was let out of Carabanchel prison yesterday. "People, every day, are being freed from the prisons. Oh, and they are legalizing the Socialist Party this week."

Later, just as I am reaching down to the ground to retrieve a bone button that has fallen off my coat, I hear Don Claudio confirm over state-controlled television that his son Nicolás escaped from a concentration camp in 1948. He goes on to explain that Cuelgamoros was a very important camp, as Franco used the slave labor from it to construct his own future tomb, the Valley of the Fallen. I hear one of the newspapermen from *Cambio 16* suddenly say, "It's started. The news about Spanish concentration camps is out, the old man said it!"

While the TV men are taking photographs for their story, Nicolás introduces me to several journalists. In a low, urgent voice, one of the men informs us that we have inadvertently "jumped" their secret agenda. The new press—*Cuadernos, Cambio 16, Triunfo*—has been trying, each week, to break through censorship. Torture is out in the open, and the next item will be the story of the concentration camps. Just during this past month, reports about the German ones have been published—Belsen, Auschwitz have been a way in for the press. They are being cautious in revealing shocking historic detail to the general public; in this period the Franco police and old guard military are still in power. The Opposition press's next objective is to topple the musty Arias Navarro caretaker government.

The press needs Nicolás to *prove* that he had been in Stalag 3 of Cuelgamoros, that the Valley of the Fallen had been built by slave labor. Nicolás points to me. "She was there, she helped us escape."

Two of the men come over to me. They want me to tell them everything I can remember: who was in the concentration camps, how we planned the escape, and what other political prisoners escaped from Cuelgamoros. They tell me they will need to know everything; it turns out that I have been witness to a Spanish past. What next is necessary, they insist, is impeccable proof.

Nicolás and his family are finally whisked away in a large black rented limousine. Marisol and I watch the car disappear. When you've been a guest at someone else's wedding, just afterward there is a lonely space. Almost aimlessly, the two of us walk over to the parking lot. Luis is already inside the Renault. Marisol says, "The Sánchez-Albornoz family has so many cousins."

"Yes."

"I explained to Nicolás that our mother couldn't come because of her bad hip, but that she would be watching their arrival on TV; Doña Teresa wants Nicolás to visit her as soon as possible."

"Yes."

I keep blinking. I feel envious of the journalists. By tonight they will have published the Sánchez-Albornoz story. *Don Claudio weeps in Madrid.* They seem quick and purposeful, the way I remembered my former self. Now I am disoriented. There is nothing for me to write about. I no longer am a cool, brisk commentator; instead, I have fallen into this odd basket of Spanish history. I have lost my bearings as a writer. On our drive back to Madrid, I gaze out the car window. *Paco said, You get stuck with a hero label, your mind corrodes, playing golden boy is not a useful occupation for intellectuals. Leave that to the dummies.* My brains seem mush, I move now in slow motion. The past has cropped up and become the big news of the present. I needed to redefine myself. What I can't avoid is that I have been one of the few witnesses to a political period most Spaniards know little about. The beginnings of the second wave of Resistance in the late forties. *Try perceiving yourself as one of those people who get chosen as a stand-in. Interesting how few of the stand-ins actually have been in prison. Stand-ins are frequently upper-class intellectuals who are able to write. The people who suffer—the butcher, the baker, the candlestick maker—remain incognito. You have never spent even an afternoon in prison; oh, you have had your share of personal tragedies, but you have never been oppressed because of a political stand. Much of your life has been lived on the high side in the safety of Madison Avenue or Central Park West. And yet here you are, a stand-in. In another country. For high-minded acts.*

Paco Benet had asked two things of me: never to believe his fellow countrymen if they told me I had been a heroine, and to keep his papers for him about his time in the underground. I had tried to do both. Now, twenty-eight years later, the Spanish press wants those papers back.

When Luis pulls up in front of the Benet house on Pisuerga, Marisol turns to me. "What are you doing this evening?"

"Having dinner with Goya, Fernando, and the usual gang."

"Like always," Marisol notes. And kisses me good-bye.

20

But I feel at loose ends. Let down. I'm meeting Fernando and Goya Chueca, Paco's cousins, and the others at a new Chinese place near Cibeles. It's a funny time for them too. I remember back to the early fifties in New York. Paco had a fellowship in anthropology at Columbia, at the same time that Fernando had been given a grant there in architecture. The four of us endlessly walked the city.

At first no one mentions this past morning—Fernando avoids mentioning Paco. His intelligent eyes reflect disappointment as he holds forth on the new politics. What he really wants is a bookish, constructive middle ground. A liberal adrift in Madrid. "And this crop of Socialists all seems to be twenty-five."

"Join the youngies," Goya snaps at her husband, a wicked, bemused glint on her face. Goya is beautiful, Basque, and down-to-earth. "What kind of democracy are they giving us? Bowing to royalty—I want the authentic stuff." She throws back her head and laughs.

His friend Paulino Garragori says, "Fernando, our old way of meeting in small clandestine groups of intellectuals is over. Spain's going to have huge political parties."

"Just like America," I add. "Don't confuse friendship with politics. It's not like the Resistance."

"But, Bárbarita," Fernando protests, "as a writer will you enjoy yourself interviewing a bunch of moronic bureaucrats? Fascists cluttering up the political panorama with their 'Viva Moscow' or 'I have always been a democrat'?"

Their friends the Canejas arrive late. Juan Manuel's paintings have the empty look, the browns, ochers, and dust of the Madrid *meseta* in them. One of the best artists here, he is always somber and silent. But Isabel is dramatic. When she has had a few too many, she sings Andalusian love songs in a deep, throaty voice. Years ago she was his model. Which wasn't at that time very acceptable in starchy Madrid society. But Isabel was good to him after he was sent to prison in the 1940s (he had an intellectual involvement with the Anarchists), and he married her after he was released.

"Bárbarita!" She throws her arms up in the air, speaking loudly so the restaurant clientele can hear her. "When I saw the TV this morning, I nearly passed out. I raced into Juan Manuel's studio shrieking, Paco, our Paco, they are explaining the Valley of the Fallen; the escape is on national television. After twenty-eight years of silence —like a ghost returning. There's Barbara running up the ramp to kiss Nicolás . . ."

"I wasn't on the ramp . . . that was some other woman."

"Never mind, she looked like you. Isabel sits down and fans herself with the menu. We are all looking at her because she has voiced what everyone has been thinking but left unsaid—about this morning being special.

Fernando looks wistful. He has everything; he's a successful architect, a leading intellectual. Goya. But there are these gaps. When I first met Fernando he saw himself as a young father to Paco and Juan. Or an older brother in charge of their education.

"When I was at the café this afternoon," Isabel continues, "a new woman at our table had the nerve to ask me if I had heard the news: Spain had concentration camps, just like Germany. Then she boasted that her nephew was involved in the Cuelgamoros escape. Something about his handing off a brown paper bag in the Atocha railway station. What gall! Listen, Barbara, *nada de* paper bags in railway stations. By next week, we will hear that half a million Madrileños were on the road giving gasoline to the escapees."

"Isabel . . ." Juan Manuel pleads.

"*Nada de Isabel.* What did you know of what went on? You were locked away in prison; isn't that right, Barbara?"

"Isabel was terrific—Paco said she was a great liaison, always ready to go to the prisons for us. And she gave us a dish of strawberries." *She made you and Barbara eat them. You and Barbara were terrified she would have no food left for herself.*

"You see, I gave her strawberries."

Juan Manuel just stares into space; it's hard on him because he was the one Paco had meant to get out of Ocaña prison. Through Fernando (while Paco was still in a Madrid *lycée*) he had gotten to know Juan Manuel. Paco had told me that from his earliest days he had been in awe of that combination: the Civil War, Art, Anarchism. But as arranging for Juan Manuel to escape from Ocaña proved impossible, Paco next turned to the idea of liberating Nicolás and Manolo from Cuelgamoros.

The evening never takes off. Isabel begins to sing "Mi Amor Perdido." *"Isabelita, por favor,"* Juan Manuel says.

"The problem," Goya says suddenly, feet on the ground, always going to the core, "is that Franco died in bed."

I look at Juan Manuel, then Goya; I don't know what to say, so I finish eating the cool, slippery, canned lichee nuts, which smell of crushed lavender. Spain is a country that always awakens in me a profound desire to be unoriginal.

POLITICAL JOURNAL

Madrid: April 27, 1976

While I was packing in New York, I went through the closet where I store old papers, and I was amazed at how much of a record I had kept of clandestine Spanish politics. Despite all the movings around the United States when Harold was a law professor, somehow I never got around to throwing any of it out. Well, I wasn't alone. Now it turns out that all of Spain has kept records. When I take a taxi and start talking, the driver frequently will pull out an old union card from the Civil War period—UGT (Socialists), or CNT (Anarchists). I will be talking to an old man, and as he shoves his identity at me, I see a young version of the same face. The old men have kept some record of their past. Suddenly those pistachio-colored anorexic Christs with the aubergine wounds running down their legs seem to have disappeared (I never did like them), and instead, forty years of scraps of paper with forgotten names, facts, dates—yellow photographs, union cards, Civil War posters, clandestine political agreements, memorabilia, accusations—are tumbling out. It turns out Spain has been just one huge left-wing storage attic. An amazing amount of information is intact; it was hidden beneath the surface by just a thin layer of Fascist smog. Day by day, old men, hidden by those loyal Spanish wives on the top or bottom floor of homes in small villages, are stumbling out into the open. Forty years is a long time to keep intelligence in the cellar.

A bunch of new Spanish glossies have hit the stands; they've gone porno wild. Very Spanish porno. They go bananas over stories involving defrocked priests or misshapen people. So far we've had a sexy showgirl who has married a dwarf (he turns her on sexually). Also, a defrocked priest who has married Lola, or Carmen, or Paloma—whoever—the glossy carried lots of frontal shots; the stripteaser, natch, had a huge, bushy pubic. Shots of the grinning ex-priest. He insists sexy wifey is providing a moral service for Spain, protecting national honor from gays. The newsstands are flooded with magazines with centerfolds of peckers, asses, breasts, young females with cats perched purring on their genitalia. Another feature is of a man who is dying because his head is blowing up into an oversize dome, a rare disease. But mostly, the modern Spanish family wants peckers and cunt. After the old boy is dead, I suppose, they feel, We've waited a long time, now can we have a little look? But the Spanish Republic still can't be mentioned.

Madrid: April 28, 1976

Cities have a smell, make a sound. Madrid goes *fffffffff brrrrr, ppsspsspsstt;* it is a Byzantine political pot continually brewing over with hysteria, rumor, crisis, and life on the edge. Favorite expression of Madrileños is, "I can't take this city another day, too exhausting." That is, when they aren't thinking, city-proud, *"De Madrid al cielo,"* which means, "After Madrid, paradise." Both extremes here are trying. Madrid has lousy politics, but it is a city where people occasionally do pleasant things in the late afternoon.

A cheerful note in this grim, sullen, confused spring: have a "good-old days" reunion with Amadeo Cuito. We know each other from Paris. Amadeo's father was a minister during the Republic. Amadeo was born in France, and got to know Pallach as a kid, during World War II, when his father was running an underground railroad out of Perpignan for Spaniards and Jews, and Pallach helped him. He is full of stories, says the police came barreling into his apartment (opposite Franco's palace), just as he, his wife, several friends, and his two-year-old son were gathered, waiting for the news of Franco's death and already quite drunk on champagne. The police asked, "Any dissenters in this room?" Amadeo replied, "My son." The men saw the champagne and laughed, and all of them drank a toast to the future. In Madrid, things happen in *pockets*. On another day, another crew of police might have been murderous.

After Franco died, the Phalangist in the house next to Amadeo's panicked. He persuaded his cook to get Amadeo's concierge to arrange a meeting between the two men. Amadeo agreed, and the guy, trembling, came to Amadeo's apartment. He had read in the newspaper that Amadeo, along with other Socialists, had been locked up in prison for a short time several months before Franco died—his very own neighbor is a member of the Opposition! Meanwhile, the man had been trying to find a way in. He told Amadeo that he has a brilliant career ahead of him, he is under forty and a great vote getter in his hometown. One of those small Spanish cities you never hear much about, Badajoz, or perhaps it was Alicante. He swore to Amadeo that he had repented; he realized he had taken the wrong path. Could Amadeo now select for him a party that belonged to the Opposition? One with a future? Amadeo made a diagram for him explaining the new parties and the meaning of the political terms now being used in the press. (Now I understand what is meant by the phrase "politics of the concierge!") Amadeo contacted a boss of one of the middle-of-the-road groups and arranged for his entry. After all, Amadeo pointed out, the man probably is a great vote getter; he might as well be put to pragmatic use.

Amadeo's visit cheers me—he and Pallach both sound so full of energy and optimism. Since Pallach returned to Spain, he has become one of the main Socialists in Catalonia. Amadeo is now living full time in Barcelona and is helping him put his party together. Amadeo says when he and Pallach get the big Socialist meetings going, I must follow them on the campaign trail. Every time I read about Pallach in *Cambio 16,* as this great Catalan Opposition leader, I feel elated. Finally recognition! I've promised Amadeo I will get to Barcelona as soon as possible. Just to see him and Pallach perform.

Everything at the moment is half baked. Including the censorship. The huge banquet planned by Madrid intellectuals to honor Nicolás's father has been canceled, as the government is demanding that the guests not mention the Spanish Republic. Meanwhile, down the street, the Socialists and Communists are beginning to hold open meetings.

When I arrive at the Wellington to visit Nicolás, the desk clerk smiles at me. "Ah, Señora Solomon, for Don Claudio." He snaps his fingers at the bellboy to escort me up to the star suite; a new regime has begun. Although I recognize him from past visits to the hotel, he shows no sign that he remembers me. I try to look cool and bourgeois as I walk through the hall.

While riding in the elevator my mind jumps back to that crazy time in 1971 with Paul, the European journalist who had wanted to swap me twenty Communists for one radical feminist. After our meeting with the women Communists, Paul became increasingly depressed. Suddenly, in the middle of a traffic jam near San Jerónimo, he screamed at me that he wanted to take off for Zurich or Rome, he was sick of covering endless trials, with no results. He wanted to go to the Côte d'Azur and do photo essays on Brigitte Bardot. Irritated, I told him the important thing was to keep cool.

"And then what?"

"Get information out."

"And then what?"

"I don't know, Paul."

"Why do you tell me to keep cool when you aren't cool?"

"What do you mean?"

"When I took you to that big Franco rally at Plaza de Oriente, you were terrified. I couldn't leave you in a bar for one minute, just to go downstairs to piss, without your hanging on me—'Paul, Paul, come back up quick.' "

"I don't like mob hysteria."

"So, I don't like being a captive journalist at these lousy trials. I've done my stint."

When we returned to the Wellington, Paul admitted to me that he had gone through my things; he had a funny look on his face; he had been afraid I might be reporting to the American Embassy, and had become worried about introducing me to his Communist friends. He had found my notes, names and addresses of official political figures in Madrid, the obvious panorama of '71. "What sort of an idiot do you take me for?" I snapped at him. "Do you think, when I get my press pass from old lovable Sánchez Bella, I tell him my plan is to interview the left? Paul, what's the matter with you? Of course I visit regime types."

He looked at me, sullen, mistrusting. "I'm not interested in being fair." Something was wrong with the door latch of the new room at the Wellington. Each time we made love, the door flew open and a new cleaning woman wheeled in her stuff. Paul was furious; he believed we were being spied on. Madrid paranoia. I thought it was just hotel dumbness. But after our door was opened a third time, Paul, in wild anger, leapt out of bed and ran naked from the second-floor corridor in the old part of the hotel, where my room was, over to the central balustade, leading down into the main lobby. In Franco's Madrid. In the Wellington! He yelled, *"Qué te pasa? No has visto nunca los cojones? Mira los.* Look at my balls!" I couldn't believe what was happening. I crawled down deep beneath the blankets, hoping to be magically transported away from there.

Does the desk clerk remember Paul with his balls four sheets to the wind?

Nicolás and Graciela looked disoriented, out of place, sitting in the *fin de siècle* suite, with the roses and free room service. I think both of them are happier in their apartment on Bleecker Street. Some of Nicolás's ex-students are with him, and several of his Socialist friends. It is hard on him, because he wants to devote the next few months to his father, whose politics are much more conservative. In Spain, everyone wants to pin a label on you. I don't think he likes being trailed by the press, especially as they rarely report his father's antiregime statements. But some things are nice, some of the mail.

A Quaker who had been sent to the camp at Cuelgamoros on a mercy mission recognized Nicolás's picture in the newspaper, and he sent him a yellowed photograph of himself and his pals. Unreal, getting these prison camp pictures after all these years. In France, a student, Jean Gabriel Cosculluela, also read about Nicolás, and immediately inquired: In 1948 did Sánchez-Albornoz and a friend (the other was Manolo Lamana) spend a night in Cosculluela's grandfather's house in Rieux Minervois on the French side of the Pyrénées? (Cosculluela is doing an oral-history thesis and wants to use as a starting point the historic significance of his grandfather's house.) His family gave shelter to two prisoners who had gotten lost that summer crossing the Pyrénées. Does the name Rieux Minervois sound familiar?

He mentions that several of the older members of his family believed that there was a significant connection between those lost children and the Spanish Republic, but the names had been forgotten and the children had vanished. Are we *they*? I am silent, I stare at Nicolás: *nobody vanished,* we merely grew up.

I remember back. Barbara Mailer and I had dropped off Nicolás and Manolo on the Spanish side of the Pyrénées in the middle of the night. (Paco remained in Spain to make sure our plan worked.) After tremendous difficulty in getting through the roadblocks, relying on our faked papers, Barbara and I finally drove into France at Puigcerdá. Our meeting point was supposed to have been a small mountain town, Osseja. Barbara and I spent days just staring across at the Spanish Pyrénées, convinced Nicolás and Manolo had been picked up by the police. I was in my teens, and it was the first time it dawned on me that maybe life didn't always work out.

The local French scrawled on our car, AMERLOK. Not long after the war; the hotelkeeper had never seen an American woman. She kept exclaiming, *"Deux femmes Yankees, dites-donc."* It was after that we drove to Perpignan, then Collioure, and met Pallach for the first time; he was Paco's mentor and handy with false papers. He learned all that stuff as a kid in the POUM, and later in the French Resistance. He told us he would go back into the mountains and find Nicolás and Manolo. Afterward we heard they had got into France through Rieux Minervois.

The next day Nicolás introduces me to Daniel Sueiro, a journalist who is planning a book on the Valley of the Fallen. Right off, Daniel grasps my hands, murmuring, But you are real, I am glad I have found you. Should I wear a sign; I live on Central Park West and am not, and never have been A VANISHED CHILD? He had heard vague stories of a fantastic prison escape, but he had never figured what was fact, what was fantasy. Living in Madrid, he hadn't known who or what he was looking for; the reconstruction of the concentration camp had been difficult. I suppose the meaning of censorship is that the truth lies, unused, slightly beneath the surface. Censorship doesn't mean no one has the necessary information. Some people possess some of the pieces, but the record is highly fragmented; no one is sure who has what, or where to find the missing parts. Until the haze lifts, history remains at an anecdotal level.

"My God, the time I spent looking for a key, a way in—it never occurred to me that people I knew could have opened the door."

At first I back off from Daniel's questions. Ambivalent, I want to help him, yet I wish to remember nothing. Spain smells of sadness, the past, lassitude. The more I am asked about the late forties, a period they know nothing about, and Stalag 3 in Cuelgamoros, of which I know not too much, the more diffusely anxious I become. The next morning I make my escape, Maria waits for me in Paris.

21

She walks toward me, dancer's gait; she is wearing a French suede jacket, her hair is done differently; a young woman, her mouth curves in a half-hesitant smile. "Maria, Maria." I run toward her, open-armed. Pull of gravity. Maria and Carla *root* me. Silky, tall, madonna-faced, her physical presence makes the unreality of Spain, too many questions about the past, prisons, and journalists, recede. Meeting in Paris away from familiar territory (at home there is time and room for Carla, Maria, and me to indulge in the pauses, the moods, the quarrels of our triangled female family life), unspoken between us is the commitment to having a good week. On my second day we walk through the Luxembourg Gardens. Maria and I enjoy our silence; we know that not often will it happen that both of us, at the right age, as a mother and daughter, will have a week together in Paris. Maria is twenty, I am in my forties; we walk casually enough, occasionally our arms entwining; people know in advance what they are stockpiling for memory.

Maria points to l'Hôtel Observatoire, just off the Luxembourg Gardens. "There's your old student place—when I first came to Paris, I would pass by—well, here I am, living not far from you after all."

"It's so fixed up—I don't recognize it." Our sentences float, disconnected familiar family knowledge. "When your grandma visited me there, it was the first time in my life I was alone with her. We did some nice things, I didn't find it so hard after that to get along with her ..."

Maria, for the short week, takes me into her life. She, Gina, and Jennifer give me the living room, which has a sofa bed. One morning a young man, an American, walks through the living room, in undershorts, just as I wake up. "Just passing through—the girls said I could bed down on the floor; you were already asleep, so we decided not to wake you."

"Oh."

I try to imagine myself at Maria and Gina's age casually instructing one of my male friends to sleep on the mat in a room my mother was using. Impossible. Those days, you left home and grew up fast, just so you could sleep with a man. But the four of them see nothing odd about his sharing a room with me. Subdued, I go to the bathroom and get dressed. When Maria comes back from classes, she takes me to the old Jewish Quarter, near rue de Vieux Temple. She's found a Russian-Jewish leather worker who converses with her in Russian. I am introduced as *la mère*. I don't know Russian so the man and I talk in French.

"Votre fille est magnifique—pas seulement belle, mais en plus elle a le caractère d'un ange. Et comme elle parle le Russe. Sans aucun accent." The man and his wife hover over Maria; he has given her a leather wallet. He pauses and sighs. He explains he has raised his eldest son in the best of French schools, David is a successful surgeon; the problem, he apologizes, is that Maria arrived on the scene too late, he has married a young French Jewish woman. "If not," he says to me soberly, "I would have introduced my David to your Maria . . ."

We glance at each other, two Jews touching home base. He had been willing to make me his best offer—his son. Outside, Maria wants me to walk with her to the rue des Rosiers. She tells me she has read Lucy Dawidowicz's *War Against the Jews* after going to a meeting at the Memorial to the Holocaust in the Jewish Quarter. "It's not at all like New York; I mean, here they really do have the swastikas on the walls . . . here you have to think about being Jewish." We do old-fashioned, obvious things in the city; Jennifer, Gina, Maria, and I picnic in the Bois de Boulogne. In one of the restaurants in the park, the Près Catalan, a special reception is being held. Conférence des Psychanalistes. Gina shrieks with laughter. "Analysts' conference. I am the daughter of one, the conference has got to be open to *me*—imagine, bumping into shrink center in the Bois de Boulogne." Crashing the conference, raiding the hors d'oeuvres, they case Freud's Paris.

Stretched out beneath the late-afternoon sun, on the wet Bois lawn, I doze. Gina is the first to report back; she falls down on the grass beside me.

"Anyone interesting?" I ask lazily, half asleep, inhaling the smell of horse, insects, spring grass, moist weather, and early roses.

"Naw, French men have *narrow* shoulders. You get a load of the tight pants they wear?" Gina says, sprawling next to me. "I like to know a man's name before he offers you his genitals. When they walk down the boulevard St.-Michel—wham! They've got them pulled tight over the basics. Tight pants and snooty, that's Paris."

When Jennifer and Maria return, we walk to the edge of the Bois, over to a taxi stand near the Près Catalan. I instruct the driver to take us all through the parts of the city I think the girls might not have seen.

"It's a different view from a taxi," Maria observes.

The driver, a Pole, joins in. We get a running political commentary.

"I thought French taxi drivers were awful," Jennifer whispers. "This one is so obliging."

"Well, he's a *Polish*-French taxi driver."

"The bill for this," Gina points out shrewdly, "is going to break you."

"But I'll be leaving Paris soon, and it's fun." From both my parents I inherit the "it's only money" principle. (True, they went from rich to broke.) "Hiring a taxi for two hours in Paris isn't a moral issue. If I took a Hertz for the day, it would strike you as reasonable, because we are used to rent-a-cars. So, if this suits me better, what's the difference? It's not a moral issue, unless you assume there is some virtue in driving the car yourself."

For her belated birthday dinner Maria has picked Chez Boris, a Russian place in Passy. The glasses lined behind the narrow, dark-wooded bar are frosted for vodka. The girls insist on a table in a dark corner, the banquette seats are half hidden by heavy velour drapes. I am puzzled why they don't choose a table in a more open part of the room, until I begin to notice the substantial number of visits these three thin young women make to the smorgasbord platters. Gina makes a quick motion with her large leather purse, which is half hidden by the velour drapes, she looks up at me, "Turbot, it was a nice slice of fresh turbot."

"Lunch," Maria says. "We'll have enough for a week."

I watch their quick, deft motions, back and forth, as they load their handbags.

"Russian restaurants," Jennifer confides, "give you more to work with."

"Maria, not a boiled potato, you're not putting a potato in your purse?"

The three of them own up to a cache of black caviar rolled in a linen dinner napkin, and then ask if we can have more frosted vodka. Suddenly the four of us laugh. Later, we drive through the streets of pink beige buildings and plane trees beneath the navy-colored sky, the cab smelling of potatoes, turbot, rolls, caviar, and even blinis, our breath vaguely of vodka, and we drive to Montmartre, Sacré-Coeur, even Pigalle, and circle back behind Notre Dame, unembarrassed tourists. I remember my childhood walks with my mother, as I strained to invent a magic world to relieve her, distract her from her phobias. "Now we are on Madison, here is Fifth Avenue, look at the horses, the ducks skimming the reservoir. Look at the tall buildings, look at Sacré-Coeur, there is the Folies Bergère." I hear the sound of my own voice, the permanent guide, and I reach for Maria, her hands on her leather purse bulging with Russian food. I put my arm around her waist, while the taxi with the four of us securely inside gains speed along the quai.

When I get back to Madrid, Juan Goytisolo telephones me from Casablanca; we have made complicated arrangements to meet at the airport. He is driving up from Marrakech. I take the early-morning Iberia flight, which makes a stop in Tangier; Barajas at that hour smells of oily croissants, oranges, and newsprint. Crowds of travelers mill in the badly organized central waiting room; outnumbering the occasional flashy tourists are the many who stumble about the airport behaving as though they've not yet been given the news that the days of Anna Magnani and *Open City* are long over. Finally the Iberia flight takes off.

My own preoccupations are with the drying of the mouth and rapid swallowing that come from anxiety. I make a careful list. If Juan fails to show, go immediately with American Express card to reservation desk, make reservation on the next plane departing for Tangier-Madrid. Leave message for Juan at desk. Alternative plan: Leave message for him at desk, go to hotel in Casablanca, wait for him there. If he doesn't show, fly back to Madrid following morning. Go swimming in Casablanca. I've also made Juan give me the telephone number of friends of his there as an alternative. I don't want to board, by mistake, a flight to Liverpool. When finally we deplane at the flat Mohammed V airstrip, I walk under the hot sun, firmly, toward the terminal. I don't look up, out of fear, until I hear Juan call my name; then I see him waving from the visitors' balcony.

I roll my suitcase on wheels through customs, relieved. The customs official confiscates one of my magazines; King Hassan's portrait is nailed to the wall. "Juan," I call. He rushes over and embraces me. I have arrived in North Africa.

We drive straight on to Marrakech in Juan's tan Citroën. Meanwhile, he cautions me, "We'll visit Ahmed next week in Casa, but I told him you took the Paris flight to Marrakech—he's waiting to introduce you to Zineb and the boys; he'll be insulted if he feels we bypassed him."

We are driving along a flat, empty road sparse with trees. We pass through small villages, whitewashed; the children and old folks stare, magnetized by the passing cars. North Africa has the familiar smell of a Mediterranean country suffering from a mysterious historic wound. I put my arm partially out the car window, I feel the hot dry sun billowing through the short sleeves of my blouse; white dusty flatlands, skinny shanked cows grazing by the road. The stillness, the buoyant dry heat, the lack of things and money, the nameless trauma, the stucco buildings laced with Fanta signs, remind me of Spain. "Of course you like Morocco—this place looks more like Castile and the Costa Brava these days than Spain does."

"No," Juan argues, startled, as though I've geographically wrongly "named" his sacred territory, Juan's North Africa.

"Yes, it does. The way Spain looked when we were kids. That vanished, empty, sad place, the *algarrobo* trees, why, Juan, it's all here now, on the road to Marrakech."

Juan frowns. "Barbara, you say things sometimes . . ." His azure eyes, framed by laugh lines just beginning to show, squint against the sun. He places a pair of sunglasses over the bridge of his long, intelligent nose. He flicks on the tape deck he keeps in the Citroën. Abruptly the wail of Egyptian cabaret music blasts the Moroccan countryside.

As we speed through the center of a North African village, Juan points to the marketplace; he informs me we will be visiting the *souks* of Marrakech. Oh yes, I say, abruptly going into a spiel about the central organizing factor of the North African marketplace. "They were the main economic institution here," I add, quickly giving a few relevant details.

Juan looks puzzled.

"I still have copies of Paco's research. I told you, he liked living with the Bedouin tribes."

I hear the sound of my own voice, my explanation to Juan as to how I learned this and that detail of the marketplaces; suddenly I pause. I had assumed, young, that life was full of definite forked roads. You take this fork, you are engaged in this sort of life; the fork to the right, on the other hand, leads to an entirely different existence. I had chosen to marry a New York lawyer, Paco had chosen to go off to the Middle East; he had married an Iranian woman, Leila, who occasionally corresponds with me. I had been positive that we had gone in entirely different directions. What am I doing here now, decades later, traveling this white, dust-caked, North African road, listening to a second Basque-Catalan Spaniard explain to me the meaning of the North African *souks*? I am awestruck by the separate travel plans dictated by my psyche. Who plots my life course? Me? Or that willful child dancing in my cranium, maneuvering the hidden scenario? At crucial moments I have experienced an acute sensation of being *given* to, of the gears of my emotional life shifting, unexpectedly, miraculously; a profound amorphous pain abruptly alleviated. The restoring occurred with the birth of each of my daughters, and with certain men. Paco, Harold, Clancy, Juan. I felt reconnected to my beginnings; my orphaned soul acquired parents.

"Paco wrote on the North African marketplaces? Ay, Barbara, I feel we knew each other in another life, we were meant to be in Africa together. *Destino.*"

"I don't believe in *destino.*"

"But, Barbara, each new fact adds to the similarity. Today you tell me about Benet's paper on North African marketplaces, the very moment I have begun to think about *Xemmaá-el-fná*. When I read your book," Juan says, agitated, "for the first time I saw verbalized my own thoughts, my own experiences. Like me that Spaniard, now dead, sought to escape the world of Paris exile politics. So many of the details were the same, leaving behind in Spain a younger brother, both of us Basque-Catalans, at the same age, one parent killed in the war. On every page, my thoughts, my frustrations. But the similarities do not end with the book, each new detail reconfirms my sense of his having been my alter ego." Juan turns to me, his voice urgent; then his eyes return to the road; experienced driver, he doesn't distract for long. "When I realized his grandfather's house was in Arénys del Mar, I was stunned. Why, *my* grandfather's summer home was probably no more than a kilometer away from the Benets'. "

"Do you remember a small casino at the bottom of the hill along the beach road?"

"Of course. Look, Arénys del Mar is an insignificant, totally unspecial beach town of maybe one thousand inhabitants. Now, Barbara, don't you think it's odd that three well-known contemporary Spanish novelists—Juan Benet, myself, and my brother Luis—are all writing about their grandfathers' houses in this unspecial Catalonian seaside town?"

"Juan, at this point you will find more and more similarities, because you are *looking* for details that mesh—"

"What are the differences?"

I am silent; *bi versus hetero.* I don't tell Juan what I am thinking, but that knowledge deeply colors my behavior to him. Had he been solidly hetero, I would be fighting to solidify our relation. No, what we share is no long-term insurance policy to be cashed in in time of ill health, a rainy day, and old age; we have nothing but the day; he has a gift for doing nice things with an afternoon.

I like being with him. I am not a woman who needs to be overly loved or flattered, but I libidinize the verbal. Certain types of men I avoid. Nix to "Hey, how about a quickie?" How I ran from so many of the wrong sentences! What I seek is to have my curiosity fully engaged, which Juan does.

Juan lives in the Gueliz, the European quarter of Marrakech, in an apartment complex of Casbah-rust-colored stucco that is built around an inner courtyard. The living room windows face the white pebbled patio, the shutters closed during the heat of the day. The cool assortment of medium-sized rooms arranged either side of a long corridor is a mixture of Mediterranean provincial comfort and dowdiness; despite its quality of emptiness, it isn't spacious; there are a few *objets du Maroc* in the main sitting room. On the wall hangs a gold-green damask Moroccan landscape, a turbulent scene depicting white-robed chieftans on snorting, long-maned horses winning a battle; in the foreground is a small mosque.

When we arrive, Juan debates for a moment; he is more used to being cared for than to doing the caring. Then he decides to switch roles. He goes into the bathroom, lights the gas for a supply of hot water, and turns on the tub spigots for me—this impresses me—and while the water in the bath is running, he finds me a closet for my clothes. He introduces me to Yasmine, a young Moroccan girl who comes half-days to do the house and some cooking. "Do you have laundry for her?" Juan asks politely. I shake my head. I unpack a terry-cloth robe and go into the bathroom; the road between Casablanca and Marrakech has been hot.

The apartment belongs to relatives of friends of Juan, Ninette and Pierre Bendraho. Pierre, a big lawyer in Casablanca, is a descendant of

Jewish Berbers, from the south. Jews have lived in Morocco since the destruction of the temple of Jerusalem, which predates the Arab arrival by almost seven centuries. Ninette's family, Juan tells me, came over in 1492. I will meet them when we visit Casablanca; the Bendrahos have invited us to stay at their house.

Juan introduces me to his friends in Marrakech. Hearing a new language intrigues me, but what I like best are my solo explorations of the city. Walking in the dryness of Marrakech in the early morning feels like floating on salt water; the dryness of the air gives a rolling bounce to my walk. So this is the way non-asthmatics feel all the time—how lucky they are. I leave the house with Yasmine near me. She carries a basket and household money. Ordinarily I am fearful, always wanting to know exactly on which street I find myself, where are the exits, how do I get back home? But with Yasmine behind me, I have the illusion I am alone, which I like. Juan remains in the apartment, mornings, studying Arabic. (Mostly it is men who experience the delicious feeling of wandering the world like Peer Gynt, careful to make sure that a patient Solveig is waiting for them. Crucial to their freedom is that the remaining partner is left behind in a fixed position. How can one leave when no one is home?)

I wander toward the markets, where the Gueliz ends and the Arabic quarter begins, and under the pretense of needing a sprig of parsley or a sheaf of writing paper or fresh coral-colored fish for us to eat, or Moroccan knit caps for my daughters, I buy small items mostly for their color, and to have a chance to practice, haltingly, my few words of Arabic. I smile and compliment the citizens of Marrakech, *"Madak Ládid. Zouina M'zin."* Occasionally Yasmine behind me calls out *"Ouakha, ouakha,"* and I make way for traffic. Knowing she is with me, I feel free to wander deeper into the city, yet trick myself into believing I am doing the exploring alone. The smells of roasting *mechoui* and fried nuts in the *souk* remind me of Columbus Avenue. The caftans, roped braids of gilt and bronze, piled near plastic bowls and pressure cookers, artifacts of modern civilization, confuse me as to place—Bloomingdale's basement, with an overshipment of Mideastern *tsatskes*. But what is New York but a great big, buy-low, sell-high bazaar?

Abruptly I wheel around. *"Il faut retourner chez Monsieur Juan."* Yasmine, wordless, turns and deftly leads me back through the maze of streets. Juan and I rarely talk about anything important. His wife, for instance. I know she is older than Juan, and that she helped him get his career going, but I know nothing of their emotional map. I assume that whatever version of their relation I would conjure up would have more to do with what I find convenient to believe than the truth, and I just let the subject sink. Although we gab endlessly about our split dream life, each of us having half of the same dream, we are oddly formal about sex. Part of the *truc*, the private game, is that our fantasies happen like spontaneous surprises. Nor do I attempt to understand the profound inner meanings and illusions of Juan's sexuality through his novels. What could I do with all those grottoes, snakes, and cruelty, the Grand Guignol effects of Spanish literature? I have a lazy tendency to ignore phenomena that are of no use to me. The unconscious, the elliptical, in modern writing frequently bore me, reminding me of my parents' youth, when Freud and Jung were very much news and surrealism was the report on the discoveries of the unconscious.

In flight against that smart German refugee world, with its big influence on my New York progressive-school childhood, I zoomed (a post-Freudian wench in rebellion) toward a celebration of the conscious. Too many of my generation have been scooped up in a net by inept therapists, forced to flap in the heavy air of the unconscious.

It is not that I doubt its existence; I just don't believe it a good idea to deliberately pursue it. Too often one ends by fishing out of those murky seas superficial fronds, known symbols of what we assume to be the depths. We are dealing, by now, with obvious goods—used merchandise, named and labeled—at the expense of remaining ignorant concerning the mysteries of a conscious world, wantonly neglected.

As no Spanish man I actually have known, to my awareness, has been turned on by slicing a butterfly's wings, fucking a grotto or a snake, or slitting open an animal's gut, I take this chamber of horrors to be a handy metaphor for Franco's children, who arrived in Paris a generation too late, with none of the aura of the original bunch of exiles; literary, pockets empty, embarrassed at not having been given soon enough the message that realism is dead, what was their new bag of tricks? American men by this time had plenty to choose from—urban Jewish smarts, the last cowboy, the last WASP, the last Beat, embittered war hero, drunk and mismated in Connecticut, SDS leftists, uppity black high style, champions of Forest Hills and Yankee Stadium, Elvis or rock 'n' roll, the cool sellout, the Watergate undercover new journalists, ethnic hotshot (*es muy* nice), the first Californian to take hot tubs; jazz; Hemingway and Fitzgerald were our young granddaddies; we blew up the world, but our men had oh boy macho choice. El Caudillo's children in Spain, until Franco joint by joint died in bed, had been invisible; the castanets and the clapping and stomping of feet were for the hoi polloi. Once more, with *Quijote?* A bad act with which to follow a musty forty years of Franco; they had to find something else.

Spaniards make bad imitation Frenchmen, and this has been a time when the French hadn't sufficient psychic breath to create a vervy new edition of themselves. (The best actors in the French cinema are the Gauloises and *le sweater*; should inanimate objects be given an Oscar? The French look so intelligent, dressed in their navy-blue pullovers, puffing away.) In the snootiness of Paris, who was to remember youth and the raw turn-on of Rita Hayworth's Gilda singing in a low-cut satin dress in the heavily censored version shown in the repressive and gloomy days of Franco? (Spanish men moaned *hhhgil-da.*)

Though Juan has his Egyptian wailing music, I stick to my own magic, zeroing in on the unsubtle, the sexually obvious; I go straight for retro brown and black silk-satin nightgowns, Paco Rabanne perfume, and a smudge of kohl rimming my eyes, reminiscent of our childhood. Juan is one of those shy, bookish men who like to be considered sexually audacious, a grand plotter of orgiastic sex and so forth. I guessed he wouldn't have asked women to sleep in black satin nightgowns—that sort of erotica was always considered the domain of the cheapo delights of the ignorant, the Catalan businessman, and the lower classes. Oh, my gifted, designer grandfather—to what ends did your intellectual, smart granddaughter, in North Africa, use your inventive, handy gifts with bolts of shiny silks. (During the next three years I make many trips to Morocco and Juan learns to anticipate the magic theater locked in my suitcase. I observe how attentive he is while the customs official inspects my packed clothing.)

The following week we decide to drive toward the Sahara; an hour south of Marrakech, in Ourika, we see a small *mansour* dedicated to St. Solomon. From the road Juan and I immediately notice the name, SAINT SOLOMON. We park the car nearby and walk over to the tomb. Next to it is a small synagogue which appears to be dedicated to a St. Solomon: it is just one small room. In one corner are three dusty, yellowed books. I pick up one; it is in Hebrew. An old Arab woman comes up and takes it from me. "Torah, Torah," she chants; then she kisses it. "Torah, Torah."

A Jewish Berber.

In Arabic Juan explains I am an American Jew. An old man, mountain-born face, joins us; he listens to Juan, his blue eyes sharpen, he appraises me. "Miami?"

I shake my head.

Juan translates, "He says he's heard there are Jews in an American city called Miami."

Then the man pushes his hands against imaginary obstacles in the air. "Israel, Israel."

"He says the young people of the village went to Israel. Now there is just himself and the two women guarding the synagogue."

I stare at the three old people; in the bare room the Torah shelf is covered with cheap linoleum; the flies have had at it, the books smell rotten. What has all this to do with me? Are they on the level, or is this the local con game to make stray Jewish tourists weep? Since when do Jews call their rabbis saint? Irrationally, I get angry. The old man disappears into another room; he returns with his arms out-stretched, carrying a tattered Jewish holy shawl. *"Talith,"* he says. I give them some money; they reach for it like Arab beggars. Then I feel sick, and I flee. In the car Juan says, "I didn't know there were Jewish poor like that—" "Shut up," I snap, and we drive on.

Much further south, on the fringes of the Sahara, Juan and I are in-vited into an impoverished Casbah. We have been walking near it after a rainfall; I haven't realized the intensity of the sun, but I see an arc of whitness above my head, then below my feet. I am chilled and hot. Suddenly Juan pulls me. "You're walking in the wrong direction, into the light." Then one of the local Arabs splashes some green tea from a leather bag on my face and leads me on his burro back to the nearby Casbah, where I am offered more green tea. They had been afraid I was about to have sunstroke. We are told not to start traveling until evening. The room in which we drink tea is empty except for the rugs beneath us. The men's wives serve us. My notions of a Casbah have been formed from adolescent moviegoing: rich Arab chiefs clap-ping for the dancing girls. But Yvonne de Carlo doesn't live in this Casbah. The men seem poor and worried. "Have you been to the Sa-hara?" I ask, in that odd tourist voice I get in alien places.

One of the men looks puzzled. *"Madame—vous êtes dedans le Sa-hara."*

"Oh?" I had imagined the Sahara to be somewhere else, less accessible. Perhaps I expected a clear demarcation of territory. *You are now entering New Jersey. Pay toll. You are now entering the Sahara. Pay toll. Have exact change ready.* After I recover from my astonishment at finding myself at the edges of the desert, I am taken into the women's section to meet the rest of the family. Although a few old men are seated on moth-eaten rugs smoking pipes and drinking green tea by themselves, the real activity is in the women's quarter. Children of both sexes, including adolescents, are milling about. The real bustle and movement from within the Casbah seems to be here. Is it the men who are excluded from the main source of life? The women are more outgoing. They connect with me. They are making bread and motion me to kneel, and laughing at my clumsy attempts to follow their instructions, they show me how they stamp and knead the dough with their feet. Meanwhile the children yammer. There seems to be no clear division between male and female quarters; maybe this is an unsuccessful casbah. Soon the Arab men bring Juan into the women's section so that he can inspect the breadmaking. One of the Arab men asks him if he carries ointment, his son has a bad eye infection. Twenty years ago this was a Jewish Casbah, inhabited by poor Jewish Berbers. Jews wear black, Arabs wear white. My people and the white sun everywhere. God, how the ghostly memory of vanished Jews sticks to North Africa! The world seems thick with places where Jews "used to live." I ask a young Arab boy who is watching my attempt to roll the bread, "What happened to the Jews from here?"

He hesitates, and says, very serious, "*Le roi*—the King of France made them leave." I gaze at the Sahara; the vistas are long, it is the end of the day and the shadows have lengthened. I assume the King of France is named de Gaulle.

The Hotel Taroudannt must have been used by the French army as a bordello when they were billeted in southern Morocco. The smell of bidet and cement dampness exudes from the bedrooms. The place has an overgrown garden, bird cages, and a mixed clientele: Arabs apologetic to the French madame innkeeper, who threatens to kick them out for drunkenness, several sharp French tourists who always seem to know the best buy in cheapo hotels, and one or two slick Moroccan women with heavily sloed eyes, who come into the small restaurant wearing sport clothes and, even in this stinking hot weather, tall leather boots. The dining room is named Café Pop, or Café des

Amoureux or Café des Amants; there is a grease-stained map of France pinned on one of the walls; the trucks of Moroccan wounded soldiers whir past us. South of where we are, the Moroccans are fighting the Polisario and Algerians over domination of the Spanish Sahara, a war about control of minerals.

The next day we drive back, past the blazing red suns of Khrouribga's phosphate plants; then, farther on, as we drive close to the Atlantic coast and I look out at the beaches, the white waves, the white-domed *mansours,* the tombs where the Arabs place their best dead in key spots with a good view of the sea; and even though it goes against my grain to be a *turista exótica* in a poor country, I am wildly happy. I have gotten my best education over a cup of coffee and consider these jaunty sprees my most serious life's work.

I want everything. We visit Fez before ending the trip in Casablanca. Juan takes me through the intricate web of narrow streets, winding turns of the intact medieval medina at Fez; my intelligence is suspended, I am all eyes to the varied levels and shaded buildings. Doors swing open, I catch glimpses of tiled interior gardens. It takes us an hour to reach the heart of the medina, the Al Karaouyne, the cool blue mosque, and the stalls of women weaving gold-threaded belts. The next day we are joined by a group of men and women students from the university. Juan has just given a lecture there. I hammer at them my endless pragmatic questions. How is furniture moved out of the old medina? How are the dead removed? The sick? In case of fire? An entire population still lives in the old quarter—what happens when you are in a hurry to get to the university?

One of the women, a Marxist engineering student, smiles mysteriously. She is wearing black pants and a Western-style flannel shirt. Finally she admits that King Hassan has slashed a road through to the Al Karaouyne. Faissi go by bus or car along the new route, but guides rarely tell tourists about it. The next morning, accompanied by the Marxists, I go the direct route. We instantly reach the center. I am disappointed. There is a flatness about getting out of a taxi and finding oneself immediately at the blue mosque.

Which means I am back from the medina much earlier than I had expected. I wait for Juan at the café near our hotel. I observe a flashy group of Faissi men seated near me. The roll of their conversation, the sudden laughter, and the backslapping are heavy with innuendo. A newcomer with a bulging paper parcel joins them; he is a tailor. The honcho of the group unwraps the parcel and tries on the jacket of a woolen suit. Then the Faissi honcho takes the trousers from the tailor and disappears down into the john, which he has decided to use as his private fitting room. When he comes back up the stairs, he is zipping his fly. While the tailor runs his hands over his customer's ass, genitals, and gut, his other pals admire the good fit. The honcho preens in the pink café mirror, laughing; he pays off the tailor. Then a second vendor comes over to the men's table. He has a selection of women's brassieres. Another one of the men, making a rippling quick motion with his hands, indicates in the pocket of air near his own chest the weight and shape of his wife's tits. The peddler sells him three pink rayon brassiers. When Juan shows up, I have become so enmeshed in this buy-and-sell, I forget, or maybe don't want to tell him about the short cut the Moroccan Marxists took to the blue mosque.

We finally land up in Casablanca at the Bendrahos'. Ninette is a small, slim woman, a fiery redhead; she puts herself out too much for her friends, which gives her a nervous, tense quality; like most well-off Moroccans she dresses French. She and Pierre met as students in Paris; she wails over the Moslemization of Morocco.

Ninette has plenty of reason to yowl with pain. It is her generation that has been traumatized by two events—the Islamification of Morocco and the mass exodus of the Jews to Israel. The spring of my arrival, the number still in Morocco had dwindled to twenty-five thousand Jews, mostly of the professional class. Ninette's generation of Moroccan Jews suffered profound feelings of displacement; they had witnessed the riots against them during the Yom Kippur War; in the 1960s, they had watched their friends and family—both the Jews and the French—desert Morocco. Pierre and Ninette's grandparents' mother tongue was Arabic.

Pierre, moodily musing on the past, at the end of a late afternoon—Juan is visiting Ahmed—tinkers with an electronic game friends have brought from New York while explaining to me his confusions of identity. "During the final years of French rule—this ended with Moroccan independence in 1962—the French regarded the Jewish community as European, a professional class to be counted upon. So we were raised in French schools, which created a schism between us and the Arabs. For centuries the Jews and Arabs have cohabited with fewer problems than in other Arab territory."

"And now that the Saudis are arriving, *merde,*" Ninette adds. "They are building out here, not long ago there was an incident at the beach.

The Saudis don't understand that sophisticated Casa women wear bikinis in public places. With the Saudis throwing around their money and their influence, soon Moroccan women will be forced back into the veil."

"Ninette—it's not that bad."

"Pierre, have you forgotten how wonderful Morocco was when we were children?" Ninette giggles. "Ooh la-la—I was one of those 'kids' during the world war that the American servicemen gave chewing gum to. One lieutenant became friendly with my relatives here in Casa; he would bring me cornflakes and Nestlé bars. Oh, how I dreamed of going to New York—I invented a scenario in which I would marry a grandson of Roosevelt." Suddenly Ninette is convulsed with laughter. She kicks off her high heels, grabs Pierre, and dances with him in the middle of the room.

> Bei mir bist du schayn.
> Oh, let me explain.
> La da deedee da da da . . .

She slaps her thigh, "Oh my, oh my—Roosevelt's grandson, but who knew he'd be Woody Allen?"

Ninette loves American movies and books. On the desk of her lush, modern living room are books by Woody Allen, Erica Jong, and Saul Bellow. She runs a tight ship, and occasionally she breaks into Arabic, letting out a guttural shout from the belly—a stream of strange vowels ensues—and suddenly the sleepy-eyed household comes alive. Tables are cleared, and we are rapidly served steaming hot coffee.

Ninette admires Juan, but she expends enormous energy trying to improve his character. She is shocked that I have never done heavy shopping with Juan in our travels in southern Morocco. *"Merde,"* she shrieks, her hand traveling rapidly through her red hair, her feet kicking nervously against the wood sofa; *"merde,* he's a good writer, but, *vraiment, c'est trop égoïste.* What do you mean, you do not do tourist shopping when you travel with Juan? Such an independent woman— and in these times. I'll take you to my special bunks—we'll get the real stuff at good prices, but Juan should learn to do what others want."

I gaze sleepily at Ninette. She fails to sense the *collusion* between Juan and me. Magical, the Morocco Juan has invented. I've joined him and added my own embellishments to his world. All mysteries, if

one looks closely, can be pierced—by a woman wearing curlers or in-
dulging in a heavy shopping spree—the allure vanishes.

"Some men give you children and security, others vacations," I answer. "There's no point trying to change people's natures."

"It's a matter of principle."

"*Your* principle."

"Barbara's right," Pierre joins in. "No one's nature changes ..."

"*Merde.*" Ninette is a small woman to have such a husky voice.
"What do they see in him? An Arab worker turned entrepreneur?"
What really perturbs her are my visits to Ahmed's house.

"Ahmed's interesting," Pierre disagrees. "A loner, a free man—for
that Berber orphan to have become a property owner, *enfin, Ninette,
pas souvent à Casa ...*"

"Pierre," Ninette contradicts impatiently—she has read all of Bellow, Roth, Malamud, and Mailer—"it is not logical that an American
woman like Barbara should come to Morocco, to Casa, and Juan
should whisk her off to Ahmed's house, always Ahmed, in order for
her to teach his wife how to make *bastilla*—that's their plan for tomorrow."

What Ninette really is yowling about is my preoccupation with
Ahmed, and my indifference toward her well-heeled friends. The *bastilla,* actually, is my idea. I mean to use it to engineer another day's
sporty adventure.

The next morning Ahmed takes me through the big Casa food market
and we buy freshly killed doves, paper cornucopias of copper- and
saffron-colored spices and almonds; the colors and shapes of what we
get overwhelm me. Zineb's family is still shocked that Ahmed has
shaped up into a first-rate provider; his relatives have gathered in his
house to watch our event. Zineb, her two sons, her young female
cousins, all become involved in the making of the *bastilla.* I show the
women how to take short cuts with the electric gadgets Ahmed has
brought back from France and America; the blender can be used to
crush the almonds; the pigeons steam more rapidly in a pressure
cooker. I adore the clatter of the day, so many people hovering over
the preparation of one dish. Tonight, in order to please Ahmed, Juan
and I will stay over, proper guests in his living room; we will sleep on
the two new, long, low, narrow banquettes that line either wall and
that are used at dinner as seats for the round dining table. On Ahmed

and Zineb's TV are two books, *Count Julian* and *Arriving Where We Started*. The child in me cries out, "Oh, world, remember me, remember me!" Ah, how sure I am Ahmed will never lose those two books; he is my most faithful reader. He will keep them forever. Ninette doesn't understand why my relation to her and her friends is less special. One year they read a new book by Bellow, another time, Updike. But for Ahmed and his family, I am irreplaceable.

Juan likes to center himself, this short, slight, apparently shy man, in the midst of the brouhaha he has created. While he sits on the living room side banquette reading *L'Opinion*, in his field of vision is all of Ahmed's family gathered around me in the kitchen, following my instructions as to the making of the *bastilla*. Meanwhile, Zineb is slowly preparing baked lamb on a spit; *mechoui*. Before glazing the *bastilla*, I make a newspaper cutout in the shape of a *J* and fill the empty space with cinnamon. Zineb, her young cousins, her two sons, understand I mean to surprise Juan. Zineb seizes my hand, gleefully laughing in conspiracy. Do I want the navy-blue dots and designs and the henna dye on my hands and arms? she inquires. How Ninette would carry on if I return to her home sporting henna Arab hands! I shake my head; then I use my skimpy Arab vocabulary. *"Zouina m'zin. Madak lādid."* Pretty. Tastes good. In our honor, Ahmed uses the souvenirs: the demitasse spoons, the cups from the Loire country, the plate Juan bought for him with a map of Texas, and a University of Pittsburgh water pitcher. All the knickknacks are arranged on the round table. Then the *bastilla* is brought forth, with the cinnamon *J* baked into a glaze. "Ah, ah," sighs Ahmed. He has proved to his family he has been out in the world and come home with the best, two writers (in his family's earshot he never says *les écrivains sont les grands menteurs*). Instead he boasts that one of them is a woman who can produce a pie made of doves. Juan, the center of this commotion, beams. "Ah," he smiles. I stare at Ahmed. Who I know will remember. Remember me, remember me. Ninette never understands why I go so often to Ahmed's house in La Villette, and I never tell her—I am seeking immortality among the Berbers.

22

"There are days," Alastair Reid had observed to me in New York, "when that mad, howling Iberian dog snaps at your heels, when there was nothing for me to do but get out of Spain for a while." After I come back to Madrid in May to write my pieces, the old Iberian dog sinks its teeth into my ankles, the mood of the city is gloomy and mean. I am living alone now, in Amadeo Cuito's apartment overlooking the Plaza de Oriente. God, how I miss Juan. It is hard to get a call through to Marrakech. I am glad when Juan Benet invites me to a dinner party.

Eduardo Chamorro, the correspondent from *Cambio 16,* is there; María and Juan García Hortelano; about five or six people I don't recognize; and a poet, Ignacio Martín Vélez. The *destape* (sexual uncorking) is in full swing. Marriages are flying apart and women are picketing with signs: I AM AN ADULTERESS. In honor of post-Franco Spain, high on hash and alcohol (Madrileños frequently combine both), Ignacio, my dinner partner on my left, is mimicking a striptease. A woman from Barcelona whispers to me: "Is it true that in New York City erotic weekends are very frequent?"

"Swingers? You mean swinging sex?"

"With more than two people?"

"Group sex, that's a more recent word for orgy."

"Oh." She thinks about it. She has heard that I am publishing a book in Spain. "Does it have an erotic weekend?"

"Well, no, it is about me as a young American woman coming of age—a sort of *rite de passage.*"

"You should fix it up and add some erotic weekends— Now, on the left, a touch of porno—*da tono.* Porno gives tone to the left."

Meanwhile, Ignacio nudges me: should he show his balls? He seems obsessed with this piece of his equipment.

The Danish journalist seated opposite me tells us about the reports of sexual torture that are being released. The methods of electric shock perfected in Latin America are also being used by the Spanish police. He describes the wounds suffered by a fifteen-year-old whom the police had attempted to sodomize, using dogs. The journalist mentions his visit with Alfonso Sastre in France. "Alfonso is in despair. There is no talk of trial or release. Alfonso is worried because there is no mention of Eva in the daily press."

Ignacio suddenly stands up and rips off the rest of his clothes. He dances around the garden-level dining room, wearing nothing but a hat he has grabbed off a coat peg near the door. Ignacio dares the twelve dinner guests: "Kiss my balls, kiss my balls." The men in the room are paralyzed. One naked person among a group of dressed people is very naked indeed. One of the men, *sotto voce,* murmurs, "Any second, *paloma.*"

María Hortelano, the wife of the novelist Juan García Hortelano, leaps into action. With the experienced gestures of a competent nurse or a fond mother, she pulls some clothing back on Ignacio. "Now, now, Ignacio—you are dear and darling, but you have had too much to drink, you are going to be so sick . . ." While María both soothes and dresses him, she calls out to me, *"Es verdad* about Eva—her situation is a calamity, Barbara; do you think you can do something?"

"Thank God, the poor American freelancer whom someone labeled CIA as a joke—then the rumor spread in Madrid—went back to Paris," Jaime Salinas interrupts.

I look up. Washington has just announced that they have been using independent journalists as a cover for CIA operations abroad. Vulnerable writers who find themselves in explosive parts of the world, generally without backup, hardly need more handicaps. Madrileños are always suspicious of Americans. "There are so few freelance writers here from the United States, do I get called CIA?"

Jaime shrugs. "I think you'll be all right, you have many friends here. Well, everyone gets named either KGB or CIA, it doesn't mean anything." He seems annoyed, it hasn't been his sort of evening. He stands up. "Children," he announces, "I am going home."

I have been invited to spend the weekend outside Madrid, but I cancel those plans as I have a Saturday-afternoon appointment to meet with the journalists of *El País.* It opened shop on May 9. The entire plant, one of the most modern in the world, was built between December (right after Franco's death) and May. It's the last essential piece of the new Spanish press, and its existence helps to cause the Arias Navarro caretaker government to crumble in July. My taxi driver takes nearly an hour to go through the commercial zones of Madrid, until finally we reach Miguel Yuste, a small street located in an out-of-the-way industrial area.

I sit down next to the journalist with whom I have the appointment and throw out a few questions. The man keeps typing, I realize I am talking to the air; suddenly he turns to me and, in a loud, conde-scending voice, asks, *"Mujer*—do you want a tour of the plant? We've received many compliments on the decoration, the color of the cur-tains."

A titter goes up in the bull pen; a real early 1950s putdown of a woman, so creaky, not to be taken seriously. Tiredly, I also smell the anti-Americanism, YANKEE GO HOME. In a low voice, I murmur that I am not interested in curtain colors and continue my questioning; the man turns to me. "Why don't you try us at closing time, after mid-night?"

"You told me to arrive at five in the afternoon. Now you say you prefer two in the morning—I gave up a weekend to meet with you." I inhale my body smell rising from my anger. I have frequently been told that I give out a misleadingly casual message. Comes from my early-on progressive-school training: "Now, children, share-the-toys and live-up-to-your-inner-potential." But who in Madrid after Franco's death knows about sharing the toys? All my cool converts to terrible wrath. I am furious at being put down, at a week of lost days, wasted by Spaniards who fail to show for appointments. Recalling complaints of other visiting writers who felt pushed into irritation and sourness makes my anger mount in group rage. I abruptly switch into high gear. I start firing, in a louder voice, the sort of specific questions on Spanish politics that only someone who had close dealing with the Opposition could have honed in on. There is silence in the bull pen. "Go fuck yourself," I say suddenly to the mocking journalist. "Why don't you go fuck yourself?"

I explode with the terrible intensity of an infrequent temper loser; once started, there is no stopping. "You think Americans have con-crete flowing through their bloodstreams? You think you Spanish have a special lien on narcissism? You people have cornered the prima-donna market?"

Still raging, I get up and walk over to the elevator. Angel Harquin-dequi, who had been out of the room during my outburst, suddenly comes rushing over. "You are not leaving," he yells at me. "I won't let you leave"—he pushes me away from the elevator. "You are going up to talk to Cebrián—our editor in chief."

I look about. The journalists in the bull pen seem more friendly now that I've indulged in histrionics, *engaged* with them, *tu a tu,* shouting my displeasure; I am worth talking to. I have proven I *care* about Spain.

A young woman, with round brown eyes and a Raggedy Ann–kinky blond halo of hair, pulls at my sleeve. She wears tight blue jeans and a big sweater. "I'm Rosa Pereda—I want to talk to you when you finish with *el jefe*. That was very good. You are getting in to see him within five minutes of arrival, I timed it." She doesn't look much older than my daughters. "Lots of men don't even get in there. He is *muy difícil* to see."

"It was accidental—I got mad at the do-you-like-our-blue-curtains routine."

"*No importan los accidentes.*" Rosa smiles. She isn't used to seeing women resist flak. "You are a woman, and you get into Cebrián's office in five minutes. Can we talk?"

"Rosa's very smart," Angel says. "She's going to be one of our literary correspondents."

"Sure." I like her.

"Lunch? I'll take you upstairs to our *cafetería*."

"Okay."

Rosa pulls me closer to her, so that she needn't speak much above a whisper. "I listened to your questions—you know about the Spanish left." She pauses. "I'm not a member of the Communist Party." She rummages through her vocabulary to find an appropriate label for me. "*Trotskista?*"

"New Yorker."

Thin, dark-haired, in his thirties, Juan Luis Cebrián, who speaks with quick nervous gestures, had been hired by Ortega y Gasset's son to run *El País*. In the final years of Franco he got a reputation for being a courageous journalist. Though I am to meet him many times after that and like him, I never feel I know much about him. He asks smart questions about the American view of developments within Spain. A thrifty journalist, he uses our meeting to bone up on information gaps. In a subdued way, he is proud of the record time in which *El País* has been born. He wants me to inspect the modern equipment used in the plant. Changing the subject, I ask him about Robert Vesco. I have kept a file of Vesco's relations with the Franco family. I had been told that a fair amount of Spanish funds had been channeled, with Vesco's help, to use in Nixon's first election campaign. "Was the Spanish financier Gil Reyes?"

"We haven't had a chance to establish our archives," Cebrián answers; then he gives me the name of a journalist at Informaciones who he thinks can help me out. He had heard the story, some of it had been published in the Spanish press. "Why do you want to do Vesco now? So many other things are going on this spring."

"Well yes, but the other stories I can follow in the press. Vesco's financial manipulations are news in America; the funneling of foreign funds into American election campaigns is important for us to know about."

Cebrián is pensive, then asks, "Do the Americans perceive of us as a potential democracy?"

Rosa Pereda takes me to the *cafetería* to have a coffee break. Small, round, and quick, she is still nervous about admitting she isn't of the Party; she hasn't nailed down a permanent arrangement with *El País*, and she is afraid her fragile connection to the paper could be subverted by one of the "submarines." Fascism produces bad mental processes. Spaniards then perceived too much as being all-powerful: the Church, Franco, the police, the Opus Dei, the army—so why not now the Communist Party? As long as the Communist Party remained underground, its rumored power seemed magical and omnipotent. As soon as it became legalized, its small voting strength—8 percent against the Socialists' 30 produced a more realistic assessment. But Spaniards like to aggrandize or devalue.

Rosa has never met an older woman who has had a writing career. She is curious about me: when I married, how many children? She wants to be my friend. I have always needed profound friendships with both men and women; Nuria's death has left a deep void, I need a new woman friend in Madrid. We send out mutual vibrations. Rosa is astonished that I belong to no political party.

"*Anarquista?*"

"No—but I've known many in Paris."

"Ahhhh!" Rosa breathes a sigh of relief; she has begun to "place" me, "*vale.*"

I explain that being a New Yorker is a special political country that can't be defined by labels such as Anarchist, Communist, *Trotskista* or Yankee-Go-Home. I don't use the term "liberal," because to them the word has pejorative connotations and means conservative. I try to define the word "radical" for her as being our closest definition of left-wing. Our lack of political definition baffles Europeans. Rosa picks up on my being Jewish—had I been a concentration camp victim? No, I tell her. Had the concentration camps truly existed? Yes. I notice her large eyes widen; this interests her.

Rosa takes me that same evening to Madrid's first legal *"verbena,"* a spring street festival in Aluche, a *barrio* where many *progres* (radicals) live. The football field is packed; a heavy neighborhood turnout. All ages jam into the playing ground, grandparents, children, workers, and *progres* sway to the rock music coming from a portable loud-speaker attached to a truck parked on the edge of the field. The danc-ing is so thick that dust rises in a gray film, creating a smoky zone over the field. We join hands in an old-fashioned conga line. Later, during "Bésame Mucho," a soldier taps Rosa on the shoulder. She pales, but he smiles. He is young; he wants to dance, not arrest her.

To Rosa the night seems wonderful. The dancing is fine; I agree, but I dislike the paramilitary trucks parked near us, their guns pointed directly at the crowd, ready to fire if some dummy yells more than just *Viva Aluche.* While Rosa delights in a free Madrid—*Ay, La Liber-tad*—I observe them and also keep my eye on the gangs of ultra-right lurking at the edges of the Aluche football field, spoiling for a fracas with the *progres.*

When Rosa learns about my connection with Ruedo Ibérico, she tells me that Luciano Rincón, who had been jailed after writing a book on Franco for Ruedo, is supposed to be here tonight. She grabs me by the hand and leads me through the crowd, shrieking almost hysterically, "Luciano . . . you'll never guess who is with me, *Luciano, Luciano.*" We don't find him, but years later, I recall her yelling for him and that night in Aluche—the dancing, the police, the ultra-right gangs—and the football fields of Aluche are fixed in my mind as the moment the Franco regime ended, the changeover irrevocably linked in my imagination with the gray dust rising in the Madrid sky as the Madrileños sway in the open air, dancing to the 1940s rumba, "Bésame Mucho."

Afterward, we go with some of her friends to a nearby bar. "You know how it is in Madrid," Rosa says. "Cliques. Those who had rela-tives on the Republican side stick to themselves. God, they are haughty. And the Communists can be heavy. But sometimes I think the Anarchists are the snootiest of them all." Rosa jumps off her bar-stool. She has the tumbled orphan look of Giulietta Masina in *La Strada* as she struts, parodying them. "With their noses straight up in the air, they never let in anyone new to join their suffering." She mimics the entire opposition and makes us laugh.

We order ham sandwiches and beer. Rosa's friends also are journalists.

"Now that all our friends are out in the open," Rosa says, "our *querida* left sounds *creaky*. To hear them makes me almost ashamed to be one of them."

"*Querida Rosa,*" says one of the men, "the left is *nada* left."

The second man turns toward me. "Rosa tells us you aren't of the Party. You aren't *Trotskista?*"

"Independent."

"Oh." He tries to place me. "Like the civil rights movement? Watergate?"

"Yes, that's about it—"

"*Caray,* Watergate was something!" Then he goes back to Trotsky. "The Communists have always been clods about literature, but the *Trotskistas*"—he pauses—"maybe their true contribution was as literary critics."

Rosa cups her face in the palm of either hand, pensive. "Sometimes I think I have in me a touch of El Trot . . ."

Inez Callahan flies in from Paris and books a room at the Sanvy. She wants to have a tour of the new politics and drop in on the old gang, who, these days, frequently are in the news. Amazing how the two of us have kept geographic pace with each other. Childhood in New York, then Paris, back to New York, and now Europe again. I wish Juan were with me—he'll be driving up from Casablanca in several weeks. But meanwhile, with Inez here, I relax. We speak in patois—Manhattan touches of 1970s Yiddish, laced with Spanish phrases, French, and made-up words. Inez is especially good at it.

When I arrive at the Sanvy, Inez throws on the extra bed in her room a dozen new tapes she has brought from Paris. We both share a secret passion for unclassy music: Argentinian *porteño* tangos, Caribbean *salsas,* Tito Puente. Both of us managed to spend our youth in Paris sublimely unmoved by Piaf. When we are together we indulge in our music.

Celebrity singers like Sinatra and Piaf produce claustrophobia in me. The notion of being forced to become the passive audience to their star performance repels me. Tito Puente, the Beatles allow room for one's own imagination and mood. Piaf's great song, "Je Ne Regrette

Rien" is ridiculous—only a cow has no regrets. How much better to concede our human lazinesses, wasted detours, petty meannesses, and wrong loves. What Piaf really means isn't that she has no regrets (she wasn't schizophrenic) but that she fucked well and often, and she is unabashed that *France knows.*

"I've brought this great shmaltzy recording of 'Blue Moon'—"

" 'Blue Moon'? Oh, I love 'Blue Moon,' " I moan in delight. "Play it on the cassette."

The two of us, at either end of Inez's dark Sanvy bedroom, are doing solo tangos, our partners being two of her silk scarves. "Blue Moon—la da da dee, oh, Blue Moon," I sing, while Inez keeps talking to me.

"So, how is our gang? Who is doing what to whom in Madrid, how goes ze bullshiteria?"

"Ze bullshiteria? Oh, everyone is reinventing some past they never had in ze first place."

"Figures. With the men, what's the current style? Imitation French? Anglo *cojones,* or is this their year for Try Spanish, it's better?"

"Some Madrid men still aim for an Anglo *cojones* style; not the Catalans, though."

Inez keeps swaying to "Blue Moon." "I don't know why in Barcelona they don't understand, for French you can do better in Paris . . . Oh, for the days in Madrid when one was young, didn't need Blue Cross, and never wore Thrift Shop recycled clothes." Inez sighs. "When the Madrileños had real *chispa.*"

"Inezka, play 'Blue Moon' again." I dance with her Lurex scarf,

Oh for the days when Madrid had chispa,
Now no more style, only chutzpa,
La da dee, la da da—

The waiter walks into the dreary room, startled at seeing two women tango; nervously he places a stainless steel tray of tea we have ordered on the night table. He assumes us nutty Americans.

"Vale, señora?"

"Vale." Inez tips him; he stands in the doorway; our music has discombobulated him.

We fall on the lumpy beds, convulsed with laughter. I explain to Inez that this spring the Madrid politicos are being introduced to the general public. "Each late afternoon there is a new happening—the

Madrileños can politics-shop. Each day a different *acto*. Speeches, a new book, it's like watching the culture stalls and new cafés go up along Columbus Avenue, after Lincoln Center was built. This afternoon we can hear Juan Benet—"

"Our Juanito?"

"Our Juan. He's doing a eulogy on Dionisio Ridruejo; a book of essays on him by his friends has just been published. It's very *triste* that he didn't live just a little while longer. Dionisio's the big hero, just now, in Madrid."

Inez balances her teacup on her stomach, and keeps talking, while sipping the tea lying down. "Dionisio, a hero of the left? Okay, true, he said *mea culpa*, and with *mucho* honor disavowed Franco, but still, Dionisio was a big-time Fascist, ye best pal of José Antonio—a high-up founder of the Phalange—Christ, he hobnobbed and colluded on a high level with the super-Nazis, demanding that he be given an important post in the blue division—and God, that crazy love poetry he wrote to Mussolini—" Inez keeps drinking from her precariously placed teacup. "Some hero of the left—shmuck-os!"

"Inez, don't be so fussy—he's the big Madrid idol now mostly because he's dead."

"The left ought to drum up someone who never was a Fascist—"

"Dionisio had enormous charm; I spent a great flirty afternoon with him, oh, maybe eight years ago—I can't remember what we talked about, except that for weeks after that I felt I was wonderful, beautiful, and so forth. He turned on men and women."

"So, what's this new bullshiteria about opposition to Franco having started in the mid-1950s?" Inez gets up, goes to the closet, and selects what she will wear. "Christ, it was the last possible date by which you could have made your conversion away from Franco and not been considered a mental retard. Or socially undesirable. Nobody was crying 'Viva Franco' then—it was 'Where's my visa for London or Paris, I want to fuck foreign broads.' By '55 you could be a café leftist and not go to jail for fancy talk."

"I can understand the way they think if I imagine Spain as a huge bubble. Within the bubble is Spanish Fascism, with Franco at the top and then the Church and the Communist Party. Their weakness here is their lack of imagination about life outside the bubble; they don't really understand people who never were pro-Franco. For them the most important part has been their own evolution away from Franco—which only occurred inside a very small group, the Spanish upper class ..." I pause. "Well, now they might shout *'Viva la República,'* but that's merely retro nostalgia; Franco is what existed here for forty years—the bubble he dominated, their true past."

"So—you are saying our gang, our pals, the Spaniards we knew are irrelevant?"

"For Spain, now, yes, for us, no."

"Are you sad, Barbara?"

"A leetle—*mais il faut se battre contre le cafard.* C'mon—the Dionisio happening is over on Velázquez; you can't bank anymore on events starting in Madrid not on time; they fool you and suddenly go punctual."

Inez rummages in her suitcase. "Paco Rabanne tax-free Calandre. Catch." She throws. "A present."

When we get to the Calle Velázquez, there is a jam of people by the elevator. Eventually we get to the second floor, where Juan Benet has already begun his performance. The head of the Socialist Party, Felipe González, looking very young and handsome in a dark, short-nosed Andalusian way (Felipe is thirty-two) is listening intently.

The main room is jam-packed; the overflow must listen to Juan through the loudspeaker system in adjoining, smaller rooms. After Juan finishes his talk, the crowd seems to thicken. I see Juan's sister and mother, Marisol and Doña Teresa, standing in the hall near Josefina and Alberto Machimbarrena; Alberto, who went to grade school with Juan, is part of the old gang. I push Inez toward the group. There are sudden cries, *"Mujer. Qué sorpresa! Anda*—how good you look—"

Josefina Machimbarrena leans toward Inez. *"Está muy divertido, Madrid, estos días*—how amusing Madrid has become." Juan is surrounded by his "fans." He looks up. *"Anda.* Now Mademoiselle Zucker has arrived." In his eyes neither Inez nor I have ever become married women.

Despite Juan's bravado greeting of Inez—the hugs, the dramatic exclamations—he seems in flight away from all his and Nuria's shared friends. In the beginning, in the way of two old friends who are determined the china will not break, Juan and I toe-danced around each other; over lunch he teased about "El Goitie," his nickname for Juan Goytisolo. Occasionally, because of Juan's fix on Morocco, Juan Benet merely referred to him as the Moor. "How is he these days? *El Moro?"*

Other times he would be more direct: "Haven't I enough trouble without having Juan Goytisolo leaving messages for you in *my* house—imagine him, using *my* telephone number." When Juan Benet's friends would kick him slightly, cautioning him to "shhh shhh," his small-boy brown eyes widen; has he gone too far?

I also want my longstanding friendship with Juan Benet to "hold." So, when his friend Rosa Regás comes to Madrid from Barcelona to stage her own happening, I make sure that Josefina Machimbarrena and I show up early for her razzmatazz political theater at the Hotel Velázquez. (Inez has already gone home.) Rosa's publishing house in Barcelona, the Gaya Ciencia, has published thirty-six booklets with essays by leading political figures—*What Is Socialism? What Is Democracy? What Is the Bunker?* Each week the Spanish public is presented with a paperback that makes the new political world more comprehensible to them.

Rosa has brought her entire Barcelona staff; she installs them at the Hotel Ritz, where she has a discount.

The Velázquez happening is clever; because of the variety of subjects in the thirty-six titles, political figures from different camps come to the meeting. Rosa arrives with her staff. Her hair is straight, carnelian-colored; her Barcelona reputation is of a modern, sexy, "free" woman. For the event she wears a stark, man-tailored, white flannel jacket, white knickers, and black boots. Rosa laughs frequently, nervously; she takes a bottle of perfume out of her bag and douses her neck and wrist. "Ah, Barbara . . . Josefina." She looks at me, and for a second remains quite still. She must be wondering, as I am Nuria's old friend, what I think about her relation to Juan. So I kiss her cheek lightly; she understands I mean well, life goes on, and in that quick gesture it is established that we will be friends.

She firmly strides up to the platform as though unaware that it is dramatic in Madrid for a woman to be moderating a panel consisting of the leading male political figures. Tierno Galván (later to become Socialist mayor), Nicolás Sartorius (whose father is a count and who is considered to be the possible next leader of the split Communist Party), and other important politicians are there. Rosa has each author talk about his book.

Josefina whispers to me that one book has remained unwritten: *What Is the Modern Spanish Woman?* The biggest revolution now is with us—you notice how they ignore it." She fans herself with the invitation. "Rosa looks marvelous."

"Very."

A young man in the audience rises to his feet and in a muffled, strangled voice announces he is here to defend Trotsky. "The Trotskista were never in the pay of Hitler." His voice is embattled. What ghosts is he fighting? "And what of the murder of Andrés Nin?" He refers to the leader of POUM, who, during the Civil War, was murdered in a Communist cheka prison. *Frozen political time. Quarrels that should have ended in '39. Old feuds, old truths left to molder in the cold storage of a dying Fascist nation. Who, now, can go rummaging in that bin?*

He sits down. No applause. The next speaker—he wrote the essay defining the Bunker, quickly points out that he, of course, wasn't one of them. Members of the audience applaud him. Laughter. Someone shrieks, "We know the Bunker couldn't write their own books. They are *analfabetos,* can't read or write."

That special Madrid cackle engulfs the Velázquez theater. An old man in the audience gets up. He shows his Socialist card, a low number, a real old-time Socialist. He tells the crowd he has waited for forty years to go public—now he wants to be listened to. "We Spanish need to be *educated* concerning what happened in our past. Don't just laugh at the Bunker, don't pretend the Fascists never existed. If we believe they truly did not know how to read or write, we are deluding ourselves. Look, they were strong and powerful and they destroyed a country; we need to understand the true nature of Fascism."

The more he pleads with them not to laugh, the more intense that Madrid nasal smart-aleck cackle gets. *Ought to be a law against that hyena laugh.* I put my head in my hands; my cheeks flush in sympathy and embarrassment for the man. His old cronies slap him on the back, muttering that he has done good, and yank him back down. He is out of sync with Madrid. I may have been a heroine about pulling people out of jail, yet I don't walk over to him. I just sit there, next to Josefina.

POLITICAL JOURNAL

Madrid: June 1976

As long as the Spanish mistake elegance for thought and romanticism for humanity, they will be vulnerable to Fascism. What they fail to perceive is that in the beginning Fascists in Spain were not a doddering, out-of-date collection of octogenarians or ultra-fanatics from marginal social groups, as they appear to be after Franco's death, but velvet-eyed, askew idealists. José Antonio's early followers had a blend of romanticism, idealism, elegance, good manners, and a bizarre confusion of left-wing and right-wing thought; these were men who answered the chaos and bad economics of the world with aggrandized heroes and idols. Dionisio Ridruejo was José Antonio's poet. True, he was sensitive; true, when he finally publicly abandoned the Franco regime in the early fifties, he did so with dignity and he went to prison—but the real question that should be asked about Dionisio, the true remarkable event, isn't his rejection of Franco but how, in the first place, did such a sensitive, intelligent man become so deluded? I don't believe that Communism, or anti-Communism, or Trotsky has much to do with the essential problems of Spain: what worries me is the failure of the post-Franco generation not to link stylish romantic behavior to Fascism; they perceive the Bunker as old men who have outlived their time. Spaniards phobically flee from what they consider dowdy, but they don't yet comprehend that democracy is by definition mundane.

Spain has never had a social mechanism for getting jobs. Which means the Church, Opus Dei, the Phalange, and the big political parties traditionally have been used as a steppingstone into the job market. This was one of the main causes for the sudden growth of the Phalange in the thirties. Is still a potential dangerous weakness.

Since 1948, I have seen generation after generation used up by the Resistance. Exhausted. Spain seems so tired now.

The Resistance reinforced the ideas of the intellectuals as an elite apart. Now they still remain apart. This time, instead of clandestine politics, they have removed themselves to an ivory tower.

23

In a secondhand bookstore in New York, I had found a book, *Spanish Prelude*, which I had brought with me to Spain. I never heard of its author, Jenny Ballou. I had shown the book to Inez, while she was at the Sanvy, because Jenny sounded so like us, but of our parents' generation. She must have lived in Madrid on her own in the late twenties, during the end of Primo de Rivera's mild dictatorship, just before the beginning of the Spanish Republic. What astonished me was how clearly, how unromantically, Jenny Ballou perceived the country in which she was living. True, Hemingway and Orwell were writing about Spain at war; and Jenny was writing about Spanish society during the prewar. When Inez read it she said, "She must have hung out with a crowd like ours."

While I wait for Juan Goytisolo and Ahmed to drive up to Madrid from Casablanca, I reread Jenny's book and devour her account of her life in Madrid, in that other time, as though it was my own, now.

Café Revolutionaries

I returned to Madrid to find practically all my friends still in prison. Only Don Alberto, the future count, was at large ... Alberto, whose house was on the outskirts of Madrid, was staying at the apartment of a friend in town who had left for London. He accompanied me to the jail on visiting days. It was like going to the theater. Limousines drove unceasingly to the prison doors.... Students played baseball in the courtyard, while inside the hall attendants hung about receiving impromptu revolutionary lessons from the political prisoners and their illustrious visitors. Our departure from jail was always sad. The Madrid streets, by contrast, were lifeless. People walked up and down the Castellana as though dreaming each other....

It was pure inertia that drove me into the patio where the so-called literary vanguard usually met. I had decided in the mountains not to get in touch with this group who, in their vulgar fear of the commonplace, had created an incestuous little bourgeoisie of their own. When José Oretega y Gasset, their patron saint, wrote *The Dehumanization of Art*, he had attempted to define a literary school, but he created a sect. The tendencies he claimed to be setting down "benevolently," with the detached eye of the spectator, his apostles, instead of following his example, took his advice. "Let us try to be Greeks as Goethe tried." And they all tried to be ancient gods, supermen, looking down on the "sub-artistic" world from their dizzy heights. The superman always appears when men feel themselves inadequate to their times.

As the vanguard group in Madrid were about ten years behind

the times, they had the advantage over the postwar generation in
other countries of being able to caricature them as well as their own
selves. The consummate symbol of these experimental souls in all
countries was enacted in the circus in Madrid, when Ramón Gómez
de la Serna, the genial demigod of the vanguardists, read his famous
Greguerías from the top of a trapeze as he unwound the roll of Japa-
nese tissue upon which they were written. Full of such fanciful
pranks, they were all beyond good and evil and the cry was back to
instinct, away with intelligence.

For intelligence was out of style at the moment, and extremely
inconvenient. "We must recover our innocence." And by force of
sheer will the advanceguardists managed to become so innocent—
an act of virtuosity on their part—that they were just about to sing
the praises of the dictatorship when Primo de Rivera fell. They had
gone a step too far in their innocence and were never to live it
down—not even after they denied shamefacedly in their weekly
that such a thing as the vanguard had ever existed.

Although their idea had originally been the laudable one of dis-
infecting Spanish letters from blood and sand, they were in such
thin air by the time the censorship was lifted that even when it had
ceased to be dangerous to write lucidly they were to find that they
had nothing new to say with their new language. For in acquiring
their agile technique, these literary gladiators had lost sight of what
they intended to do with it. They carried their vanguard burlesque
into the new Republic, of which they were destined to become the
playboys.

In their game they had learned that what is left unsaid is of far
greater importance than what is said—and that it had far less con-
sequences. This "impartial silence" praised by Mallarmé had stood
them well during the reign of the dictator's censor; but after they
were given portfolios in the Republic it was too late to stop the
impetus of parody. They were to prove too enervated by their rhetorical debauches to make more than a light opera of the beliefs for
which men had rotted in prison. Victims of their own jest, they
were to become easy tools of the deadly reactionary forces they had
pretended to despise.

For when faced with the real problems of innovation and change,
they allowed themselves to be hypnotized by such slogans as "In-
justice is preferable to disorder." Hadn't Goethe himself said this?
And were they not all studying German, emulating their patron

philosopher, José Ortega y Gasset? If they had known how to read plain Spanish, they would have found hidden in the depths of Ortega's own writing these words that could have guided them where their master did not dare to go:

"I, who am professor in the University, need the thoughts of the people much more than they need mine; because of the spiritual absence of three fourths of Spain, our life is an inept fiction, and as great as my efforts might be, I know too well that three fourths of my ideas are condemned to remain pure artifice. . . . I believe that the people will triumph, and that we shall return to them to restore our soul that the large cities are rendering sterile."

These experimenters of New Spain—so they considered themselves—did not know how to listen to their own master. And even then, when in Madrid I did not yet understand the true significance of their vagaries, I had an innate loathing for these "martyrs of the circus" with their knight-errant culture, and for their imitators. Surely even my boardinghouse loneliness was preferable to renewed contact with them . . . I was overcome as I approached the table, with a cruel languor, a horror of the fate that made me a spectator among spectators. And a mortal boredom overhung the group; it was as if their very soul had been blocked out by the censors.

I semidoze, outstretched on the bed in the small bedroom overlooking the Plaza de Oriente; in my sleep the characters in Jenny Ballou's account of Madrid in 1929 come alive. The poet who declaims *When are we going to forget Don Quijote—The dead kill the living—We must forget Quijote with the other nightmares of our history. That is the first task of revolution. Without a clean break with the past there is no hope for the future* melds with the poet I meet Tuesday night, spring 1976. *When are we going to forget Don Quijote, the dead kill the living.* I have become Jenny. Jenny Ballou, presumed dead, has been resuscitated—spring 1976—no more boardinghouse; now Jenny is Barbara living in Amadeo Cuito's apartment in the old part of Madrid, where the streets still smell of acid, wind downhill, and at night the sky is lit with the outline of domed churches, instead of crosses electric lights flash *banco, banco.* Then the downstairs buzzer rings; it is Juan and Ahmed.

Juan is sunburned from driving; his darkened skin has turned his eyes pond-blue. Ahmed comes up behind him, carrying more luggage upstairs. When I am with Juan I feel as though a laser beam is directed at me. In the presence of the two men, I become more alive, my skin takes tone, I feel I've become better-looking. Later that night the three of us walk between the Puerta del Sol and the Calle Mayor. Juan has rarely been in Madrid during these last twenty years; he shows me the top-floor pension he lived in as a student at the University of Madrid. Nearby, on the next street, is the third-floor pension-hotel where Inez and I had stayed several weeks during the late forties. That part of the city then was full of funny small hotels, really just a floor-through, generally located on the third or fourth floor, and very cheap. I am astonished that such ancient artifacts of old-fashioned Madrid still exist. I had forgotten about the Puerta del Sol.

I point up. "In that pension there, Inez, Juan Benet and I found a signed copy of Ernest Hemingway's *The Sun Also Rises* just lying on a dusty Victorian ebony piano—nobody in the pension had the remotest idea of who Hemingway was. We were too young, too innocent, too stupid, and too reverent to have the wit to know when to steal. We looked at the book and just put it back on the top of the piano, just left it sitting there ..." Ahmed, Juan, and I walk past the Puerta del Sol with all the cheapo pearl shops and places with Grandma's tablecloths and plastic mats for sale, and we keep walking until we get to the Plaza Mayor, and we sit down at one of the outdoor tables. Juan and I order coffee; Ahmed, who is looking about, wants a Coke.

Juan is listening to the conversation taking place at the next table; he pokes me and whispers, "Did you hear what they said? That couple just dined with relatives—returnees. Listen to how casual they sound." Juan mimics the people seated at the table near us. "Can you imagine? This is Don Jaime's first visit in forty years." Ahmed is very quiet; to me he seems sad. Once he was the center of Juan's life. Now, if Ahmed makes the request, Juan takes an occasional trip with him, but Juan never asks Ahmed to join him anymore. I observe him; his silences are very loud. *You can't say to Ahmed you are sorry he has been half kicked out. Because you are not sorry.* Suddenly I take Ahmed's hand; he seems surprised at my rare gesture of affection. He looks at me intently; his eyes meet mine. *As if he is thinking, Well, you waited until you were safe, until Juan no longer wanted Ahmed.* Juan is oblivious of my show of affection toward Ahmed or Ahmed's ironic acceptance of it. Late that night, after Ahmed has gone to sleep, Juan whispers to me that he no longer likes to be alone with Ahmed, as the sexual thing is dead. After Juan loses interest in him, I become more tender to

Ahmed. It is I, much more often than Juan, who says, Oh well, let's spend the day together.

Ahmed joins Juan and me the next day to have lunch with the sales representative from Juan's publisher, Seix Barral. Antonio has just moved to Madrid from Mexico City—and arrives at the restaurant with a black eye and a cut lip; accidentally he had found himself in the middle of a fight in the Madrid subway. "Every day is a new experience here," Antonio remarks, while the waiter brings him cotton and alcohol. "People in this city either give you too much or too little of themselves, never the right quantity. I ask a woman a direction—she insists on walking twenty blocks out of her way to be sure I reach my destination. The next time, *paffff!* For no reason, you can end up needing three stitches on your face. Unpredictable—"

"Like New York."

"Juan," Antonio continues, he is in charge of shepherding us about, "you must be at the Seix Barral stall at seven-thirty to sign copies of your book. You'll see—you are a tremendous success here. Everybody is waiting to meet you." Then Antonio finally turns to me: "At the next book fair it will be your turn." At Seix we are looking forward to publishing your book."

"The period Barbara writes about, the late forties, is completely unknown here in Spain. It's very important that *Arriving Where We Started* be translated. It will cause a tremendous stir."

I like Juan's enthusiasm, although I feel a little disoriented, amputated, that the American parts of the book probably will be ignored. Here it will be read as being *about* Spain.

"Everything now in Madrid is causing talk. Day by day we get fresh news of the past. And now all of Juan's banned and censored books are being openly sold at the book fair in the Retiro."

Juan interrupts Antonio, he wants to see a revival of Visconti's *The Damned*. "Don't forget," Antonio warns us, "this book fair is special—the first uncensored one in Madrid in forty years—"

We promise to be in front of the Seix Barral bookstall promptly at seven-thirty.

The three of us sit huddled in the dark movie theater near the Madrid-Palace; I am seated between Ahmed and Juan. Occasionally Juan leans over and explains to Ahmed why the Brown Shirts are beating up and murdering the other Germans. Ahmed doesn't understand what Nazi Germany is all about. Behind us movie patrons exhort: "Shuush! *Cállate!*" Juan is mesmerized by the film; the cruelty, the morbid incest, the bloody deaths get to him. "Juan," I remind him, "it won't be Fascists singing 'Cara al Sol' lining up at the Seix Barral stand but ordinary people like you and me." He is silent. I nudge him. "I know why you wanted to see *The Damned* before making your first public appearance—it helps get you in the mood, fleshes out those old Fascist phantoms of your youth that are still dancing around inside your head; Visconti's Germany is your ancient Spain—but it isn't *now.*" Juan stares at me in the dark; suddenly he blinks.

We walk through the Retiro, directly to the Seix Barral stand. Soon we hear Juan Goytisolo barked through the park loudspeaker; they are announcing the group of writers who will be signing books in their publishers' stalls. At first nobody comes. Then quickly a crowd materializes. Relieved, Juan says to me, "I've forgotten—nothing in Spain starts on time." He pauses. "They told me my only audience in Spain was the sergeants who tore up copies of my books in the police station."

"But you didn't believe that?"

"No—but how was I to know? I never realized Spain had so many secret democrats."

Rosa Pereda, strolling with friends, sees us. "Barbara!"

One of the men approaches Juan and extends his hand. "Imagine, Juan Goytisolo in Madrid. I've waited fifteen years for such a book fair—"

A young woman journalist accompanying Rosa exclaims excitedly, "Marcelino Comacho, Nicolás Sartorius, Communists, Socialists, all these mythic people we've heard about—why, everyone is *real*. It's history."

Despite the police, who walk in teams in front of the bookstalls, the mood in the Retiro has the natural gaiety of a spring Sunday in the city. In order not to provoke incidents, the *progres* are skirting the small ultra-right stand. While Juan remains inside the stall, signing books, Antonio joins Ahmed and me; he brings each of us a bottle of Fanta. Jaime Salinas, inspecting the fair, walks over to me. When I turn to introduce Ahmed, he quickly disappears.

Jaime watches him recede into the crowd. "Juan's Arab friend?"

"Well, yes and no"

"I would have expected an Arab boy—" Jaime appears puzzled. "He seems much older than Juan."

"Oh?" I never confuse friends with too much information, which means I frequently say, Oh. Just then Carlota Bustelo comes rushing over. This is before she becomes a Socialist deputy, and before her brother Paco Bustelo (who represents the left faction of the Socialist Party) becomes rector of the University of Madrid. "Barbara," Carlota urges me, "take down what just happened to me, now be a jounalist. The bookstore I help manage, Antonio Machado, has just been smashed in by gangs of ultra-right. They came in with those iron chains. Barbara, write down the details—'Despite the first uncensored book fair, destruction of Madrid bookstores by thugs and gangs continues on a daily basis—' " Carlota is breathless from running, as she loads me down with handbills and manifestos; her face reddens to fever-pitch. While I am taking notes, Marisol walks over. We move inside the stand. "I've just autographed a book for a count, and a third cousin of mine, very conservative, came by to congratulate me," Juan tells me excitedly.

In the next booth, Nicolás Sartorius, recently released from Carabanchel prison, is autographing copies of his book. Juan introduces me as an American, "who really has done good things for Spain." I take it as a short cut implying that I shouldn't be subjected to anti-Americanism. "Where's Ahmed?" Juan asks.

"He went for a walk."

"He's not happy?"

"Well, things are different now—"

"For you, too?"

"No—for Ahmed." *Explain to Juan that now he has become famous, but Ahmed has remained in place, just a Berber small-time entrepreneur. Juan doesn't realize Ahmed's not dealing from the same deck of cards.* But more crowds gather, and I say nothing. Soon Ahmed comes back along the dusty central path, still carrying his bottle of Fanta. He notices I have joined Juan inside the stall; he hesitates; then he sits down on a nearby bench and just waits.

"Ce n'est pas chic," Ahmed tells me the next afternoon when we are alone in Amadeo's apartment (Juan has gone to his publishers) in answer to my remonstrations about his sitting alone the night before on the park bench drinking his Fanta. *"Il y a chic* and *pas chic,"* Ahmed

knows what is elegant. Juan has come home. He is the great man, "only him and you should be in the stand, no Ahmed. *Pas bon*. Barbara, there are rules in life; I tell my boys, You don't want to be a *petit* dark *merde*, caca on the streets of Casa, you learn from Ahmed the rules—I want my boys to have a French head or a Jewish head; *then* they become architects, engineers in Morocco. And you will become a great lady—the Jeanne d'Arc of the Resistance. Now only you and Juan, no more Ahmed."

"But, Ahmed, it was you who wanted to take this trip—"

"Ahmed was wrong, my head was fuzzy-wuzzy. Last night, my head cleared, I heard his name called over the loudspeaker, *comme un roi, Juan Goytisolo, Juan Goytisolo . . .*"

"All the writers' names are announced over the loudspeaker; that's just publishing business . . ."

"The line for his books was the longest—I am *fier de Juan*, but I know what is chic and what is not. Juan creates disorder in my head, I tell him *pas normal*, man-man; normal is man-woman. Juan plays a crazy game. Niki-Nikki between men no good. But didn't I take care of Juan? No more kif for Juan, I said, kif was what made fuzzy-wuzzy, *petit caca merde* of the dumb Maroqui, the bums of Europe and North Africa. You, I got off of those cigarettes, no more Koolies for Barbara; bad smell stink up a car; now you have no more asthma." Ahmed rests his head on his elbows; he leans on the TV table in Amadeo's apartment. "Not fair—in another world it would have been me who loved you."

"Ahmed, you are a wonderful looker," I add to his litany.

"You are humoring me. *Je ne suis pas un bébé*—Oh, *je comprends tout. Todo*. Because Ahmed is not a *grand menteur* writer, for you, *je n'existe pas*. I am not a man. So tell me, if Juan was not a big-time *grand menteur* writer—would you put up with his fuzzy-wuzzy head? I ask you, Barbara, answer me, *ta parole*—"

"Ahmed,—I am immune to those sorts of claims." I take a deep, firm breath. "When I was a kid I was given the business: My proletariat boyfriends complained, 'So, you think you are too good for me—I, who was the son of poor immigrants; I, whose parents suffered through the Depression; I, who am a mere country boy and you a slick city chick. I, whose skin is black, while you are Miss Lighty-whitey.' Look, Ahmed, sex is no CARE package you can ship off to the starving masses in China. And American men are specialists in the line you are giving me in your Casablanca *Belleville* French, I have been inoculated against sexual blackmail by the proletariat, or by those self-appointed male representatives of the proletariat. Okay, Ahmed, you are right. Technically, you are more macho-looking than Juan, yet Juan attracts more women because he has writing talent. That's the way it is, Ahmed, *la vie n'est pas juste*. Besides, you have plenty of girl-friends in Casa—"

Ahmed stares at me. "Ahmed never wanted Juan, Juan wanted Ahmed. He told me he gave up everything for me—his wife, his life. Now Juan says, only Ahmed and Juan. So then, suddenly, why is it that Madame Barbara shows up? Only Ahmed, Juan says. Ahmed is king—but then there is Madame Barbara. Ahmed is very clever, he asks and asks until Barbara gives in. But then I ask myself," he continues, "why is Ahmed so lonely? If Ahmed is king, and even Barbara loves him, why am I so lonely? Then suddenly, one day, no more Ahmed, just Barbara and Juan. And I *capiche*. Ahmed was not clever, Ahmed was a stupid man." He stares at me. "You made love with me not because you wanted me but to cut off my fingers, render me powerless, impotent; you make me want you, and you make love to me, and soon Barbara has Juan all to herself. Ahmed is gone, pushed away. Now Ahmed sleeps alone."

Ahmed is on to you. He's figured out your handiness at knowing how to reject, discard, while appearing to be Ms. Warmth.

I observe Ahmed as though seeing him for the first time, taking in his tall stride—always in motion. I smell the odors of his beige skin, intense, intelligent, he stares at me angrily, he knows he's been had.

"Ahmed," I say in a low voice, "Ahmed, I did always want you too"; the late-afternoon light dapples through Amadeo's living room windows, turning Ahmed's eyes camel-colored. "But you were a rival, come on, you understood that—and, I guess, I loved me more," I admit in a small voice. "I wanted Juan for myself."

"So that was why you slept with me—to get rid of me?"

I stare at him, unblinking. "I wanted Juan, and you were, well, *extra*."

"So—you are as crazy as him! As fuzzy-wuzzy. You say always, Oh, Ahmed, remember me, remember me. Why should Ahmed remember you? Makes no sense to remember a woman who makes you lose being king. Who doesn't recognize the smell of your manhood? I carted your suitcases—I was like putty in your hands."

"Don't be melodramatic, like Juan said, women prefer a dry style."

"Remember you?" He continues his own line of thought. "Why

are you so concentrated on being remembered? All day long in Madrid, in Spain, they do nothing but snap your photo and ask you questions and write down the answers. Ahmed observes, Ahmed knows. You have a whole country remembering you, why do you need me?"

"—a miserable cinder, a *petit* piece of caca from the streets of Casa." I finish his phrase, mocking him. "Ahmed, don't you be a *vieux con*. Media doesn't remember a person, media devours. Ahmed, Ahmed, to be stuck off in some small, musty corner of Spanish history means, at most, some student, say five years from now, will be doing his thesis at the Sorbonne or the University of Salamanca or at Santa Cruz in California and they will write: *Valley of the Fallen, see footnote: Solomon (Probst) prison escape, 1948.* I will be filed away in a computer bank. But, Ahmed, that isn't *memory*. You, Juan, and I, we have lived now—that is what is real—not what gets said in the click-click camera interviews; we don't exist in those interviews. They are DEAD. But we were alive, Ahmed—" Suddenly I am yelling at him, "Ahmed, you *knew* we existed, you knew the three of us were alive—ALIVE. NOT FUZZY-WUZZY. NOT A COMPUTER BANK." I look at him, and suddenly—I don't know why—I run out of the living room and down the four flights of stairs, out, by myself, to the Plaza de Oriente. I walk rapidly through the old streets, toward the Plaza Mayor and back over to the Puerta del Sol. Ahmed's pissed because he's figured out he never mattered for me as a man. He's furious at Juan and me. We no longer need him. I walk quickly; suddenly I bump into a tall man, he's wearing a navy-blue sweater and gray flannel pants. I hear Ahmed's insistent voice, You never saw me as a man—and instead of moving on I stare at the man; I take the time, mentally, to undress him; he smiles slightly at me, as though guessing my thoughts; lightly he touches my shoulder, *"Perdóneme, señora . . ."* Then, slowly, I move on.

When I walk into the Plaza Mayor, I count the number of men in the square, and slowly, man by man, I undress, mentally, each one. I've walked out without a jacket, without a purse; I keep walking, hands in my pockets, casual and intent. *There are many men in the world. Almost as many men as there are women. How much energy do you use to limit the ratio of men you perceive of as sexual objects to such small stuff numerically? You are operating on a narrow cloth, sticking to the same old stand, a narrow belt of intellectuals. Suppose you changed your mental processes, suppose you didn't limit? Ahmed, Ahmed, I wail, petit caca of Casa, promise you'll remember me.*

I walk back home. I have become confused by the constant interviewing of Juan Goytisolo and of me that goes on in Amadeo's apartment. History becomes fresh news when a country becomes psychologically ready to absorb pre-existing information. Am I interviewer or interviewee? The tape recorders the Madrid journalists use frequently break down. I lend them as backup my Sony. Their machines are big and bulky; my minature Sony is much admired. One of the young journalists tells me he has become very disoriented. Before Franco died, he hated the upper classes. Now, as news unravels, it would appear that the Resistance had in it an astonishingly high proportion of them. The journalist confesses that all his preconceptions have been turned inside out.

It is hard for them to keep track of so many different generations of anti-Franco Spaniards. Because they have no clear image of Spaniards who were roughly my contemporaries (they would have been very young children during the Civil War), they use the symbols from a previous, more familiar generation to define us. My father was exactly Hemingway's age; my friends *read* Malraux, went to the movies and watched Humphrey Bogart; Paco's father was killed in the Civil War. We were a transitional generation.

"Do you consider the legendary prison escape from Cuelgamoros as being the end of the Maquis or as the beginning of the post-World War II Spanish political resistance to Franco?"

"We didn't consider ourselves to be part of either the Maquis or the Resistance. Just students in Paris. We thought of the Resistance as having to do with World War II; by the time we came along the war was over. We felt we had been gypped by being too young, and had missed the real drama. We were in awe of those people like Pallach who had been in POUM and the Maquis—but they were much older."

I think I am making myself clear, but the journalist shakes his head, he disagrees; he says we were in the Resistance. Well, it no longer matters who we thought we were in '48. Now, in 1976, we have become the Resistance. Or is it that when you are very young the Resistance always appears to be one generation away?

Daniel Sueiro, who had briefly talked to me with Nicolás, now comes to interview me for his book, *The History of the Valley of the Fallen.* I explain to Sueiro about Manuel Amit, that the Anarchist Secretary

General (and member of the Galician executive) had been in the Cuelgamoros stalag along with Nicolás and Manolo, and had escaped willy-nilly after finding out that the Spanish authorities had discovered his true identity. The Anarchist underground knew of his whereabouts and appealed to Juan Manuel Canneja, then stuck in Ocaña prison, for help. Juan Manuel asked Isabel to get Paco to take Amit back with us to France when we did the prison break. Paco, Barbara Mailer, and I went to the caves on the outskirts of Madrid; Gypsies and the poor lived in them, near the Guadarramas, where Amit was hidden. We brought him medicine. He had a rifle in the cave; it was the only time in my life I ever saw a loaded firearm close up. Amit was sick; he lay on the bed, under a blanket. I didn't understand Spanish then, but I realized Paco was trying to convince him to come with us, that we were capable of getting across the border into France. I tried to look intelligent because Amit kept staring at Barbara and me, as though he could determine by the expression in our eyes a secret clue to his eventual fate; finally, he declined to come with us. Instead, he joined a massive Anarchist prison break, which included about fourteen older men. All but two were arrested; they were apprehended in their meeting place, a football stadium in Madrid. Ejarque, who was one of the two men to escape, had a wooden stump for a leg. I met him after he arrived (traveling across borders on foot) in Paris. But Amit was recaptured. Juan Manuel Canneja told me that he died years later in Puerto de Santa Maria, a prison near Cádiz.

After that, whenever I was in Madrid, suddenly I would see Amit's phantom face; Barbara and I must have looked too much like nice, young American girls to be able to convince him to join us. If he had come with us, he would have lived. I try to explain to Sueiro the connecting links then between the Anarchists and the students. "You, Barbara, and Benet reached Amit—an Anarchist leader in a cave near the Guadarramas?" Sueiro is incredulous. He can't get a bead on Spanish and American kids reaching Anarchist leaders in Gypsy caves outside Madrid.

But isn't his confusion at your description of events a mirror of your own disorientation? Sueiro doesn't completely understand that the abortive Anarchist prison break from Cuelgamoros crisscrossed with our freelance student break, which did work. He sees the two events as being separate. He fails to make the proper connections because he has no previous knowledge of connections between the Anarchist movement and left-wing students of the upper class of that time. The period is too remote, too hazy.

But the Anarchist prison break must once have been important to you. Your first attempt to write a novel, done when you were twenty-three, has an odd beginning. The opening chapter begins in the outskirts of Madrid where an old man is running; he has just escaped from prison. Nearby are the caves. Then the next scene is in a fashionable Madrid apartment: a spoiled, chic, intelligent young man manages to put together a package of clothing and medicine. He goes to the cave, meets the man; he realizes he has no connection with this wounded Anarchist; he helps him and is disgusted with himself for recognizing that what is survival for the old man for him has the thrill of adventure. He loathes himself; but the older man is very grateful for the help given. That was the way you started your first novel, and in it were all the details of the football stadium and the failed Anarchist prison break. When the young man learns of the failure, he is on a train headed for Paris; he looks at his handsome reflection in the mirror and says, I am already a hero. But you ran into the same trouble as Sueiro. You really didn't know how to put together or sustain your upper-class world, which you had started off in that strange way, by having your protagonist wandering in the mountains, bumping into Anarchists. Then there was the problem of the young American girl. You didn't know where to locate her, so you left her out until midway through the novel. You made her a nihilist because nihilism was fashionable during the time you wrote that novel, but you never were remotely nihilist. You picked a style, an overused metaphor out of confusion. You hadn't a clue as to how to integrate Anarchists, mountains, and New York City schoolgirls. Like Daniel Sueiro you noticed that nothing fit; when in doubt stir one nihilist into the bouillabaisse. In reality you were just one more serious schoolgirl living the time of life between graduation and motherhood and grownup career. When you understood that, years later, you wrote Arriving Where We Started.

After Sueiro leaves, an *El País* journalist and photographer come to the apartment to interview Juan. Rosa Pereda has scheduled a talk with me for the following week and has asked the photographer to take some pictures of me as well. Which disconcerts Juan. While he is discussing his novels, the cameraman is rolling up the window blinds and making a great clatter moving furniture around. Juan stops in midsentence and glances our way.

"Can't this wait until Juan finishes?"

"I'm late for a conference at the Eurobuilding."

After they leave, I make us some tea, which I bring into the living room. "I'm sorry he messed up your interview . . ."

"No, it was fine. Madrid irritates me—I promised I'd be in Barcelona by the end of the week."

While Juan was in Morocco, I met his younger brother Luis at a Madrid party. He seemed nice and offered to show me his version of Barcelona. I had planned to drive there with Juan, but his tone is off-putting; I sense he doesn't want me along.

In Times Square, while we waited for Franco to die and planned our party to hail in the new era, it had seemed understood that we would go to Barcelona together. I hesitate. I am not good at pointing out that the rules of the game have been switched.

"Come, if you like."

But his voice is cool; I feel as welcome as poor Ahmed.

"No—I'll go there in the fall; by then we'll know more about the election calendar," I point out, asserting my own history, "and I'll be ready to join Pallach in his first political campaign." I am hesitant. "Look, Juan, we are both free as birds, honest Injun. Do you want us to go on?"

He stares at me intently. "Yes," he answers abruptly. "Very much."

But when he leaves for Barcelona, two days later, joined by a pensive Ahmed, I recognize that his return to Spain is a solo flight. Barcelona, not Madrid, is his hometown.

24

After Juan leaves for Barcelona, I become depressed. The odd rumors circulating concerning Nicolás's escape from Cuelgamoros don't help. An Oviedo newspaper publishes a bizarre version in which Franco (due to Don Claudio's international prestige) gets American authorities to spring Nicolás from jail. The idea that Franco, in 1948, could have contacted Norman Mailer and gotten his car, his sister, and her friend (a recent Dalton School graduate: *me*) to plot a phony escape of leftist students is mind-boggling!

The real reason for the *Alice in Wonderland* stories is that the Opposition press is beginning to succeed in their efforts to get rid of the old guard, and stories about the existence of slave-labor camps inside Spain are important. As soon as Nicolás's father leaves for Buenos Aires, Nicolás gives a long interview, with many historic details, including the real names of those involved, to *El País*. The newspaper wants me to corroborate the facts with Rosa Pereda. I am hesitant. Technically, what I did was against the law, and Franco's government hasn't been overthrown; the political picture remains murky.

Pepe Martínez and Ruedo Ibérico are still marooned in Paris; the publishing house hasn't yet been granted official permission to return to Spain. I have never *publicly* in Spain admitted to my past involvement—Sueiro has promised me not to use our interview in the daily press. But Nicolás is upset by the rumors, so finally, when Rosa comes over, I say okay, print it, you can use my name, it's true. His account, with the first uncensored photographs of the slave-labor camp, is published in *El País* in mid-June. The demythification of Franco's monument, the Valley of the Fallen, has started; the tomb is shown in its true light. My own, much briefer statement would appear several days later. Then a week after that the Arias Navarro caretaker regime would collapse and Juan Carlos would appoint Adolfo Suárez prime minister. Which is when the post-Franco era really begins.

That same week Manolo Arroyo Stephens, the publisher of Turner Books, pays me a visit. Manolo adores Dickens, Lewis Carroll, *Middlemarch*, and British tweeds; he seems very proud of the Stephens and has an amiable, reflective nature to go with his British surname. Very low-key, he casually hands me a long report on torture, especially of the Basques—would I give it to British Amnesty, to the *New York Review*? Oh, of course, I say.

This spring is crucial. I am astonished that the Opposition is ignoring what will be their most thorny problem, the Basque separatist movement. Morally, it is indefensible of the Socialists and Communists to push aside the members of the Basque Resistance (they have had the highest number of prisoners), as though their efforts and the extreme repression within the Basque country had never existed. The isolation of the Basques by the Opposition comes from their unwillingness to irritate the army or the police. The Basque issue is delicate. Both the Socialists and Communists are firming up their positions for the first election campaign. The Communist Party and the Basques have always competed for first place in the Resistance, and the Communists still face the problem of getting their party legalized. The Socialists definitely could be doing more. In letting the Basques cool their heels in prison longer than any other group, and by not including them in the post-Franco political panorama, they were losing a real opportunity.

The Opposition has ignored the most effective Resistance group in Spain. Where is their sense of cause and effect? What do they *think* will happen next? When the situation with the ETA eventually hardened into a tragic cycle of repressive police torturers and increasingly aberrant terrorist acts, the Spanish looked puzzled, as though there never had been a point when a more intelligent solution could have been tried.

But after Manolo leaves, my depressive panic resumes. I have trouble sleeping. I am glad to get a telephone call from Jaime Salinas. A sensitive man, he has appointed himself cultural cruise director of the post-Franco era as it chugs its slow way to democracy. Jaime is very much a product of the Spanish Republic. His father was Pedro Salinas, the poet, and Jaime grew up in the United States; out of ancient loyalties, he tries to keep an eye out for stray Americans like me. "Barbara, are you all right?" He worries his friends will get hit by the anti-American feeling in the city.

After Jaime does his daily morning head count, I open the shutters onto the small balcony overlooking Plaza de Oriente, where the ultra-right had forever shouted: *Viva la ignorancia!* While balancing a cup of Nescafé, I breathe in the fresh Madrid morning air. I am always grateful Jaime calls me, though I never tell him. I continue my political journal.

POLITICAL JOURNAL

Madrid: June 17, 1976

After Franco's death none of the new political parties had much real strength—after all, the opposition never did overthrow the regime. The real war is between the emerging Spanish press and Franco's old crowd. This spring the press has unprecedented power. I doubt many Spanish themselves recognize the degree to which the press is shaping, arbitrating, and "naming" the post-Franco political map. By now a large part of the Spanish press is in the hands of the Opposition (this doesn't include the government-controlled radio or television). The press is testing right-wing forces by running these daily explicit torture reports, making public the acts of a frightening, amok, diehard police. *Cambio 16*, which has a format something like *Newsweek*, is very politically savvy. Juan Tomás de Salas, its director, seems to understand that in this present confusion a temporary political referee is needed. He runs weekly columns advising the Opposition and Juan Carlos what to do next. *Cambio* not only reports the news, it is architecting the post-Franco era. Salas chastises the Opposition when they get out of hand, and praises Juan Carlos for an unexpected piece of moderation. He cajoles, flatters, and scolds the new political class like a headmaster. Salas names the problems, the political parties, and week by week, he outlines new issues the Spanish public and politicians should be thinking about. At the same time that the new politics is unraveling itself, or, indeed, *revealing* itself, Spain is being bombarded with forty years of past news. A heavy spring. On the torture issue the big weeklies—*Cuadernos*, which is Socialist and literary in its orientation, *Cambio 16*, *Triunfo*, and *Doblón*, as well as several other magazines—are publishing reports in tandem. When *Cuadernos* is recalled from the stands and fined by the government for having been too explicit in revealing torture data, the other weeklies band together, and the following week carry similar reports. Day by day the press is pushing harder, inching its way out of censorship. Slowly the Socialist Party is being "named" in the press. The letters "PSOE" begin to appear; Felipe González, the new head of the party, is getting a lot of exposure. The reconstitution of Spain's old Socialist Party (with many changes) has virtually been created overnight by the Opposition press. And the decision has been made to openly mention the Communist Party. Although Carrillo, officially, is still in exile, the newspapers are constantly carrying stories about returning Communists; now it is no longer so necessary to refer to the umbrella organization masking the CP, the Junta Democratica. The new journalists model themselves on Watergate, as in Dustin Hoffman and Robert Redford. Now that *El País* has gotten rolling, it will be impossible to maintain an uncontrolled police *and* a decontrolled press. The press reads like daily notes from the underground. Although the Minister of the Interior, Manuel Fraga Iribarne, can't control the police, the government no longer bothers to deny torture reports. Eight months out, the Juan Carlos regime has failed to provide a quick and complete amnesty for political prisoners and exiles, legalization of the Communist Party, and control of the police. The Opposition isn't yet in power; but their press is in control and has won over the Spanish public.

The press, I believe, has unwittingly filled a vacuum created in a time when neither police, army, king, nor newly emerging political parties, on their own, have had sufficient power to dominate the country. Had the process been reversed, had strong political parties abruptly emerged in a country with a weak, ineffective press, I suspect there would have been more bloodshed and less of a chance for the peaceful formation of a working government.

Manolo's report is on the dining room table—probably the last thing on torture I will be taking out of Spain. Yet my hands tremble. Why the anxiety now? Why not ten, twenty years ago? But small things these days worry me. Abruptly I decide to cut short my trip by a week.

I take a taxi over to the TWA building and buy a ticket for the next flight to New York. In my anxiety, I want every detail made easy; I've run out of psychic energy. *A TWA 747 has nothing to do with torture.* After I board the plane the next morning, I begin to relax. The sun streams in through the small window as we glide through the clear skies over Portugal; while we are heading toward the Azores, I leaf through the torture reports. Electric shocks on the genitals, forcing prisoners to eat their own vomit, and so forth. Then I close it. I promised to make the report available, which I do, not to read it, which I never do more than is necessary to be able to include some of the details in a piece. I ask the stewardess if she has a copy of *The New York Times.* I glance at yesterday's ads and make a list of what I need for the summer. *Look at me, I am so serious, I write about prisons, I have done extreme and risky things; therefore, I am entitled to frivolous love affairs, trips, and a great view of Central Park.*

Weeks later, with my daughters and some of their friends, I find myself sitting on the early summer grass in Central Park. It is the night of the Bicentennial, the park is jammed, we listen to Lenny Bernstein play *Rhapsody in Blue* and watch the fireworks shooting off in the direction of the Battery; I feel rooted. Spain temporarily fades in my mind, as a jagged, unreal dream. But the following morning I get a letter from Nicolás. Carmelo Soria, one of the old student gang who had stood trial with Nicolás in 1946, has been murdered by right-wing fanatics in Chile. He was strangled to death. His daughter was forced to identify the corpse. *El País* has now added Carmelo's murder to the story of Cuelgamoros.

During the spring, while Carmelo was visiting in Madrid, he had begun to obsess to Nicolás that he had gotten off "scot-free"; unlike his friends, he had managed to get out of Spain before being sentenced to prison. In the replay in Carmelo's mind he blamed himself for "deserting" Spain and perceived of himself as having been overprivileged (his grandfather was the urbanist Arturo Soria, the inventor of the linear city). After the putsch in Chile he felt history was repeating itself. Many of his Chilean friends had been murdered. But Carmelo remained invulnerable because he worked for the United Nations. Nicolás had desperately tried to convince him that these were dangerous distortions: who would have been helped if one more Spanish student in the 1940s had served a prison sentence? Hadn't Nicolás himself managed to escape? But Carmelo was firm in his scenario: desertion versus non-desertion. Despite warnings, he went back to help his friends and within weeks was murdered.

I walk over to the living room corner window, which has the park view. The city sanitation officers are cleaning up the junk paper strewn the night of the Bicentennial. I can't get it through my head that Carmelo has been killed. *In the fall things will get better. You'll visit Teresa and Pallach in Barcelona. Catch some of Pallach's optimism. You'll make plans, I'll cover him on the campaign trail* . . . But I keep thinking about Carmelo. I don't know what to do.

The next time I see the New York City skyline combined with *Rhapsody in Blue* is in Woody Allen's *Manhattan*: we New Yorkers are beginning to stumble through our town like a bunch of extras living out dreams designed for us in Beverly Hills.

VII

*Days and
Nights on the
Spanish
Election Trail*

25

After a trip to Morocco I fly to Barcelona in November. I register in the Colón, in the old Gothic quarter, and telephone Amadeo; he's euphoric. Because Amadeo's friendship with Pallach dates back to his childhood in World War II, to the time when his father and Pallach ran the underground railway near Perpignan for Jews and Spaniards, this campaign is very special. Now he and Pallach are working around the clock to organize Pallach's party for the spring elections. I feel wonderful. My original political mentor has come back to Spain, and is going full-blast as a big Catalan Socialist leader! Selfishly, I like my friends to do well, it makes me feel more alive. And I feel stale from sitting so long in a cramped plane. So I have my hair washed in the hotel beauty parlor. A mother and daughter team takes care of me; the mother washes, while her daughter gives me a manicure. "We Spaniards are abnormals," the daughter comments. "You've got to be nuts to kill your own."

"Amalia, it wasn't like that."

"Hitler killed others. Mama—we murdered ourselves." Later, when I make some telephone calls to Madrid from my room, the telephone operator, chatty, remarks, "Too early to phone Madrid, all your friends will still be asleep—nobody works there. So stuck up, Madrileños believe from *los Madrilos* straight to paradise. *Fascistas, todos.*"

Barcelona had gone Catalan in a big way. When I walk outside the hotel, Catalan flags are everywhere. Pictures of Luis Companys (the head of the Catalan Generalitat executed by the Phalangists during the Civil War) have replaced Franco's in all the hotels and restaurants. Too Catalan for my taste. I don't go for the Spanish *geographical* notions of good and bad. In Josep María Castellet's essay *What Is Catalonia?* he wrote that the most important fact about Catalonia is that she lost the war. Now, this is very convenient bullshit for those Catalans who like to think of themselves as victims, always ignoring the economic fact that, one way or another, Catalonia is one of the richest industrial areas in Spain and under Franco boomed economically. Catalonia didn't lose the war; *the Spanish Republic* lost the war.

Some Catalans lost the war, *some* Catalans won the war. There were many Catalan Fascists. Many of the Catalan left, Franco's children, are children of conservative industrialists, and especially fond of this image of left-wing Catalonia pitted against "Fascist" Madrid.

When I first came to Madrid in '48, and it was still a sleepy, clear-aired town, I was struck by the sadness of the defeated city. The oppression was worse there *because* the Franco government was located in the city. In that pre-jet time, plop in the middle of the Sierras, Madrid seemed isolated and poor, horrendously poor. The workers had no protection; there was nothing between them and Franco, no fall-back position. Barcelona was then so bustling, so near France, such a rich uncle to poor Madrid. The workers in Catalonia had a little more protection, as their bosses, like themselves, were Catalan. Franco frequently ignored Catalonia, never Madrid. But in the Catalan equation it is the Catalonian *people* who are the victims of Madrid's government. The problems of the *inhabitants* of Madrid are eliminated.

I feel like a kid on a spree when my taxi driver describes Pallach as the big Socialist leader in town. He drops me at Calle Canudo, where Pallach's new headquarters are located. When I walk in, he is winding up a meeting. We fall into each other's arms. "How are the girls?" he asks. Those were happy summers spent on the beach at Collioure, Harold and me, Teresa, Pallach, and their daughter, Titona; Carla and Maria buying stick cocoa-crème biscuits on the beach. Grinning, he shows me his new shiny setup, the posters of his party, rows of modern file cabinets, a slick beige telephone system—the works.

When I first met the Pallachs in Paris, they had no money. Carfare, coffee, diapers for Titona were all major outlays. For me, Pallach's energy and optimism is living proof that deserving exiles don't always end up with musty, third-rate fates.

A mutual friend rings him up. Pallach says, "Guess who is here—Bárbarita."

It takes us some time to stop being just old friends who date back to the year one, to adjust to our new roles. He as politician, me as journalist. I fiddle with my Sony cassette. "Pallach, what I write about Spain gets printed in the United States. Really."

"I've known that for years."

"You do?" I revert to being the kid trying to impress the adults.

Pallach is critical of the American Embassy's stand against the legal-ization of the Communist Party. "They just don't understand Europe. Or, for that matter, Communists. The Communist Party is going to be legalized. And the sooner the better." He pauses. "I was con-demned to death by them, my friends in POUM died in their cells. One day I will ask them about the death of Andrés Nin, but now they must become legal; the Americans are wrong. I have gone through many political evolutions in my life, but thinking it over, I still feel I was right to have admired Bakunin. In many ways he was more pro-phetic than Marx . . ."

Very casually I ask: "And what about the Middle East?"

Pallach stares at me reflectively. "Israel was formed as a democracy, an imperfect democracy . . . Their position on the Palestine issue is too intransigent, but their lack of flexibility is understandable," he says. "I know of no Arab countries I consider even an imperfect democracy."

"Then you think the Spanish position on Israel is wrong?"

"*Wrong?* It's nutty leftover Franco policy, of course Israel should be recognized."

Until I spoke to Pallach, I had begun to feel I had wrongly imag-ined my past; perhaps I had given my allegiance to anti-Semites, per-haps my judgment had been off, perhaps I had been blind. Pallach vali-dates the choice I made; his moral map is familiar to me. I am excited about his political future, his great success in Barcelona, and late that night I talk animatedly to Teresa during our dinner in a wharf restau-rant by the docks.

But Teresa is tired; she is indignant at some of the mud-slinging Pallach has received from rival groups.

I try to cheer her up. "Oh, Teresa, everyone in Spain gets called Facha, CIA, or KGB—that's par for the course. Of course you weren't a Fascist or rich in France—that's local wild talk."

I feel Teresa's vulnerability. She keeps asking me if I remember how poor they were in Paris. I wish she could step back and laugh off the ridiculousness of two refugee schoolteachers being called rich Fascists by the offspring of Fascist industrialists. I wonder about Pallach and Teresa continuing to teach during this next period while Pallach will be campaigning. The years of being a refugee teacher in France as well as active in the Resistance probably have become a habit. Felipe González is thinking travel-by-jet; he isn't planning to teach school *and* be a Socialist leader. He is getting his money and his guidance from West Germany.

After visiting with Pallach and Teresa, I interview other political leaders. Miguel Núñez, number one or two man in the PSUC, the Catalan Communist Party, which operates independently, comes over to the Colón, and we have drinks in the bar. I get the feeling he is a Party man through thick and thin. We get on well in that casual way that professional Communists generally do with American journalists; they leave the anti-American barbs to the amateurs.

Over drinks Núñez, a tall, affable-looking man, says that the only way the PSUC was able to get out of its clandestine ghetto was by making friends with some of the right. I smile slightly as Núñez boasts about the aristocrats who had acted as emissaries for the Communists with members of the Spanish govenment just before Franco died. In Spain Communists love to trot out *aristo* names. "We also had the best architects acting as intermediaries."

"In Barcelona, the architects draw like angels and love to dance with politics," I add, still smiling. "But, Miguel, how do you feel about the Communists always knocking down their siblings on the left, I mean, that's not so great." Finally I ask him to explain to me the circumstances in which Jorge Semprún and Fernando Claudín had been expelled from the Party in '64. What did Núñez think about Semprún's book about his years in the Communist underground, *The Autobiography of Federico Sánchez*?

"Oh, you know about that book?" Núñez hesitates; I don't think he wants to discuss Semprún's impressions of the Party; then, finally, he says it depends on the *tone* Semprún uses. "We live with a sad and terrible truth, many comrades went to their death shouting, 'Viva Stalin,' and never realizing what that implied. Doesn't that strike you as tragic? I don't care what happens to the PC or the PSUC, but I have promised myself never again will Spanish Communists be led and lied to by another country. Whatever our sins, they will be fabricated in Madrid, in Barcelona, not in another universe three thousand miles away."

"When did you become aware of Stalinism?"

"Not until the 1950s; it was after I got to Paris. It wasn't easy for a Spanish Communist to know what to do with that information ..."

After we get up to leave and exchange the usual addresses and telephone numbers, I ask him what his prison dates were.

"People will tell you that the Resistance started in '55, '56, whenever the person talking became active. But the prisons were full in the 1940s. Those were my dates."

"What did you go to prison for?"

"It was complicated. I was in a student organization, the FUE. They were important during the Republic and the war. Later they went underground."

"Then you must have known Nicolás Sánchez-Albornoz, who was in the FUE and escaped from Cuelgamoros?"

Miguel Núñez stares at me; finally, he pieces it together. "Oh—you are *she*." We begin all over; we sit down again at the bar and have a very different talk. Núñez is quiet for a moment; finally he says, "Perhaps we should phone my wife." He wants me to have dinner with them, but I am leaving Barcelona within a day. "Next time."

We share no political position, no similar field of vision, but our lives at some prior time had almost crossed. A mutually remembered past has a stronger hold, frequently, than a political point of view. Núñez continues to talk about his wife. "She went through worse troubles being a Communist than I did, paid a bigger price, but in the end, suddenly, unexpectedly, there is this afternoon at the Colón, and I am here at the bar having drinks with you. I am a big man in the PSUC, and in the end, she isn't asked. I have to think about that; the Party hasn't done much for women."

Meanwhile, the bartender at the Colón has been glued to our conversation. Núñez is a leader, after all, of the Catalan Communist Party. After our long-lost mutual FUE identification, the bartender simply stops serving drinks—great parts of the changeover take place in the lobbies of the best hotels. After Núñez leaves, there is a political incident in the Colón. One of the employees, standing on the curb in front of the hotel, makes disparaging remarks about Franco in front of the police. A brawl begins, and other employees of the Colón hurriedly push the man back inside the hotel. The policemen rush into the hotel to arrest him. The desk clerk holds off the police: "As of this week, Spain is a democracy. Where is your search warrant?"

I like sitting in the bar observing events happen. An old man carrying roses walks through the lobby, followed by a big crowd.

"He's a big Communist from the Civil War," the bartender tells me. "This is his first day back from Rumania or Bulgaria." When you see tears, old age, and bouquets, it generally signifies returnees.

It wasn't so easy for the Spanish exiles to be given the freedom to return home. An old-timer, Antonio Mije, one of the leaders of the Communist Party in Seville who had lived out most of his life after the Civil War in exile in Ivry, France, died of a heart attack as soon as the Spanish consul in France granted him his Spanish passport. His body was placed in a casket which was flown back to Seville from Paris. As the Communist Party was not yet legal, they buried him there with silence and roses. Spain has a new problem: transitional deaths. The Socialist leaders are carefully planning their first nonclandestine congress, which will be in the Meliá Castillia, in Madrid, in December. (Exiled leaders had held several in France.) Heart attack units and medical emergency-aid centers are being set up inside the hotel, so that the older members of the Socialist Party can be immediately treated if, like Mije, they succumb to shock.

Later that evening, when I go for a walk through the back streets of the Gothic quarter, I bump into a shootout between the police and a group of dissenters who are mad at the mayor. I duck into a corner rare-map-and-book store and watch the fracas through the window. My Barcelona friends consider me odd because I ask taxi drivers and people in the street questions; they feel there is nothing, politically, to be learned that way. I disagree.

One of the drivers explains to me, "When you see the letters CNT, UGT, PSUC, you know you are dealing with the regular ones." Those guys are *auténticos,* the new groups aren't *de confianza.* The chic radicals underestimate folk history, the familiarity of the average Spaniard with their fathers' and grandfathers' past. As soon as one *talked* to people, the old union cards would be flashed and the stories would come out, most families seem to have remembered their own political trajectory.

Overlooking Barcelona, at the top of Tibidabo, there is an amusement park with a roller coaster perched on the edge of the mountain. I get out of the taxi, and walk over to it. Joyriders shriek as the cars zoom out over Barcelona, above the Mediterranean.

An odd piece of memory nags me. During the early morning, while Nicolás, Manolo, and Barbara Mailer were asleep in the ratty hotel near the Barcelona port, Paco woke me up and insisted we drive up the mountain to Tibidabo. It was deserted. Paco had said, In normal times this is the best amusement park in the world. Was the place shut down because it was early in the morning? Or for repairs? At the time I thought it had something to do with Franco, but I thought then that everything in Spain worked or didn't work because of him. *"Could you explain to me why the Tibidabo did or did not work as an amusement park in '48?"* I watch the cars speed downward and listen to the thrill-scare screams; the park is jammed with people. *Maybe these are the Spanish normal times Paco was referring to, it's already here, normal times at Tibidabo.* Then I walk back over to the taxi, and ask the driver to take me to the Colón.

Some days I doubt 1948 ever existed. At a party, I am introduced to a man who tells my friends the Cuelgamoros escape story is false. "Impossible," he snaps. "And it is of no importance—prehistory." For a moment I passively acquiesce. I am prehistory, don't exist. But why should I oblige so rapidly, collude in my non-being? I stare at the man. "Oh, prehistory—that's a misuse of a Marxist term." He looks away, he understands I have realized he was a Fascist youth.

Just before I leave Barcelona, Juan's brother Luis Goytisolo drives me to Montjuich, (Jewish mountain). He wants to take me through the Miró Foundation, an almost mystical place. An extraordinary daylight fills the museum. Strange, this building is what moves me most about Barcelona. After forty years of exile, José Luis Sert must have come back home from Harvard and *stretched* himself to build this monument to memory and desire. Luis says a fortune was spent in getting the right pink-beige cement for the outside walls; Sert had insisted no materials or colors could be used that evoked prison. It had been difficult to get the *Algarrobo* trees of his childhood to take root in the museum courtyard. The first few died, but sturdier plantings took to the soil. I stand in that magical space, all the paintings alive, bathed in the natural light; I watch workmen carry upstairs crates of Freud's papers for a Freud exhibit being planned for the Miró Foundation. Freud in Barcelona. Well, and why not? When I fly with Iberia out of Barcelona, I look down at the sea and the mountains, and I think about Montjuich, the Tibidabo, José Luis Sert, the Miró Foundation, and Franco's Valley of the Fallen. These other, lighter places have outlasted his grotesque tomb.

POLITICAL JOURNAL

Madrid: December 1976

The Communists are at a disadvantage. They are not yet legal, though the elections are scheduled for spring. They need to push their way out of semisecrecy. I am invited to a "coming out" meeting of Communist journalists. "Look, I don't want to show up and then hear rumors that I am working for the CIA." "Oh, come on, Barbara, nobody's going to label you CIA." "Hah," I reply. "That will be the day." But I decide to go. It is a cold December day, and I wear the family mink coat, recycled from my mother's collection circa early 1950s during our family's palmy season. My worry about being taken for the CIA provokes frivolous behavior. I want to stand out as being an American, no lurking about trying to pick up pieces of information that are of no use to me. (If I discovered all the secrets of the Spanish Opposition and buried them in a bottle in the middle of Central Park, and announced it on the *Today* show, America is so sleepy about Europe, nobody would disturb the bottle.) I go to Calle Libertad. (Is that street a deliberate choice? One of the Communist headquarters is on Peligros. Liberty. Danger. Sounds like a political game of Monopoly.) My journalist friend looks furious. "Why are you wearing that mink coat? After forty years the Communist Party is becoming legal—and *you* come to the show in a mink? We are having our photos taken ..."

I shrug. "I can wear it because I am an imperialist capitalist; it's *you* people who have taken the vow, *you* can't have mink. Besides, in Barcelona, the Communists consider luxe positive."

"Madrid isn't Barcelona," the journalist snaps at me. "You know perfectly well those PSUC people are bizarre."

"Well, I thought we were all in this Euro-Communist thing together," I continue meekly. "A sort of bourgeois happy Communism?"

The crowded apartment—wine in paper cups, potato chips, young couples milling about, tired mothers in black turtleneck pullovers calming down screaming offspring—reminds me vaguely of Greenwich Village gatherings in my adolescence. The posters, the emotional speeches, the collecting of small amounts of money, the enthusiasms. I loathe crowds; emotional political speeches embarrass me. What bothers me most is the possibility that the meeting will be broken up by an onrush of police. I position myself near the back door. The business of being well dressed is a habit I picked up in America during the civil rights demonstrations; it is one way of keeping at bay overenthusiastic policemen. I generally do have a practical reason for my behavior, but always let it pass as just flighty. One of the women gives me her card; she works for one of the big Spanish weeklies and tells me to contact her. "The toughest thing here is to get *through* as a woman; the men on the left just don't understand that." I agree. Then I buy a poster of La Pasionaria, because she has a great profile and astonishing eyes, and leave.

Josefina Machimbarrena, the wife of Paco and Juan's childhood friend Alberto, who has a generous heart and conservative politics, admires the poster of Dolores. "*Madre mía,* she's a real looker." We settle into a lazy Sunday afternoon of gossip and lunch in Josefina's white sunlit apartment, near the old *belle époque* promenade off Princesa.

"*Bárbarita,* what did you think of *El Desencanto?*"

The documentary is about a dark Spanish literary family apparently beset by madness, drug addiction, homosexuality, and semi-enacted incest. In it, the official poets of the regime are bitingly satirized. Feeding on the Spanish delight at debasing official images, the film has been a big success.

Josefina, long-legged, lanky, tosses the straight brown hair out of her eyes as she walks back and forth, getting lunch on the table. She talks excitedly of the new Spain, gesturing with her hands as she makes clever observations. She is wearing a sweater, blue jeans, and moccasins. Josefina goes to the hall closet and takes out a wonderful silver-fox jacket, which she throws over her shoulders. "Well, *Bárbarita,* what do you think of this? Isn't it great? The jacket's mine now. Years ago my father did some legal work for Queen Victoria, the one who was Juan Carlos's mother, well, queens don't get billed by lawyers, so she had this jacket made up by her furrier in Switzerland and gave it to my mother."

Josefina tells me tales of the terrible tragedies and errors that happened to families she knew. By mistake the right-wing families frequently were murdered by the right, the left-wing families by the left; there had been awful mixups. Suddenly Josefina laughs hysterically at the unfunny. Soon I join her. Each new death seems more absurd, more unnecessary than the previous one. We make lists of families leveled by tragedy and political mistakes, and yet we keep on laughing. "The *desencanto,* the *desencanto,*" Josefina exclaims. "It's all of us." It is one of those quiet afternoons that later in my memory is etched as the CHANGEOVER. Josefina, laughing, dressed in blue jeans and the Queen Victoria silver fox, sitting on her sofa, the dusty sunlight coming in through the window of her second-floor apartment.

That night we see Martín Patino's *Canciones para Después de una Guerra—Songs for After a War*. The montage of newspaper clips of the Civil War and the immediate postwar are juxtaposed with the Spanish rose-in-the-teeth hit songs that were popular during that time of short food supplies and overabundance of death; the film sums up Fascist culture as having been a mélange of bullfight, patriotism, vapid films, and musicals. Forty years of Fascism produced no culture of its own. This December, even the civilized right has begun to talk of "our inheritance from the Republic, our García Lorca, our Picasso." When I board the economy section of the TWA 747 this time, I don't feel the need to breathe easier; Spain has calmed down.

26

But I never do go on the campaign trail with Pallach. Six weeks later, in Rizzoli's, I am leafing through *Cambio 16*, at first delighted to see his photo featured (I am getting used to reading about many of my friends, who had previously been anonymous, in the daily press). CA-TALONIA HAS LOST ONE OF HER SONS. He is dead of a heart attack. I lean against the foreign-magazine stand in Rizzoli's, steadying myself; for a moment I am blank. Dizzy. Then I go home.

I telephone his wife, Teresa; she sounds awful. *Cambio* had criticized the unfair attacks of segments of the Catalan left. He died being called a Fascist. But in death once again he seems to have become a hero. According to the newspaper reports, the entire Opposition marched for him in Barcelona, and another procession took place in Palafrugell, where he was buried. The funeral was televised.

Teresa says she is sorry, she was too confused to call. I reply, I am calling to comfort *her*—I promise to send her the cassette I made with Pallach.

The newspapers refer to his charisma, his appeal to the common man. Born of modest origins in Figueras, he understood the essentially conservative, workmanlike nature of his fellow Catalans far better than the Barcelona *Devine Left*, which is radical chic. Catalans like his *bella historia:* In 1946, the night before he was to have been executed in a Figueras prison, fellow members of POUM raided the jail and sprung him. Now the press adores telling about his exploits in both the Spanish and French Resistances. I can't make it out. In Barcelona his popularity swings like a pendulum. In future years, when I go to Barcelona, I hear the same groups who called him Fascist for not wanting his party to join a popular front with the Communists prior to the first election refer to him as the great missing dead hero of the left. Yet I don't believe the name-calling caused the attack: he was in great physical shape, had never been sick a day of his life, and was much too much of a political animal to be put out by battle. He thrived on it, and expected it. His was a transition death.

When Amadeo is in New York for a few days, I almost hurl the cassette I had made with Pallach at him. "Give it to Teresa for her archives." Much later I think, Now, why didn't I make a copy for myself? Why didn't I take the time to listen to it?

Juan Goytisolo and I speak by phone, and we make plans. I am going to Spain to cover the elections, and we will see each other then.

What I notice first in Madrid is the classy visual effects. The Communists have attractive matchbox covers, the Socialists expensive record albums, all the knickknacks of the many competing parties are wonderfully designed. The drama of the Civil War is being reborn as SOUVENIRS OF JUNE FIFTEENTH, 1977.

The two strong parties expected to emerge from the elections are the UCD, Unión de Centro Democrático, headed by Prime Minister Adolfo Suárez, which is a new amalgam of conservative centrist parties, and, just left of center, the PSOE, the Spanish Socialist Workers' Party. (During the Spanish Republic it was the party with the largest electoral following and constituted the single largest bloc in the Spanish parliament.) I am assuming that the many small regional and splinter Socialist parties presently on the ballot will eventually be absorbed into the PSOE.

To the right of the UCD (which is an uncertain mixture of Opposition liberals as well as the modern wing of former Francoist followers) is the Alianza Popular, headed by Manuel Fraga Iribarne. (He was a Minister of Information under Franco, and therefore in charge of censorship.) After that comes the *uncivilized* right: the *ultras,* Los Guerrilleros de Cristo Rey, led by Blas Piñar.

To the left of the PSOE is the Spanish Communist Party, which was finally legalized in April, the same month that the Movement (the modern name for the Phalangist party) was abolished. Santiago Carrillo is the only party leader whose history goes back to the Civil War. Suárez, Felipe, King Juan Carlos, are all men in their thirties or early forties. Because of Carrillo's insistence on maintaining leadership of his party, perhaps beyond his "time," there have been many internal battles within the PC, and the PSOE has picked up some of their defectors, including a group of leading intellectuals. In Spain, now, it's Socialist chic.

The problem of home rule in the Basque country and Catalonia makes the political panorama in these areas even more complicated. (Though now all kinds of tiny regions—the Canary Islands, Andalusia, Galicia—are clamoring for home rule. Several small ultra-left groups, ORT, LCR, and PTE, have succeeded in getting on the electoral ballot. After the elections these groups would disappear, their membership absorbed by either the Socialists or the Communists.

I have spoken to Alfonso Sastre, he believes that Eva will be released from prison and flown directly to Holland. The arrangements are under way.

End of May

I go to Barajas to welcome Pepe Martínez. He had gone first to Valencia to visit his mother. She seems to be dying. We wait in the small domestic-flights waiting room. With me are his friends, the Naredos, and their young daughter. I say to them I don't believe Pepe has ever been in Madrid. How could he? After prison in Valencia, he went straight to Paris in '48. The Naredos think I am wrong. But after Pepe deplanes, he mumbles that I am correct, he has never been here before. "Hóla, Bárbarna." His jaw and neck lines are tense. He says he is in a hurry to see one of the Madrid distributors for Ruedo Ibérico. "So," I say, "can't we have a cup of coffee together?" Pepe says sure. Juan Manuel Naredo drives us back to Madrid; on the way we stop at a nondescript café, and standing up, we have a beer. Which is the way Pepe returns to Madrid. Figuring we would celebrate that night, I had left the evening free. But Pepe telephones and says he is busy for the next several days. At first I feel hurt; so do Marisol and Luis—we are his closest friends. Then we figure coming back is hard on him, and we will wait and do things his way.

Rush of political meetings. Go to hear Ramón Tamámes the economist. He is one of the Young Turks who are trying to oust Carrillo from Party leadership. Speaks at drafty school, Calle Filipes. His problem is lack of charisma. I don't think he could ever win *new* followers for the Party. At the PSOE headquarters I bump into Carlota Bustelo; she runs down the staircase screaming, "Eva is out of prison. They've released her here in Madrid!"

Beginning of June
Go to a dinner given by the Communist Party for government employees. Very elegant, somber banquet. Carrillo reassures the white-collar bureaucrats that no workers will replace them in the government sector. Tables decorated with rose-colored carnations; the menu is equally soothing: smoked salmon, shirred eggs, veal, *bombe glacée*, an assortment of wines, champagne, and cognac. Looks like a Westchester fund-raiser.

June 2
The first Spanish political campaign in forty years is being limited to three weeks; an entire country needs convincing that voting isn't the equivalent of going to war.

Such a smorgasbord of political parties, drama, intrigue! I want to be everywhere. With the workers in Andalusia, in the small towns of Galicia and Asturias. Spain's on a binge, a political fiesta, fueled by porno adrenalin. *You are one person. You can't compete with crisis news teams rushed in for the big moment. Remember Pallach. Stick to the familiar. Do one or two things. Pallach misgauged his energies and died. Pick two places: Madrid and the province of Toledo, which is the poorest part of Spain, the area that had the bitterest battles during the Civil War. Besides, Fernando is running for senator there; stick close to your friends.*

When I tell Juan Benet I have decided to cover the campaign from Toledo, he asks quizzically, "Back at the old stand?"

"What do you mean?"

This time Juan Benet has outtrumped me; outmemoried me; he fishes a biggie out of our barrel of the past. We are sitting with his friends, Juan García Hortelano and his wife, Maria, in a Madrid café, Juan is gleeful. "Ha, ha. You have forgotten your own inventions. Remember your first story, 'Day in Toledo'? Naturally it was all about me—where would you be if I had never existed?" The story was published in a paperback in the mid-fifties: *New Campus Writing*. It was about Juan Benet as a reluctant and bored private billeted in Toledo.

He has given me a beautiful opening. "I would have found another Spanish writer named Juan."

The García Hortelanos laugh; this time I've touchéed him.

"I'm moved that Barbara is going up to Toledo," Maria says. "My family lived in Toledo at the end of the war. It was awful seeing my old father led off to prison in chains. *Traumatic.* He went into prison a Republican, came out seven years later a Communist, then he died." Maria pauses. "A child remembers things like that." Then she orders orange juice, which is a Madrileño dessert.

Friday night, June 3

Fernando Chueca is running on the liberal ticket for senator of Toledo. He has a home there, and has been passionately involved in the preservation of Toledo. Fernando; his son, Fernando *hijo;* Goya, and I are going to Talavera, which is about an hour away from Toledo. Toledo province stretches like a long boot from the center of Spain; near Madrid, down toward the south, bordering Ciudad Real, just north of Andalusia. It is Cervantes country.

We are caught in a traffic snarl inside Madrid. The Spanish never have been overly fond of letting their arms dangle quietly. First the Fascist salute, copied from Mussolini; now many Madrid strollers are tentatively raising their fists each time a Socialist, Communist, or splinter-left caravan rolls by, with the loudspeakers blaring the just-legalized Internationale. Spain's politics happen in the fresh air. You can feel the city turn from right to center and left, just by taking a stroll.

Our car is trapped behind a caravan of a splinter Trotskyist group, CUP. We get stuck inside their drama. The CUP vehicles sport red flags and loudspeakers playing: ARISE YE PRISONERS OF STARVATION. ARISE YE WRETCHED OF THE EARTH . . . Fernando yowls in frustration, "Why are these amateurs blocking traffic? Why are we in their caravan?"

I am convulsed with laughter; Goya screams at Fernando *hijo* to make the first left turn.

Fernando, meanwhile, reads me his speech. He sounds too scholarly, too much the architect. I suggest he eliminate some of his allusions to aesthetic values and concentrate on economic problems. "And give a nod to women."

Fernando gazes at me.

"You'll see. Women's rights will be one of the big new issues." I remind him not to be reticent about his past. "Look, you were on the side of the Spanish Republic, all sorts of trash want to wipe their own slate clean, you are now a moderate centrist, which makes you a sitting duck—you have to be prepared for attacks."

In my heart I would have preferred him to have gone with the Socialists, but their style is too young, too freewheeling, for Fernando's temperament. His party, the Liberals, is a small group that has been absorbed by the UCD coalition. Fernando isn't too comfortable being part of UCD, there are too many leftovers from the Franco regime, but there is no other large party in the middle that he could have joined.

A good-size crowd has gathered in the Talavera stadium. Uncertain about her own role in the campaign, at first Goya just stares at the handbills with Fernando's picture. She isn't a woman who is used to making pals of strangers. Then abruptly she does a turnabout and passes them out to the crowd.

At two in the morning we reach their home in Toledo. In the huge stone entry hall twenty political helpers are seated at makeshift tables stuffing envelopes. The marble floors are strewn with political posters. A Fanta bottle nestles precariously in the outstretched arms of a medieval Madonna. Sandwiches, Spanish junk food, noisy cassette radios, and demographic lists are tossed over the statues of the Virgin; the place looks like a West Side Democratic Club hangout. The real impact of Fernando's political race dawns on Goya. She gasps, puts her hands to her cheeks; her home has been violated, *"Qué lío, qué lío. . . ."* she mutters angrily. Fernando quickly steers her upstairs to their own living quarters. He looks at me nervously. I tell her, "In the U.S. the wives campaign with their husbands." She is silent. The next morning she comes down to breakfast wearing a white T-shirt and pants. On the top is printed: FERNANDO CHUECA SENADOR. She had gone down to the main hall and asked one of the helpers to give it to her.

Once Goya decides to throw herself into Fernando's campaign, she becomes a dynamo. As the legal time allotted for electioneering is three weeks, the efforts of the new political class are highly condensed. Newspapers don't count for much in the provinces; the next afternoon Goya goes off with her son, several buckets of paste, and cartons of posters; she intends to paper the walls of all the small towns with Fernando's picture. Most of the population here consists of the aged rural poor; their children have gone to work in the cities and in West-

ern Europe. The old people are scared. Toledo is *cacique* (boss) country. For hundreds of years the will of the *caciques* has been law. Toledo
also is headquarters for the hardcore ultra-right. Their leader, Blas
Piñar, is also running for a senatorial seat. It is impossible to gauge
just how strong is this group of fanatics based in Toledo. On a national level, it is crucial that Blas Piñar and his group, Warriors of
Christ the King, be knocked out of the running. No one wants his
party to gain a toehold in the newly formed senate. So, on a local
level, during the first election, there is slightly more cooperation between the UCD, the Socialists, and the Communists here than else-
where.

Saturday night, June 4
In the small towns the political meetings are held late Saturday night,
after the workers have come back from the fields. At ten p.m. Goya
and I set out in her small Citroën, while Fernando goes with his political aides in another car. Fernando has a habit, when he sees an interesting Roman, medieval, or Arabic ruin, of stopping the car in order to
inspect it. He smells the stone and pats it to see what needs to be
done. Fernando is an admirer of beauty. He has been the person most
responsible for preserving Toledo during the bad years.

The sky darkens as Goya drives through La Mancha. The local government administrators, mostly Franco's leftovers, won't allow special
lights to be used to help those on the campaign trail; only the actual
meeting hall can be lit, so soon we are deep in the countryside and
traveling along bumpy dirt roads in total darkness. To our right are
the shadows of the Sierras; we are passing through poppy fields; in the
night, infused with the odors of the olive trees and the damp earth, a
sweet smell fills the car. "Look, Goya," I cry, pointing, "a windmill,
it's turning!" I go into mild shock whenever I bump into a cliché—
what are these Gypsies, flamenco dancers, and bullfighters doing in my
modern Spanish landscape?

"*Madre mía*, Barbara, you're right, it's a windmill."

After driving slowly another hour in blackness, we finally meet Fernando in Consuegra. The mayor of the town has just been suspended
for having permitted the local *caciques* to menace the small population.
When the entire population unanimously voted *no* to the pre-election
referendum, the new political parties demanded an investigation, the
scandal hit the national newspapers, which made Consuegra famous as
the "no" town.

After a brief stop there we zigzag east, toward Quintanar de la Orden. We meet up again with Fernando in Villanueva de Alcardete, a town of under a thousand. Several hundred people are waiting for us inside the local movie theater. We are the first members of the political class to arrive here in forty years. The old people just look at us; they don't know what to expect. The hall clearly is used for all occasions; the green paint on the walls is peeled back to dirty stucco, only a few light bulbs are in use, several rows of seats are missing. Goya and I sit down near one of the few young couples seated in the theater; they have brought a child. In the rural parts of Toledo the inhabitants have stamped on their faces the mark of the Almoravide invasions: the facial structure, the round raisin brown eyes are Mussulman. The males congregate in small groups; they just stare at the politicians who are seated on the platform behind a desk covered with purple crepe paper. It is hard to see clearly, due to the lack of light. One of Fernando's aides, a man in his late twenties, comes over to Goya and me. He leans over. "Did you have any trouble? Meet up with the ultra-right?" We shake our heads. The theme is: Vote in the Election, preferably liberal, but vote. In towns like Villanueva de Alcardete, where we are the first group to arrive, it is hard to get the audience to ask questions. But during the three weeks, day by day, the change is swift. The people in the provinces gain confidence. In places that have already had a visit by the Socialists or Communists, it is easier to make contact. Finally, one man gets up and asks a question: "The river is so dry, it's hoarse—when will we get a dam?" Then another man asks about hospitals.

The big job is convincing them to go to the polls. The old people had fought in the Civil War. In the small towns everyone remembered who did what to whom, the savage murders, the mean-spirited political betrayals for an extra acre of land; nobody had bothered about the inhabitants of La Mancha for forty years. Would voting be a preamble for another war? A fresh massacre? How could they be assured that the *guardia Civil,* which would be manning the polls, no longer had the power to punish in case of a wrong vote? Elections in the big cities and industrial areas bore no relation to the problems of *cacique* country. In the end, many of the older inhabitants had to be taken to the polls by their children.

There would be only one more Saturday night, June 11, before the elections. Although it is well after midnight, we have to go on to meetings scheduled in other small towns. Several of the local men gather in front of the movie hall and watch us get into our cars. Then they wave good-bye, pointing the good road out of town, as we are driving in total darkness.

We head north to Noblejas, not far from Aranjuez. One of the women in the bar where we meet asks if we have had supper. She brings us cold tortilla, ham, and wine. In the next town, three hundred people are waiting outside a local football field, because the mayor had refused to light the field before the political caravan arrives. Later, on the way back to Toledo, Goya and I pass a small Socialist car; we can hear it coming toward us in the darkness because they are playing the Internationale. We clack our horns in recognition and keep on going until we get back on the main highway. When we reach home it is five in the morning; the dusty beige early light turns the city walls Roman, Arab, Goth: the color of nasturtiums.

Sunday, June 5

As Carrillo is holding a rally here this afternoon, I drive over to the Communist headquarters. I glance out of the car window at an El Greco view of Toledo. In the front room licking envelopes are several rows of old-timers. During the Civil War Toledo was split between left and right. The Socialist Party is a newcomer in this region, most of their people are young.

I tell their pressman that I want to be able to sit up in the grandstand with Carrillo. I explain I am claustrophobic and heavy crowds make me panic. I am sent to the back room to meet Luis Lucio Lobato, who is assumed to be the man who has spent the greatest number of years in prison. He was born in this region. Behind his desk, hanging on the wall, is a huge campaign map of the province, with flags stuck in various towns indicating those places where meetings have already taken place: Tembleque, Talavera de la Reina.

He is a small man with chiseled features, intense light-colored eyes, and close-cropped gray hair. He has the slow movements of a person who has recently recovered from a shock, who doesn't want to make any errors, no verbal slips that would point up the blanks, the lack of street knowledge. After I am identified, he is quiet for a moment, then asks: "Have you heard about the troubles in Talavera? The PSOE headquarters had their windows smashed by the Fuerza Nueva."

"No." Though technically Lucio Lobato is running for the Senate, the Communists are planning a low profile in the province, as Toledo is no longer a Communist stronghold. They want to build slowly while avoiding trouble with the ultra-right. At the last moment they plan to throw their votes to the stronger parties in return for future favors. He complains to me that the PSOE people in Toledo are uncooperative, they refuse to "pactar" (make a deal with the Communists). I am silent. It is obvious the PSOE are under instructions to join no one; they will use the first elections to prove they don't need a coalition. Lucio Lobato promises to get me onto the grandstand; then he asks me to come by another morning, to compare notes on the progress of the local campaign.

Right near the Communist headquarters is the Sinagoga del Tránsito. Abruptly I decide to walk in. I wander through the synagogue, suddenly remembering that in medieval times Toledo was the capital of three religions: Christian, Jewish, and Mussulman. About twenty years ago, after Franco officially asked for the symbolic return of the Jews to Spain, the synagogue was restored and a museum of Jewish history was added to it. There is a time map and a story of the Jewish golden age in Spain. After 1492 the Jewish calendar stops; the Diaspora began the same month, and from the same harbor as Columbus setting sail for America. (How many Jews joined him and landed up fighting the Indians?) Jews never were good proselytizers. *Do independents, precisely because of their ambivalence, always lose?* On one wall is a map with Toledo at the center of the Diaspora; the Spanish have starred the cities with a heavy population of Diaspora Jews who the Spanish (at least those in charge of the synagogue map) believe at some future date might wish to return home: Los Angeles, New York, Moscow, Chicago, Buenos Aires, Casablanca, and Toronto.

I stare at it. Though I don't fancy myself as a self-styled proselytizer. It isn't in the name of some higher moral good that I am in Spain, or have become a scribbler, or travel, some of the time, with another woman's husband. I am doing all of this merely to please myself. I look at the map for the longest time, only half remembering why I need to commit it to memory; then I turn and walk out of del Tránsito. *Breathe deeply, take a few whiffs of fresh air.* Can't help any candidate with the Jewish vote; there is no functioning Jewish quarter left, just knickknacks for the *turistas.* I walk a while, then hail a taxi and ask the driver to take me to the Socialists.

In the headquarters an aide I know tells me that a few blocks away Goya is having some trouble with Fuerza Nueva kids. The two of us walk over. She is standing in the middle of the street, a hand on either hip, a cigarette dangling from her mouth; strands of her electric-black hair are falling from a loosely pinned bun. Goya, looking awesome and wonderful, is berating a group of ultra-right kids, "You will NOT scrawl your lies on my husband's posters."

"Goya, please, come away, the ultras smashed up the Talavera head-quarters this morning." The Socialist aide steers her back into her car.

"And you will not remove or defile these billboards. I pasted up these handbills myself." Goya can sound very imperious. "Now, go away. Away, away."

The Fuerza Nueva militants seem confused by her. Abruptly, like a group of naughty children, they turn and run down the street. The Socialists and I exchange glances. It would never have occurred to us to *talk* to Fuerza Nueva, but even if we had, we could never have conveyed Goya's stern authoritarian message.

Sunday afternoon, June 5

The football field is jammed with crowds of local people as well as Party members from adjoining towns who have been busloaded in to hear Santiago Carrillo. While we are pushing our way through the mob scene up onto the grandstand, I feel an anxiety attack coming on. The sun is strong; I start to sweat and am trembling slightly. Goya tells Carrillo's aide, "*Nada*—nervous," and he goes off and brings me back an orange soda to sip. The Communist security police firmly lock hands, the special guard completely encircles the field, the car carrying Carrillo and his wife unloads in the area directly behind us. One of the local Party leaders is a construction worker who works for Fernando. He is amazed and moved that Goya has come to meet Carrillo. He whispers to her not to worry, he will instruct his entire family to vote for Fernando. Carrillo also seems startled that a rival candidate's wife is lending her support to his Toledo visit. I overheard his aide mumble: "Chueca's wife is *muy Basca,* very Basque." I assume he means high-spirited. I don't know whether it has occurred to Carrillo that Goya came with me out of curiosity rather than political sympathy. But Fernando is a well-known cultural figure. Carrillo motions the TV cameras to follow him; then he walks over to Goya and she holds out her hand like a queen for him to kiss, while Carrillo appears properly humble as he welcomes her to his meeting. In the distance, groups of Fuerza Nueva are hooting their motorcycle horns. Carrillo's wife looks very tired; she is wearing a typically French white blouse and serge skirt (the cut is different in Spain) and moves back from the front row to a more sheltered spot on the grandstand. I am a dopey coward; why should I die in Toledo for the Communist Party? I take a third-row seat next to her. I introduce myself, and we discuss doing an interview when things calm down. During the playing of the Internationale neither Carrillo nor his wife gives the raised-fist salute. Carrillo runs a more conservative campaign than the Socialists; he has a lot to overcome, and will permit his fragile party no left-wing flimflam, no mention of the Spanish Republic. During the Internationale Carrillo glances at Goya, who, braver than me, is standing next to him in the front line, and she gives him a direct stare back.

In front of Goya and Fernando's house: *Monday, late morning, June 6*

Two women in charge of the UCD campaign truck are bickering in front of the main gate. Flor Gómez, a Galician woman, the granddaughter of Anarchists (Anarchists like naming their children Flower, Peace, or Liberty), is arguing with an Italian woman executive who has been imported for her expertise. The Italian, a veteran of many political campaigns, pulls rank: What could a Spanish woman who has never seen an election know of such matters? Flor insists that the Italian is making a mistake importing help from Madrid; the Communists and Socialists are building up their local parties on a grass-roots level. When Miss Italy insinuates that Flor is a country girl from Galicia, Flor's skin tone mottles. In order to stave off her anger, I invite her to lunch.

We have a quick sandwich in the main square, near the cathedral. Before the elections Flor worked for a hotshot advertising agency in Madrid.

"A descendant of Spanish Anarchists working for the moderate wing of the UCD?" I tease her. "What are *your* politics?"

Flor laughs. "I like Fernando . . ." She gulps her Scotch and grins at me. "I'm *Anarquista,* moderate, independent, agnostic, romantic, and liberal." She pauses. "In my *heart* Anarchist." Flor asks me if some of the *chicas progres,* the new Spanish left-wing girls, don't strike me as oddly nunnish. "People are always accusing the Catholic Church of the obvious, its repressive, authoritarian legacy—but one of the big vacuums they've really created in Spain is that we have no models for civic behavior. People associate doing good, when it doesn't carry a political label, with the nuns' charity baskets. We don't see civic action as dynamic." She confides, "I hate to admit it, the Catalans are so impossible, but Barcelona is the only city with a strong civic tradition." Flor looks at her watch; she is in a rush to get back, as she doesn't want *La Italiana* taking over.

With Toledo Socialists:
Monday afternoon, June 6
After Flor leaves, I go to a meeting with several Socialists in a hotel opposite the cathedral. The atmosphere here is different from Madrid Socialist chic. I climb up a steep flight of stairs to a small hotel room where a group of men are sitting around a small table. There is a jug of water and a neat stack of round, dry biscuits. As Toledo is off the beaten track and, except for special occasions such as Carrillo's visit, not in the news, everyone likes to gab with me; I am the only resident writer on the block.

A former union organizer who has just arrived after forty years of exile in Argentina keeps interrupting the younger men. He calls them kids, wet behind the ears. Assuming I know nothing, he makes me a primitive graph of the major political parties. The younger men are mortified. Politely I listen, and every so often I ask an appropriate question. I feel awful. You can't give a person back forty lost years. Abruptly one of the younger men says, "She has an appointment with Haro." He takes me by the arm and we leave to meet with one of Toledo's new Socialist leaders.

Dr. Tomás Haro lives with his wife, Maite, and their small son in a modern apartment complex in the new part of town. He is a psychiatrist at the main hospital in Toledo. He emphasizes he is a doctor first; if the Socialist Party means more hospitals and better medical care, fine. But he isn't committed to an abstract allegiance to the party. "My profession radicalized me. We have only one real hospital in Toledo, and one in Talavera. Not enough. Technically, social security pays for hospital beds, but most doctors hoard them for private patients."

"How are your patients handling the elections?"

"As soon as the elections became a reality, the psychosomatic symptoms of the general population grew. Many people don't realize they are suffering mentally, because, as you know perfectly well, Spaniards avoid thinking about mental problems." Haro puffs on his pipe. "It's much too early, and no name has been put on the ailments we are treating during this period, but there is definitely a higher death rate, more accidents, fear,"—he pauses—"obsessive rememberings of the past. Insecurity about the future."

The driver of a Socialist campaign truck honks his horn. Haro goes to the window and waves. "The loudspeaker works fine."

"Can you hear the Internationale?" the driver shouts up. (How could we not?)

Haro continues, "In obvious terms, Bad Daddy is gone. During election time we doctors are being deluged with patients. But it will take years for the psychological scars created by this emotional upheaval to be sorted out. In addition to this new sickness, in Toledo I have to deal with the effects of an overly accelerated rate of industrialization." Haro is reflective. "Not all problems have good solutions, I can't very well recommend to my patients that they go backward and start firing their own pottery, now can I?"

I am surprised to find a textbook by Joe Goldstein in Haro's bookcase. I tell him Joe and Harold were law professors together in Yale.

"Joe Goldstein," he says, "is one of my heroes."

I promise to send him a copy of the medical profession protest for Eva Sastre published in the *Times*. He wants it for his archives.

I used to think of censorship as a deprivation suffered by those living inside Spain. But it worked two ways. The views of intelligent Americans also were muffled, and remained unheard. That, too, is a form of censorship. Unheard was the small, lucid voice that pleased neither Franco, the authoritarian left, nor the American Embassy.

Monday night, June 6

If the head of the Socialist Party, "Speedy" Felipe González, can air-taxi from one campaign drop to the next, I can hire a taxi to get myself back to Madrid. The driver is garrulous, "It's abnormal for the rich to vote left, abnormal for a worker to vote right. As the workers have more votes than the rich, it is logical that we will have trouble." He tells me that his parents are terrified of a confrontation at the polls. "Old people remember incidents. People were stuffed down a well in Tembleque, packed tight like loaves of bread, and shot. So I will have to go with them. I am telling them to vote Socialist. With the Communists, it could be out of the frying pan into the fire. I figure we won't get much, but maybe Felipe will pay the bill for education."

Madrid:
Tuesday, June 7

Last week, after Carlota Bustelo told me that Eva had been freed, I went straight to her lawyer's office to greet her. She was giving a press conference when I walked in—she had no idea who I was, never had seen a photo; when I gave my name, she stopped talking and threw her arms around me. We agreed to meet as soon as possible. This morning, she and her daughter come for breakfast. Again, in the lobby of the Wellington, we hug each other.

Eva whispers, "I gave the desk clerk my maiden name to avoid attracting attention."

Doesn't Eva realize that as either Sastre or Forest she is one of the most known women in Spain? While Eva talks and looks me over, her teenage daughter stays pasted to her side. She keeps looking at her mother.

We sit down in the dining room of the Wellington, and Eva says, "Croissants, *bollos,* and lots of good coffee."

She talks in an animated way about solidarity inside the prison, her gratitude to her friends. Doesn't seem to be aware of how many of her friends spoke out against her or did nothing, so I make no comment. The waiters recognize her, but these days so many people have come into prominence for one reason or another, prison fame is taken in stride. Finally, I ask, "Did you write *Operation Ogro?* Were you 'Julen Agirre'?"

She nods.

"Well, well. Something about the way the tapes were put together; the tone, I thought, was female, but I wasn't sure."

"So," says Eva, "it turns out that both the author and the translator of *Ogro* are women." *Eva was nearly killed for going the one step further; if you had lived in Spain, would you have become Eva?*

She is explicit concerning her three-year imprisonment, and the psychological and sexual-physical torture to which she was submitted; she insists that her most terrible deprivation was never seeing her reflection. Eva looks at herself in the dining room mirror. "I keep doing that now—I feel more me. It is awful never to see your own face. You begin to think you have become grotesque, a monster, deformed. Who are you without a face? I lost my sense of time."

She regards herself as being in the center of a political struggle, I doubt if she understands, now that things have changed, how extreme and frozen in prior time some of her views might seem to her friends.

She is an oddly appealing mixture of adult wisdom, childlike devotion, and wonderful optimism. Hope she halts her political voyage this side of fanaticism.

Hotel Colón, Barcelona:
Wednesday, June 8

With the election a week away, I have made a dumb move in flying to Barcelona. Transportation strike here has thrown city out of whack. Massive PSOE and PSUC rallies, but so much confusion I don't think I'll be able to get to them. Teresa Pallach is campaigning for Pallach's seat in Girona. Can't locate people I want to see. The hotel clerk is helpful; he drives me on his lunch hour over to a few appointments. Just as I am sitting in my hotel room beating up on myself for not anticipating the snarl, Juan Marsé comes over in his car to take me home to have lunch with him and his wife, Joaquina. I had met him during the Madrid book fair and we instantly took to each other. Clearly some forty-odd years ago all the mothers of future kings and novelists decided to name their son Juan. Juan Carlos, Juan García Hortelano, Juan Marsé, Juan Benet, Juan Goytisolo. Juan Marsé's novel *Si Te Dicen Que Caí* is wonderful. It's about the zany adventures dreamed up by Barcelona street kids during the late forties. It is all very evocative (the title is a line from the national anthem, "Cara al Sol"). The kids dream of joining the mythic anarchists in Toulouse and meanwhile invent erotic stories about a famous Barcelona whore who was mysteriously murdered.

When I tell Juan I adore his book, he grins in relief. "I thought you were going to attack me for not writing my novels in Catalan."

I burst out laughing. "That's the last thing on my mind."

"The atmosphere is so thick here; every group is split into a Catalan wing and a non-Catalan wing. But it's really hard on writers. They want us to write in Catalan. We've gone from a dictatorship to *this*? A mess."

Barcelona was the most cultured city in Spain under Franco. Now the repressive measures the Catalans are taking against those who do not speak or write in Catalan are unreal. Because of the political instability in Latin America, Barcelona has become the international publishing capital of the Spanish language. And Spanish is being forbidden in the city. Wild. Barcelona, whose morale was so good under Franco, now seems bent on destroying itself.

Juan Marsé is one of the few writers here who actually comes from a working-class background, and he has a brash, easy charm, as if he were the first kid on the block to get himself some street smarts. He has tousled Gypsy hair and the open smile of a man who knows he is appealing to women.

"Let's talk about Stendhal."

"Stendhal?" Juan likes that idea. "He's my man, and Fellini too. Yes, let's talk about him. That's a nice thing to do a week before the elections, eh, Joaquina?"

Spanish culture is wacky. Since in the last five hundred years Spain hasn't had more than a few years here and there of healthy government, and no reformation, no French Revolution, the culture has had a long history of existing in spite of, rather than because of, official Spain. The arts have foliated like a slightly mad, eccentric, orphaned stepchild of the gloomy bourgeoisie. After all, this is the country that invented the picaresque novel, the story of the marginal man, odd man out. Which they are.

Thursday, June 9

Cut your losses, okay, you made a dumb move, don't compound wasted time. Make plane reservations and get out. Before I leave, I stop by Luis and María Antonia Goytisolo's apartment. (This also takes special arranging with hotel clerk who drives me there.) Luis is away. I am very fond of María Antonia because she has a way of making me feel good. She has a musical voice and graceful gestures. She has her hair done up in a scarf; while Luis is away, as she puts it, she can really get at the apartment. María Antonia is so elegant I can't imagine her scouring. She has this lilting, dreamy way of being interested in the down-to-earth. She opens her large dark eyes, points her slightly aquiline nose, and says delicately, "Don't you prefer the family gone when you attack your apartment?"

I agree.

María Antonia says that male novelists are thin-skinned. "They put on a big show, but they're enormously vulnerable, don't you think?"

I give María Antonia a present, a small Venetian-red lacquer box the color of her living room door. María Antonia gives me wonderful compliments. When she remarks on my color sense, "It is the exact shade—very few people have such precise color memory," the child in me is delighted. Some profound nerve is satisfied when my visual awareness is praised. Could it be the deep need to identify with my artist mother, rather than with my intelligent, astute father? To make peace? My earliest childhood memory was of irritation and desire. I think I was under a year old—I was propped up in an enormous black carriage. Faces, women's faces, were looking down, admiring and clucking at me. I was covered with a serviceable navy-blue woolen blanket with gray edges and, I think, a gray monogram. I remember turning slightly and watching another carriage being wheeled past me with a wonderful white fur cover. I yearned for it. I actually recall being jealous. What greed, what infant sullenness!

Madrid:
Thursday night, June 9

In Madrid again. A billboard sign reads: WORKERS' COMMISSIONS TREMBLE. THE ANARCHISTS RIDE AGAIN. During the Civil War, at its height, the Anarchist trade union, the CNT, had two million members. The Communist nightmare is: will their ghostly enemies emerge again? Ninety-five percent of the present CNT is under thirty; a certain number are the children of Anarchists. These days the word *"Acráta"* or *"Anarquista"* might mean anything from the CNT, which is a trade union and espouses mild, libertarian ideas, to simply nonconformist. The Anarchist ideology has been discovered by ecologists, feminists, gays, and other freewheelers of the counterculture. In April twenty thousand young Anarchists held a rock 'n' roll jamboree celebrating the old traditional Anarchist movement in San Sebastían de los Reyes, near Madrid. I don't think the traditional left knows yet what to make of this "sing along with Anarchism" routine. The older lefties are nonplused. It is hard for conventional Marxists to empathize with a younger generation that feels smothered by outworn dogma; the children of the left are tired of it all.

Madrid:
Friday, June 10

On the way to Juan Benet's house, the taxi passes an elegant men's shop, *Fancy Man.* Spanglish. *No he tenido ningún chance con mi boyfriend. Me gusta un buen aftershave. Quiero un relax con Scotch on the rocks.* The election campaign uses a lot of Spanglish. Meanwhile, Madrid has been ravaged by Mexico's revenge on *los conquistadores*: the Aztec-modern architecture pops up everywhere.

Juan is slouched in a leather chair in his living room listening to Brahms. He smiles craftily, very Anglo in his English gray flannel shirt, drinking his coffee and cognac. Should he add another story to my repertoire?

I egg him on. "Don't be a holdout. Oh, I know I am a pain in the neck for you. I know too much of your real history. You are pissed off that Paco blabbed all the good family stories. But, Juan," I bargain, "didn't you use some of my sacred territory? Daniel, his house in Darien, the boiler room in his basement? After all, he was *my* boyfriend. In *Sub Rosa* you helped yourself to him without asking. My Daniel from Darien is cluttering up the pages of modern Spanish literature. Is that fair? He has no business in Iberian *belles lettres*—you just grabbed him, so now talk up."

He gets his you-are-going-to-owe-me-one look.

"Besides, I could pull a mean trick."

"What?"

"Not put you in my book."

He leans forward. "When I was a mere schoolboy, stuck in Madrid, I had a wonderful mathematics professor—this was long before Jorge Semprún and his crowd reached town. He was an early Communist organizer. As he conveyed such worldly urgency, I enrolled. While I was waiting for my first assignment, my mentor had the bad luck to be killed in a train accident. According to newspaper accounts, the police identified him, from the contents of his suitcase, as a Communist liaison. My luck was up. I waited for them to arrest me. One month, two. At the same time I expected the Party to claim me. Who would arrive, I wondered, first? Which group possessed me? Then it dawned on me—perhaps I was his only follower and he hadn't bothered to record my name. After half a year I realized I was free, an escapee from them both. I never went back," he pauses. "The guilt trip, the rhetoric—think of the starving miners—works only once. I received an early dose. Now, since the old boy's death, that sort of emotional blackmail is over . . ."

I have a vision of Spanish males of roughly Juan's age always running away from something. If the Church doesn't get you, the Party will. If they don't claim you, Opus will. If they can't convert you, the army will take you. Bizarre, but Franco's death has liberated many intellectuals from the Communist Party.

That same day I have supper with Josefina and Alberto. When I leave them, Alberto walks me to a taxi. The weather is unusually foggy. Alberto gives his twisted smile and, puffing away at his pipe, says, "Malraux weather."

"*Cómo?*"

"Not the real Malraux, but the one we grew up with. Mist, Paris, . . . *symbols* of what we yearned for as kids . . ." Alberto muses, we walk up to Princesa. "Well, well, well. Spain is in *plena corrida política . . .*"

"Two weeks to the DAY."

We keep walking. "A sort of a victory—we have outlived him. A very happy campaign, very professional. But don't you feel the past?" he asks, as he shuts the taxi door. "In times like these, there is always the deaths of old friends, *las memorias.*" We kiss good-bye.

Toledo:
Sunday morning, June 12

Sleepy from campaigning all night. At four in the morning one of Fernando's aides offered to drive Goya's small car back across the mountains while we continue in Fernando's car. He drives, Fernando never tires. Is animated by contact with the people in the towns. Now that the campaign is ending, marked change in local population. More friendly, more jokes. The questions come in a steady stream. Later in the morning the local taxi driver, used to my going back and forth, again drives me into Madrid.

I join Rosa Pereda and Marcos Barnatan. We want to go to the big Communist rally in Torrelodones. Half hour out of Madrid torrents of rain flood the main highway. Rosa's car has a very low wheel base and we have to turn back. We are disappointed. Later we hear that Carrillo's helicopter nearly crash-landed due to the heavy flooding. Over two hundred thousand people are there, mostly those who had left Madrid earlier in the morning.

We are unexpectedly free this lovely, lazy, wet Madrid afternoon. Marcos invites us to a small Argentinian restaurant, El Locro, on Molino de Viento. Later we go to a movie. In the darkened theater the audience goes wild at each new reference; *Unfinished Degree* is one of the first uncensored films to evoke their time and place. Wild laughter at the shots of the bored modern couple lying together in bed as the radio blasts the news that Franco is dead. Delighted cackles at hearing the wife use *cheli,* a new apache-style slang popular in Madrid. Rosa pummels me. "Look, the hero is reading *El País.*" She is exuberant at suddenly seeing her own generation *named.*

A labor lawyer bumps into his first love on a busy Madrid street. Both of them now are married. After the lawyer sends the woman flowers (signed Robert Redford, as in *All the President's Men*), the two start an affair, determined to live the life that years before had been truncated. Meanwhile, our dashing lawyer is busy defending imprisoned trade union leaders. Clearly the movie has in mind Marcelino Camacho, the trade unionist, and the Carabanchel 10 case. Audience breaks up—the lawyer's Woody Allen-type pal is nicknamed Trotsky. Although the lawyer becomes an enormous success at defending members of the Opposition, he informs his mistress that he still believes in the bourgeois sanctity of marriage. The new woman is ditched; in the last frame we see her making herself a cup of tea and staring off into space. A dedication flashes across the screen: TO THAT GENERATION WHO NEVER FINISHED THEIR DEGREE, AND TO THOSE WHO GREW UP NEVER KNOWING WHO MIGUEL HERNÁNDEZ WAS OR WHY HE DIED IN PRISON. Silence. Wild cheers. Hernández is one of the best modern Spanish poets. In the 1940s he died of TB in prison. Eva had said, If you cannot see your own face, you begin to believe you are deformed, a monster, or you simply do not exist.

Outside the theater the Madrid streetlamps are still wet, their round vague moons a light fuzzy amber. What about Juan Goytisolo and myself? Aren't we truncated pieces of each other's youth never properly lived out? The film makes me uneasy. Then I turn to Rosa. "The car is parked across the street, remember?"

The driver of a rain-drenched caravan returning from Torrelodones yells: Melina Mercouri was there. The cars roll along the Gran Vía playing the Internationale. Suddenly our small car is grid-locked between the Communists and the Fuerza Nueva. A fight breaks out. "Marcos," Rosa says, "we're stuck." We hear the police sirens yowling along the Gran Vía; there is nothing to do but wait it out. Marcos locks the doors, rolls up the window. Soon the police are at it with their clubs. Later Rosa admits to having been scared. "Me too," Marcos says. I feel less isolated now that it is okay in Spain to express fear at ordinary things. Before, people lived through horrendously dangerous situations and said, *"No es nada, nada, nada. No tiene importancia."*

Hotel:
Monday morning, June 13
Juan telephones from Paris, says I am mumbling and sound funny. I realize I am behaving as though he were the labor lawyer in the film and I the housewife-mistress staring into space. I am very impressionable about movies. Abruptly I stop reacting to the fantasy and tell

Juan about the new changes. After the elections, street names like Generalisimo will be changed. José Antonio once again will be called the Gran Vía.

The two television channels are now giving visual instruction on the use of the polls. During the last few days the major political parties are each allowed a certain amount of time for television campaigning. Many people don't read newspapers, which is one of the reasons Spain from sea to sea is plastered with handbills. In a Madrid traffic tunnel is a Charlie Chaplin scene: At the entrance, one man carrying a bucket of paste is putting up posters; at the other end, a man carrying a bucket of water is ripping them off.

Madrid:
Monday night, June 13
I have arranged to meet Juan Cruz, one of the *El País* journalists, at the press gate at the Rayo Vallecaño stadium. The Socialists are winding up their campaign with a huge rally.

To be on the safe side, I decide to get an early start. Many of my friends will be at the stadium: Nicolás and Graciela, Manolo Arroyo. I hail a taxi and ask the driver to take me to Rayo Vallecaño in Vallecas, the working-class district. A half hour north of the stadium, we get stuck behind the political caravan. Felipe González, in contrast to the Communist policy, has made a point of not separating the Socialist Party from its symbolic commitment to the Spanish Republic; the Socialists are under orders to march through the streets with the old-time UGT trade union banner. In fairness to the Communists, as they were legalized just before the campaign opened, they are in no position to take risks.

The crowds lining the streets quietly watch the caravan drive by. Then suddenly, as the political procession nears Rayo Vallecaño, masses of people start to run toward the stadium. I am a creature of the 1950s, I have no memory of the mass rallies of the 1930s, this sort of stampede is unknown to me. Windows along the street open, people rush out of buildings with their children, and they just keep running. The crowd swells, like the Russians running down the steps in Eisenstein's film *Potemkin,* but that was grief in motion; here I am watching hope. All of us engaged in the campaign had assumed that the Socialists would emerge the big party, but now during the march toward Rayo Vallecaño, the real returns are in. Campaign planes buzz overhead. When my taxi reaches the stadium, the two policemen in charge of parking are convulsed in laughter. They have pinned on their lapels the Socialist insignia. How odd, in Madrid, to see police giving the Socialist salute. At the press gate, confusion. A Socialist aide has my name on their press list. "Just get inside quick and grab a seat, you'll never find Cruz." I race up the stairs, for once not allowing myself an attack of claustrophobia as I push and shove my way toward the benches. A journalist from *Cambio* finds me a place next to him. It is jammed. "Keep the press section clear!" "I can't," yells back a second aide. "I need to seat this batch—we can't ask the oldies to stand." On either end of the football field, instead of score cards, are the magic letters: UGT and PSOE. Felipe, thirty-two years old, brash, ambitious, enthusiastic, and well trained by the West Germans, stands there; a true political animal, he gains adrenaline from the size of the crowd. The crush thickens, security breaks down, and the entire playing field is covered with the overflow. The Internationale is sung; the crowd raises their fists in salute. If only Spaniards weren't so easily tempted to salute *this* side or *that* side. When the crowd calms, Felipe, in the hot accents of Andalusia, voices the cool reason of Willy Brandt. We are all stunned by the intensity of that rally. No, not just because of the purported half million who stampeded the stadium or remained just outside listening to the speeches via loudspeaker. Later, after we leave the stadium, we see Vallecas spontaneously going wild, street meetings bursting like stray firecrackers into the early hours of the next morning. Many things would happen after that in Spain, but all of us who were there for years always said, Remember Vallecas, remember the crowds running.

Fernando's house in Toledo:
Tuesday morning, June 14
It is quiet now. The campaign is over. Tomorrow at the polls. Flor Gómez knocks and comes into my bedroom. "Well, I've done it—all the political parties are coming to dinner." As a loyal granddaughter of Anarchists, Flor has made her own last-minute statement apropos the campaign. She has decided that it would be "nice" to have all the political parties celebrate the first general election with a joint private dinner. "It was rough going—I spent yesterday dashing back and forth, persuading them not to be touchy. Lucio Lobato kept insisting that if we invited the extreme right, Alianza Popular, he wouldn't show. Face it, he has a point. Breaking bread with the same crowd that kept him in prison all these years. His aides had to convince him that

what counts is the spirit of the thing. I mean, we can't not invite the Alianza people, can we?"

Legally the press can't make any further mention of the campaign. So the dinner will be private. As Flor says, all of us have lived through, one way or another, these last three weeks together; we ought to be allowed to honor its specialness.

That evening we meet at Viento del Aire, the best restaurant in Toledo. One of the leaders of the Christian Democrats remarks sheepishly that they expect such a poor showing at the polls they aren't sure they belong at the fiesta. (They poll almost no votes.) We don't know whether Alianza will show. But they do, looking very perky; they seem anxious to make a good impression and not be called Fascists. At times during the campaign the PSOE turks could irritate by behaving with the smugness of *nouveau riche* relatives, but tonight they are on good behavior. Flor anxiously watches the door. Finally Lucio Lobato appears. "Well," he says to her, "here I am." The waiters are bug-eyed; the mixtures of people assembled at the banquet table must seem unimaginable. He motions me to sit down next to him. Champagne toasts are drunk. Arias Salgado, who later would become one of the leaders of the Suárez liberal wing of the UCD, gets up. He says that the most savage fighting of the war occurred in Toledo; it is historic that men of opposing beliefs can now, in 1977, sit down and dine together. This is the spirit that needs to be preserved. His father was one of Franco's key men. Looking at Luis Lucio Lobato, Rafael Arias Salgado says that he is ashamed that a man like him had spent nearly thirty years in prison for having been on the other side, for holding another point of view. "We can never, never let this happen again." The two men glance at each other; then Salgado sits down.

Armando Rubén Puente, who is covering the elections for a French magazine, happens to be in Toledo, and at the last minute, he and a French publisher join us at the banquet. The French publisher mumbles *sotto voce* to Armando, "*Dites donc, ces Espagnols sont beaucoup plus avancés pour la démocratie qu'on aurait cru*—Say, these Spaniards are much more advanced in democracy than one would have believed."

It is late when Goya, Fernando, and I return home. I walk up the stone stairs to the second landing; they call good night, then disappear down the hall. I open the window and look over Toledo, the mountains in the distance. Twenty-five years I've been coming to this town ... Downstairs, leaflets, campaign debris have been cleared away; the madonnas' outstretched arms no longer are holding half-empty bottles of pop. I brought my daughters here after Harold died. They played Inquisition in the basement. Carla and Maria would cover their faces with white dust, hold tightly to the window grills, while outside on the street Fernando *hijo* yelled, "I am the bloody Moor— Attack, attack!" Images kaleidoscope through my head. Juan Benet billeted in Toledo in the 1950s, as a scrawny private in Franco's creaky army, the hot *churros* for Sunday breakfasts, Lucio Lobato, Sinagoga del Tránsito, the movie theater in the mountain town, rising out of the blackness, campaigning at three in the morning, then daylight over the June poppy fields. I fall asleep.

Election Day, June 15

Armando comes over with his friend. The caretaker dutifully gives them a tour of the remodeled palace. The French publisher is very direct about voicing his opinion of the price of this and that. "This is the real stuff," he says. Near the second-floor landing is a refectory table with many photos: Paco at twenty in Chartres (I took that one), Pepín Bello (who was García Lorca's lover), Lucia Bosé and her husband, Luis Miguel Dominguín. I think, How interesting that the bullfighter's brother—Domingo Dominguín—was one of the chiefs of the clandestine Madrid Communist Party. I hesitate, then explain nothing, as the man is more involved in furniture. Most people walk right past history because they won't permit the most obvious news to penetrate their consciousness; rarely is much of the stuff hidden.

Armando has offered to give me a lift back into the city. A young French woman, a reporter, joins us. On the way back she tells me that she is really covering the elections *"pour Papa,"* a Spanish exile. She says it would be too much of a shock for him to return; she has come in his place. Armando takes the main highway into Madrid. As soon as we hit the industrial outer belt, the turnout at the polls appears to be heavy. No incidents. Each of the major political parties is doing its own monitoring, its own tabulations. The publisher wants us to stop in a town that has a particularly good El Greco. He keeps making odd remarks: *"Dites-donc,* these Spanish exaggerate, a very first-namey bunch. I hear in Madrid even those around Juan Carlos *tu-toi."*

"Different strokes for different folks—in Paris *vous*, in Madrid *tu*," I mumble.

Puente whispers to me to find common ground with his friend so that we can have a good ride to Madrid. "Have you ever sailed?" he asks desperately. "Talk about the sea."

He is flying over to the Newport Cup races after the elections. I rise in his estimation after revealing I will be summering near there. I fish out of my past Daniel's Bermuda 40, which I remember not to call a boat, and soon the two of us are doing fine. Certain Europeans prefer global pigeonholes: the Spanish are difficult, Americans naïve, the cheese in the next town too soft, and so forth. Their comfortable point of departure is familiar generalization, while Americans are more haphazard. We might begin with a free-floating tale of our family origins, a run-down on Oedipal difficulties; we start with the intimate and abruptly cool off when aggressed upon. Europeans start with the insult and eventually calm down. Habeas corpus versus no habeas corpus. The Frenchman hasn't a clue that the reason I have taken a small place in Stonington is cheap rent. He becomes more sociable, and we spend the morning of the first general elections chatting about the Newport Cup races.

Wednesday afternoon, June 15

I am puzzled by a message at my hotel asking me to come to the Socialist headquarters. I take a taxi to García Morato 165. Inside the last door, sitting behind a large office desk, is Carlos Vélez—part of our original gang; we were students together in Paris. "Carlos!" I am astonished and delighted. While hugging me, he says he had telephoned my daughters in New York. "I figured I'd find you in Madrid."

He looks wonderful; the most responsible and least dramatic member of our group. For a while we talk about the death of his son in an automobile accident. Nobody should have a child die, but Carlos least of all. He has always been a good family man. Carlos winces about that. "We're all right now." He means his wife, his daughter, and himself. Typical of Carlos, at the last minute, with everyone scattered, to be coolly manning the almost deserted Socialist headquarters just doing what needs doing. Carlos used to tell us stories about his life in a refugee camp in Morocco with his mother and sisters. Carlos busied himself by teaching the Moroccan kids to read. At first his family were told that his father, a UGT leader, had been killed in Paris by the

Germans, along with Luis Companys, but the report was false. The family eventually were reunited and went to Mexico.

There is a mild bomb scare: a man identifying himself as a Cuban brings over a suspicious gift. Carlos orders him to return it to the Cubans; it turns out to be a gift of a case of white rum sent by their embassy.

Carlos shakes his head. "Those Cubans ought to be more careful with their presents, this is no time to send over unidentified men with heavy packages."

More interruptions: A pair of teenage runaways have come here to seek protection from their parents, who are opposed to their Romeo and Juliet romance. Carlos very patiently asks them if they are aware this is election day. The telephone rings constantly. Carlos keeps giving instructions: "Madrid is coming in much too heavy, we are in no position to win. Ward off the latecomers. Tell them to throw their vote to the Communists or one of the small groups."

Carlos turns to me. "According to our tabulations, we could go over thirty percent. Which means winning Madrid." He shakes his head. "The party has grown too fast. We need more time."

"Are you happy, Carlos? To be here?"

His slanting nostrils flare; he runs his hands through his hair, sandy streaked lightly with gray; Carlos always had a "young" aura to him. "Whenever I came to Madrid for professional reasons, I used to rush. Never even saw the Puerta del Sol. Maybe I didn't want to see the city. Imagine, vacationing in Spain. As a nuclear physicist I have no career problems. Really, the only bad thing that has happened to me in all these years is the death of my son. But now I'm not sure where I belong. Part of me feels I have an obligation to return because of my father..." Carlos walks me to the door; we embrace. Tomorrow night we will have dinner together.

Wednesday evening, June 15

Throughout Madrid many parties have been planned for this evening. Three of the big ones are at *Diario 16*, *Cambio 16*, and *El País*. Graciela and Nicolás are starting the evening at *Cambio*, and we make promises to be together for some part of the time. I am on the *El País* list. About nine in the evening I take a taxi to Juan Benet's house. His children are checking the television reception for the election returns. Juan telephones Rosa Regás, who is watching the returns in Barcelona. He tells me he has just bought a new car, an extraordinary vehicle, and he has chosen this night to test it out. Juan is laughing and cracks many jokes. I wait outside for him. He drives up in a white Daimler; I am quiet. In Paris Paco told me that the clearest image he had of his father was sitting next to him while he drove a white sports car. "Driving with him meant Madrid before the war, comfort, paradise." Juan honks the horn, he yells at me to hurry; I climb in, nervously knotting and unknotting a silk shoulder scarf. He teases: "You will never guess the car's secret."

I am silent. Still in shock. Does Juan know? It must be a pain in the ass for him that his almost twin brother was such a confider of their blurred childhood. Instinct cautions me to keep my mouth shut about my opinion of the magic white sports car; years pass before I casually ask, Wasn't Juan's father also a sports car aficionado? When we drive up to the gate the newspaper plant is surrounded by guards. After Juan parks the Daimler, we walk inside and take the elevator to the top floor. The party has already started.

El País:
Night of the elections, June 15

Todo Madrid. Rosa Pereda is covering the dinner for *El País;* she is asking all the guests for quotes: the movie director, Carlos Saura; Fernando Claudín, the theoretician of the Spanish Communist Party (he broke with it in 1964), the economist, Ramón Tamámes, and *El País's* publisher, Ortega Spottorno. Javier Pradera's wife, Gabriela Ferlosio, kisses me; she is giggling and romantically dressed. "I've got on my bullfighting gown. You don't go to them, do you? Javier says that now that bullfighting is no longer stylish, those who understand it should make a point of going . . ."

I am seated at one of the round tables covered with a damask cloth, with several friends. An elegant spread.

After dinner the doors of the banquet room are thrown open. I am astonished to see Felipe sitting on a bench outside, flanked by his followers, patiently waiting for us to finish dinner. Takes my breath away, always, always, the way Spain goes suddenly snobbish. Why should one of the main political leaders in Spain cool his heels in the corridors while we finish our mousse? Spain, Spain!

The election returns are being flashed in. Rosa Pereda runs over to me. "Fernando has won, he and Peces Barba (the Socialist candidate) have senatorial seats in Toledo. Blas Piñar is defeated." The returns are following the pre-election pattern predicted by the polls published in the Spanish press. I am watching the Madrid vote. Socialists are running ahead of predictions at twenty-nine percent. But at 2:30 that morning, "difficulties" develop in the tabulation of the Madrid vote. Between 8:30 and 2:30 of the following afternoon, the Madrid vote mysteriously vanishes from the news. The phantom Madrid vote reappears in the news a week after the elections. The UCD wins Madrid by a tiny margin. Neither the Socialists, UCD, nor the military want the Socialists, eighteen months after the death of Franco, to carry the capital.

Early morning, June 16

Everyone at fever pitch. The combined vote of Socialists, Communists, and splinter groups means that left of center has won Madrid by a healthy margin. Although Adolfo Suárez (the head of the UCD) is premier, the Socialists have emerged the strong party of the future. Manolo Arroyo, Paul Preston, a British historian, and I, euphoric, drive over to their headquarters. I want to find Carlos Vélez, but the Socialists, afraid of angry demonstrations by the diehards, have already put an end to their fiesta. A few stragglers are whooping it up in the street. Manolo insists we go to the student café in San Ginés. They go there for hot chocolate and *churros* after drinking all night. Paul is very funny; he is a Liverpool boy, he tells me he met John Lennon, and because of the Beatles, he didn't drop his Liverpool working-class accent when he became a historian. On the way to San Ginés, Paul sings "Lovely Rita." Manolo parks his car, and the three of us walk into the place. Raucous students have hoisted the Socialist flag, yelling, "Felipe, Felipe." Meanwhile, several policemen drinking hot chocolate before their morning beat are watching them. The students are quiet. Suddenly they realize the police can't arrest them; the Socialist Party *is* the legal establishment. The policemen keep drinking their chocolate. It has also dawned on them that they can't make a move; this is one of the new flags the police from now on will be asked to defend. "Well, luv," says Paul in a Liverpool brogue, "Liberty Hall." It is seven in the morning when I get to bed.

Afternoon, June 16

Juan Goytisolo telephones me from Paris. He says that I sound elated. I will be back in New York several days before him. I promise to meet him at Kennedy.

The three strongest figures to emerge from the elections are Adolfo

Suárez, the new President of Spain and leader of the UCD coalition, Felipe González, leader of the Opposition in the Parliament, and the King, Juan Carlos de Borbón. The ultras on either extreme got nothing.

June 23
The summer heat has set into Madrid; this morning I fly via TWA for New York.

Juan Goytisolo flies to New York on June 25. The city is hot; we spend evenings walking along Columbus Avenue, eating at Victor's, and with his ex-students at Ponce de Leon on East 116th Street. Late afternoons in my Central Park West living room, he gabs with Maria, listening to her various scenarios for her future. After July 4 he flies to Ann Arbor. When I arrive, several weeks later, he has a bad cold, and his new friends from there tell me he visibly cheers up after I hand him tea with cinnamon sticks and we go for good picnics in the lake district.

Their program is informal; sometimes Juan has me visit his classes and give his students my opinion of contemporary events in Spain. A sweet lazy summer. I return East, and by the beginning of August he joins me in the house I have rented on the outskirts of Stonington. I want to show him New England. I need no maps, no direction signals for this part of the country; I feel profoundly attached to this place. The earliest summers of my childhood had been spent near Essex, Ivoryton, and Saybrook. We drive through Watch Hill where there is that run of Victorian hotels and wide beaches. He is astonished at the light, the long empty stretches of low sand dunes. What most surprises him, on the way to Newport, are the cheap beach stands where you can get lobsters, mussels, clams, and corn. "Well," I say, "we do have Maine lobsters and summer space here."

VIII

///////////

Common
Passage

27

Now it's my turn in Madrid. I have a month until my book comes out in February. January of 1978 is so cold and bleak, when I arrive here, I decide to do myself a favor and check into the Wellington. In December Jorge Semprún's autobiography was published; battles between Communists and ex-Communists are sizzling; the question of the Resistance from the 1950s on has come up, my own book—which seemed to have been unaccountably stalled—has to come out now. It takes me about two minutes in Madrid to realize that I have been removed from the Barcelona calendar. Although I see the book as the story of an American girl's coming of age, from a political point of view I had known Pallach, and I had portrayed him in a favorable light. This accounts for maybe five pages of the entire novel, but for Catalans those are the crucial pages.

I do fairly well, though, with the business head of Seix Barral. I convince him that if we bring the book out now (it is already in galleys and there's no real need to hold it over for June, which had been someone's lousy bright idea), we can make money. Ángel is apolitical and we hit it off fine. But everything else coming out of Barcelona smells like a barrel of rotten fish. A wild Argentine woman, sent by a Barcelona magazine, arrives at my hotel to interview me. She comes dressed as Castro's girlfriend, with two photographers, and immediately yells at me for my hatred of Latin America and nefarious influence in the Civil War.

"How come Latin America has crawled into my act? Have you read my book?" I ask sharply. "Nefarious? I was barely born."

Despite her threats, screams, and hysteria, I rapidly extricate myself. After finishing with *La Argentinita* I go on a fishing trip. I telephone a member of the Barcelona publishing claque and indulge in a breezy chat. *Spaniards think American women are slightly crazy. Naïve. They won't know what to expect, what is normal behavior for an American. So turn that to your own advantage. You can do and say anything you want; they won't be able to figure it out.*

I have noticed that in each culture men attribute to women the traits they don't value for themselves. In America women have always been allowed to be sensitive and aesthetic. In Spain women are presumed to be practical and soulless. Literature is left to the men.

When the man asks me how things are going for my book, I become chatty. Breezy. "Look," I say, sunny-voiced, a regular Girl Scout, "this book represents my own special view of politics . . ."

"Yes, Juan Goytisolo explained that."

"I would hate my point of view to become mixed up with the ideas of others—that would only cause confusion, and could irritate people. I suppose this sounds very American female to you," I continue, breathy, into the phone, "but I want to go it alone. Do my own publicity. Be myself." (*So, have you a choice?*)

I hear his laughter. "Your agent has pegged you wrong. She described you as Goytisolo's friend on Cloud 9. As if you couldn't find your way out of a Spanish maze—you don't sound so lost to me."

Spaniards always think Spain is so complicated, all foreigners will lose the map; then, if they create sufficient confusion so that people ignore them, they complain nobody is interested in their country. I make a mental note to fire the agent from Barcelona. Her I need like a hole in the head.

Annoyed at her negative buildup, I telephone and peevishly ask her to show some interest in the publication of my book, as, after all, I am a foreigner here.

"But, Barbara," she trills in her thick Catalan accent, "we are only poor people from the *meseta*, what do you expect?"

"Since when have you lived in the *meseta?* Madrid is in the *meseta*. You are a rich Catalan." I am amazed at my own aggression.

Smoothly she gives me some dopey reasons why my book will have a coming out only in Madrid. Ordinarily some sort of event is organized for writers in both the cities. She suggests that four or five people at a small dinner will be more tasteful for Madrid, as big publishing parties have gone out of style.

"Since when? Try good taste on some other writer—I want the Hotel Velázquez." I slam down the phone.

I am risking my heart. If I fuck up in Madrid, I would be crushed, but it's bad to be too cagey. I want my book to be read; I have to go after public recognition. Once I make that decision, I refuse the luxury of depression; I sense that at this moment I have unusual psychic energy. I feel amazingly free. No man I have cared for stands in my way. My father, Paco, Pallach, Harold, Clancy, Dr. Schur, Juan. I feel that the men I carry around inside my head have given me permission to go zoom. I have their benediction. No, I don't feel alone or powerless. I don't perceive the literary and political mafias as being all-powerful. Sure, I could fail a little, or be made to appear foolish or ludicrous, and my heart would smash, but not permanently, and what could a few small groups of people really do but throw up several annoying roadblocks?

The Communists, or ex-Communists, all formed by the same authoritarian glue, attempt to guard history like priests preserving dogma. A ritualistic bunch, they feel they have dibs on the left, freelancers make them nervous. So who is this New Yorker horning in?

Certain people with certain credentials are allowed to take prescribed positions against the Party, but they are permitted to be an enemy because it is understood their criticism stems from their desire to reshape it into a purer vessel. In medieval jousts, opposing princes stand on opposite hills overlooking the prescribed battlefield. At dawn, a Shakespearean knight gives a yell, the black army charges the white army in a straight line. Now, none of this jousting would be fun if a pack of ill-assorted, unannounced Gypsies straggled into battle from a third hilltop. History, as I pointed out to Inez's mother, doesn't let in just any class of people.

Well, I am the Gypsy from the third hilltop messing up a clean fight. What class of enemy I am eludes the authoritarian left. But how could the orthodox left locate me? I come out of Miss Hogan's drama classes for the gifted child. During the beginning of the Second World War, over on Lexington Avenue, if your father paid your tuition, you were considered a gifted child. The neighborhood—East Side, Upper Eighties—was dismal; there was a small dusty beauty parlor with wax mannequins of young women with marceled hair and pink dots in the middle of either cheek, and next to it a medical supply store with trusses and torsos in the window. Mentally I joined the wax marceled heads onto the trussed torsos. The third shop was a funeral parlor.

Miss Hogan loved being avant-garde. All of her pupils were highly artistic. "The Voice of History," she would boom. "The Voice of History . . . is theater." Awestruck, I was mesmerized by her droning voice, the way she salivated while letting her young charges in on the real lowdown of the world of the theater. "Dialogue, emotion, improvisation . . ." She enumerated her private litany of the steps to the sacred gate, which opened on to the higher calling to which we, her twelve, aspired. "The Voice of History, as exemplified in the Living Newspaper production of *One Third of a Nation* . . . is true Art."

The end of each spring Miss Hogan would persuade our parents to chip in extra money, and she would rent for one night a Polish beer hall that possessed a stage made out of a rounded platform—other nights small, unknown jazz bands played there. We, her charges, performed solo routines in what she called Miss Hogan's Program of Individual Improvisations of the Gifted Child.

For one month I worked on my act. Miss Hogan impressed me— but what was she trying to teach me? Was this Voice of History some omnipotent offstage God? What was the living-newspaper theater? I didn't have a clear bead on what I was being taught. When was I a newspaper? A person? A feeling? News, fact, the Voice of History? My mother lived in London. I turned on the radio. Hitler had been in Vienna for what then seemed all my short past life. Hitler, the Polish Corridor, Europe, war, London Blitz. The Voice of History and me.

I bought glue from Woolworth's that smelled of flour and stuck to my fingers like pasty soured milk. I collected copies of the *Herald Tribune*, the *Times*, the *Sun*, the *World Telegram*, and *Collier's* magazine. LONDON EVACUATED. BLITZ CONTINUES.

Who is the Voice of History? Am I a feeling? A newspaper? A living newspaper? Hours before the big May evening, I turned myself into a newspaper collage, pasting up my entire body with scraps of newsprint and war stories, leaving four holes—eyes, nose, and mouth— for breathing and seeing. I filched my father's black top hat, one of Mickey's creaky red-label records. When it was my turn to perform, I raced onto the stage, flapping my arms rooster-style. I am a newspaper. I am a war. I am the Voice of History, the Voice of History. I cued my acting pal, Sara, waiting in the wings; she started the record going. And I broke into my version of a cakewalk, singing funky-black style:

> *Down by the riverside,*
> *I'm gonna lay mah weepons down*

Down by the riverside.
I'm gonna lay mah weepons down
And ah ain't gonna study wahr no mahr.
Down by the riverside,
Down by the riverside,
I'm gonna meet my mother thyuh—
Down by the riverside, I'm gonna meet my sugar thyuh—
Down by the riverside, I'm gonna meet my brother thyuh—
And we ain't gonna study wahr no mahr.

(The Communist Party wants to locate me?) "I am the Voice of History, I am a feeling, I am a newspaper, I am a person, I am the Blitz. THE LONDON BLITZ CONTINUES." I flapped my arms, grinning madly at an unseen audience in the dark of the Polish beer hall auditorium. I continued my frenetic cakewalk while barking out daily reports I had learned from my current-events class. EUROPE IS IN DARKNESS. The newsprint and glue had combined and made a suffocating smell under my nose. But triumphant, my newsprint-covered body continued to whirl on the stage platform. "Bunny, now, Bunny, Bunny, please, that's enough." Miss Hogan's tremulous voice calls to me from the unsteady cardboard wings of the stage. She sounds hysterical. But firm, I wait on the stage. Until the curtain fell and I came out front, to get my applause.

My room in the Wellington—in the old part of the hotel—looks over the patio and swimming pool, a home away from home. After a burst of energy to organize the party at the Velázquez, in spite of my messages to myself, I suddenly depress. I bury my head under the covers and stay in bed until noon, listening to the canned music piped in through the radio near the bed—a nasal mixture of *Cante Jondo* and Rolling Stones. The housekeeper finally knocks and asks if I am all right, she isn't used to me staying in the room so long. Prodded, I dress and get moving.

Pepe is flying in from Paris for the party and Nicolás from New York. So is Inez, who works for BA. So why am I so profoundly crushed? Mentally I put a scalpel inside my head, determined to examine in a clear light my fantasies. *All your life you have attached yourself to certain kinds of men, aiding and abetting them, hand in hand, while you applaud their moral stance. Brightest girl in the class with the brightest boy. And Spain was first-rate territory. But the little girl's original dream was never the solo act. If Juan Goytisolo had wanted to be with you at the Velázquez—which is symbolic, not literary—like your being at the airport when Nicolás came back to Spain, then you would have maintained the illusion of the two of you being together. Instead, he wants you to visit him in Casablanca because he can't decide just how open is an open marriage. But you can't get hooked into his ambivalence now. Let go of the myths or you will end up with nothing. So maybe you would have made a nifty mistress and saloonkeeper to some bright, lofty-ideas guy; you would have typed up his ideas, read what he wrote, and passed the brandy on time, but that was another century, other dreams and schemes. Now, Bunny, you are solo. A considerable amount of what you did in Spain you did on your own, you write on your own, and you think on your own. Paco, Harold, Schur, Pallach—all of them dead now, as well as your old man. Have a temper tantrum, but none of them is going to reincarnate and show up at the Velázquez, so get on with it.*

Once I get it clear in my head that I care desperately about what happens to my book in Spain, I move rapidly. Realizing that there won't be copies of it available in time, I Xerox the galleys myself. I have also brought with me, for just such an emergency, copies of the American edition. I have certain advantages. As an American I can't be shamed as easily as a Spaniard, who would be embarrassed to actively promote a book. I write a flier on myself and my work, which I also Xerox. The Seix Barral salesman (another Juan) stationed in Madrid is intrigued with the way I go about things. I tell him, habits picked up in the civil rights movement and among the feminists. I take a huge stack of the fliers over to a Socialist conference and explain to the woman seated at the desk in the main lobby that I have a book coming out; several of the people in it are Socialists. I calmly tack one of the sheets on the memo board and leave a nice pile nearby, with the date on it of the Velázquez happening. The woman appears surprised, but makes no objection.

Willy-nilly we plan the Velázquez evening. In Spain books are presented; usually several of the author's friends talk about the work. Juan Benet will talk about Paco and growing up in Madrid during the late forties; Nicolás will describe Cuelgamoros and exile life in Paris. I want to avoid, though, a sentimental situation. I insist that we keep the atmosphere "light." Juan García Hortelano offers to round out the panel with comments on my style. He also promises me to let fresh air into the proceedings. "You want frivolous, frivolous. Yes, yes, I understand."

What is missing is a woman on the panel. Rosa Pereda helps me go through the files in her office at *El País*. There are very few literary ones from my generation, or younger. There is still an enormous vacuum of women in the arts. I turn to Rosa: "How about you?" She is delighted. "I'll bring Marcos's mother. You can put in a good word for me with Naomi—before I marry him I want her to understand that I, Rosa Pereda, am not personally responsible for the nutty Inquisition—" She sighs. "I wish she would *like* me."

"She will when you have a child."

"She's promised to help pick curtains for our apartment."

"Your mother's in Santander, you want to continue working—so let her worry about them. Rosa, travel light."

I had given one of the Xeroxed galleys to Juan Tomás de Salas, the publisher of *Cambio 16*. When I get back to the Wellington, Xavier Domingo, now Salas's right-hand man, telephones me from Valencia, where he is covering a story. The book has moved him tremendously; it rings true to his own experiences in Paris. When he arrived in France—just a few years after the period covered in my book—he had heard stories of the terrible sufferings of his compatriots, but the details had been hazy. The account has jolted him. "It's the story of the independent left, what they did, who they were, and what happened to them." Xavier is excited. He tells me he has talked to Salas, and unless something big breaks, they plan to use the book as the cover story for the week of February 28. Could we meet in the hotel the following morning, and can he have the exclusive? I agree, and the next day he comes over.

No longer the poor bohemian writer living on the fringes of Left Bank Paris life, Xavier seems sharper and infinitely richer. Metamorphosis. He sits in the large armchair in my room, glasses on, and reads quickly. Abruptly he looks up. "You do realize what you have here? If a twenty-year-old Spanish student in Paris could publish in a home-made magazine—*Península*—so much information on the Russian trials, what happened to Radek and so forth, well, then all the facts were in—"

"Xavier, *of course* the facts were in. There were debates then between Sartre and Camus about the Russian concentration camps. In Paris everything was known, it was just a question of picking your favorite church."

"Here almost nothing was known, which is why so many intellectuals became Communists as a protest against Franco. But why did men like Semprún—a fair amount older than Paco Benet—remain blind to the Communist Party until so late? Until they were expelled in the sixties?" He has begun to interview me.

"Oh, Xavier, so much has been written on this . . . why people fail to notice the obvious, what finally triggers them. I suppose it's like a bad marriage. You keep pouring more and more energy in, in order not to admit you've devoted your life to the wrong cause. What's interesting is that, in nearly all accounts written by ex-Communists, their defection almost never comes from some outside information. Almost never do they say, I happened to be reading Koestler and eureka. No, nearly always it is a slow, painful account of a dawning awareness of savageries within the group. I've never been a joiner, but groups that can mobilize people's instinct to do good, plus their natural ambition and need for group protection, obviously can exert a lot of power. Defectors have to be strong enough to undergo some loss of identity."

Xavier is intrigued with the symposium Paco published on the Spanish left in Paris. "Why, it's early oral history." There, in neat order, is a lengthy account, answers to the many questions Paco had asked: where each group on the left stood, where they had been, and where they were going. The answers of the various leaders are interesting. I had remembered that Carrillo chose to ignore the symposium, but probably due to my own prejudices, I had forgotten how difficult Rodolfo Llopis, the head then of the Spanish Socialists, was, and that he had also refused to participate in our symposium.

"How did Paco go about it?"

"He took me along with him, and he just badgered and argued with each of the exile groups until they answered his questions."

"What did you think of the exiles?"

"The truth is, I felt I was talking to old men—but now I realize they might have been only forty or fifty—I think they found Paco odd because he belonged to no political group. Spaniards then had no idea what a cultural anthropologist was. And then his bringing me along . . . It all seemed to them very un-Spanish. Paco was fond of saying that the real revolution in Spain needed to start in the kitchen . . ."

"Why did a Spanish student with a safe berth in Paris, during the worst of times in Spain, decide to turn around, go back into Spain, and start pulling people out of camps? Especially as he had no political ties."

I hesitate. I could describe my own past, but I don't want to use my 1970s tone to explain Paco Benet. I explain to Xavier that I can answer only for one brief period in Paco's life. Leila, his Iranian wife, occasionally corresponded with me. True, their marriage belonged to a later period, but managing not to trespass on someone else's territory is a tricky business. I certainly didn't want Harold's ex-girlfriends overstating their perceived claim on him. So I am reserved. I think Paco's motivation came from his father being killed in the Civil War; it was unclear which side had killed him, and Paco *wanted* to believe he had died on the Republican side. When you are twenty, how your father died matters.

Xavier finally picks what Paco had written in *Península.*

> Neither youth nor history can pardon failure. In order to prevent the next generation from losing their way in a Stalinist quagmire . . . we need to overcome the past, forget those Spanish liberals who were unable to convert their energies towards a productive future. We must create that future ourselves, with our bare hands, all, now, we possess.

The style seems more rhetorical than I remember it, lacks Paco's wit, and doesn't indicate his desire to be politically eclectic, not fall in the Stalinist or professional anti-Communist camp. What it does recall is the mood of 1948; the remains of the old Spanish underground, left over from the Civil War, had finally been overwhelmingly defeated. There was an enormous need to do something new, to prove one's manhood and that France was not all powerful.

"Was Mailer in Spain?"

The question surprises me. Frequently I had been asked how many wives Mailer had had, what had he thought of the success of the escape, what had been his relation to his sister, Barbara—but never, had he gone to Spain. Like all good journalists, Xavier intensifies the story. "Yes, the winter before Barbara and I came to Paris. He went with Bea, his first wife, and Paco. They were making connections for the eventual prison break. I've never focused on that because it happened before I arrived in Paris."

"Can you call Mailer? Can we interview him on his own trip in

'47?" Xavier talks rapidly. "Look, these photos you've brought—they seem too contemporary. Can Nicolás bring over pictures from '48, the car, yourself, the Spanish crew?"

Schur was right. You always leave some part of the past obscured. If those photos are lost, you have no copies. Schur would say, Don't waffle. Don't hold back at the last minute. Xavier can't lose all the photos; take the chance, give him some and keep some.

"You don't trust me, you think I'm going to pull a number on you—look, if I have my way, you've got the cover story in *Cambio*—how many writers get that? Barbara, you don't understand. I was that poor Spanish exile kid in France who cared about the Anarchists and got pushed around by the French. I promise you I won't pull a fast one."

This is your chance. All the magazines, the pamphlets, the record of the left Paco made, you can dump all of it on Spain, where it belongs, and new people will come along and make a fresh history out of it, whatever they want. And you go free.

I stare at Xavier. "I'll call Nicolás—and Norman."

The next morning we do the interview with Norman. At a prearranged hour we telephone him from the Wellington. I am on an extension in the bathroom, in case Eduardo Chamorro runs into a language problem. Years ago Norman had pointed out to me that the important thing in an interview is to decide in advance what you intend to say, and to keep going. "Don't take time out to listen to the other guy's argument—by the time you think through his point of view, the program will be over. Just slough ahead—let the other guy worry about the non sequiturs."

Norman means to do me a favor. Ignoring questions on Spain, he rapidly says several attractive, quotable things about me. There is no way an interviewer could cut out those remarks and still land up with a coherent statement. A lesson for me in how to give the interview *you* want, rather than be dominated by the interviewer.

After Eduardo hangs up, he cracks up laughing. "You mean a New York Jew was lurking in Spain in '47? Five years before the French Communists? *Madre mía!*"

He makes me feel less strained—more my zany self, less Ms. Politics. It's good to hear Jew mentioned and not mean Zionist imperialist or six million dead; it's good, simply, to laugh. A private joke wildly unfair to Jorge Semprún, who had, after all, spent twelve years in the un-

derground in Spain. But I know why Eduardo is making fun—the left
has begun to hang over everyone's head like a large, damp cloud.

The next afternoon Xavier invites me and several of the *Cambio* staff
to the most expensive French restaurant in Madrid. All those grim
years in Paris the heart of a lavish man had been beating in Xavier
Domingo's breast. Cash short in France, he had opted for outrageous
bohemia. Frequently what passes for eccentric behavior is merely people with no bucks. The seven-page story he writes on me is headlined:
BOOK BREAKS THROUGH WALL OF SILENCE ON FIRST ANTI-FASCIST NON-
STALINIST OPPOSITION INSIDE SPAIN. He uses my book as a point of
departure for reappraising the Opposition. During the following
months *Cambio* will run many interviews with different groups on
the left. I was in luck: just at the moment *Arriving* was published,
political fashions in Spain abruptly changed. The Communists have
just finished having at each other; they've dragged out their own skele-
tons, and in the new whirligig "independent" suddenly has become
okay. So here I am, a dark horse with great timing living in the Wellington!

I have begun to feel that Casablanca-Madrid is reached by a jitney bus,
I have done the route so often. I take two weeks off just before the
book comes out—and fly down to visit Juan. We had planned this
trip since last summer; I now feel at home in Morocco. Juan recently
has moved from the apartment in the Gueliz to a small house with a
patio inside the Casbah in Marrakech. During the last five years we've
learned to travel well with each other; we even share the same allergies
to cats, smoke, and feather pillows. But the publication of *Arriving*
causes strain. It was Juan who discovered the book in America, he
had emotionally responded to it, he had insisted that Seix Barral publish it. Now, suddenly, with the Velázquez event less than two weeks
away, he is acting very laid back. As if it didn't exist. During our
trip we simply don't discuss what is going on—or not going on—
in Madrid and Barcelona. Then, just before I fly back, we spend a
night at Ninette Bendraho's house in Casablanca, and Ninette
lights into me. "*Merde*, Barbara, you and Juan are awfully oblique
with each other—it's his business to be at that party for you in
Madrid."

"He's writing a long article for *El País* about the book—he says he
prefers doing that."

"*Merde*, that's intellectual, not personal. You're awfully dumb about knowing how to accomplish small things. Sure, you'll use tons of energy to move mountains over some principle, but you haven't a clue how to get a man home for dinner by eight. I think that's why you've made so many changes in your life," she observes shrewdly. "Once the romance is gone—and after they've failed you a few times, Achilles heel showing, you haven't the foggiest idea what you want your man to do for you."

"I certainly don't intend to drag him to Madrid."

"You have to let him know you care. Look, you know Spanish men have been very badly brought up when it comes to women. And they are not used to women who indulge in sensitive double thinks within their own heads—silence means nothing to them. Their women kick, scream, yowl, and put up a tremendous fuss. However much they complain about that style, they really aren't attuned to the over-subtle."

"Juan is plenty subtle."

"Well, you're not doing him or you any favor with all this high and mighty—after all, it isn't just the book—some moments can't be repeated; it is, symbolically, everyone's homecoming. You should never allow things to happen that people can later regret. *Merde*—sometimes you just get down on your knees and give a flamenco scream. And everyone's better off."

But I don't know how to do what Ninette wants of me, and she seems pensive as she watches Juan drive me to Mohammed V to catch the Iberia flight back to Madrid.

I am late. I run toward customs, and briefly turn back. Juan is waving at me. Then I think about Madrid.

The day before the Velázquez party my bedroom unexpectedly converts into a meeting hall. Journalists come and go, friends wander in, waiters keep bringing up fresh platters of small sandwiches. Manolo Lamana, who had been the other student imprisoned in Cuelgamoros whom we had helped escape, is also in Madrid. Manolo and I want to talk to each other—we need to catch up, it's been thirty years. But a Madrid theater critic is holding forth: "My sons think my wife and I have been cretins for remaining Communist. They throw in our faces ecology. What the hell do they **mean** by 'acráta'? Taking off their clothes and fucking in public? Well, Barbara, you certainly are lucky to be publishing an off-beat book now."

Inez arrives the night before the event; she shares my room at the Wellington, and the two of us have a last-minute gab.

Inez is putting turtle cream from the Caribbean on her face and blow-drying her hair; I am lying on my bed in a loose red terry robe and clipping my toenails. Meanwhile, a waiter brings us up supper, lots of scrambled eggs and Scotch and water, with tea for dessert.

"I don't believe the Communist Party is where the real flak is coming from," I say. "I'm simply not important enough. Carrillo is busy making love with Juan Carlos; the level is different. Besides, I do reportage. They would want to convert me into a friend."

"Come on, I'm sure that the wise guys who voted you out of the club never read the manuscript—everyone here, one way or another, is nervous about their past. Maybe some of Juan's pals thought you were pumping him for some supersecrets of the left, about which nobody in America could care less. How could the local paranoids figure that all you and Juan were doing was joyriding and cooking Moroccan pigeon pies?"

"I think I got egg on my face, in Barcelona, from his pals in the rump party—the good guys."

"Three good guys is a crowd—maybe they felt you were horning in on their territory." Inez sighs. "We read Koestler and *The God That Failed* in high school—do we have to do that all over again? Which reminds me, did you bring me those gold-braided belts you can pick up cheap in Fez?"

"I've some nice ones—brown twisted with gold, which will look first-rate in New York, less *ongepotchket* than some of their more glitzy ideas."

"Loewe leather prices are out of sight."

"Goya has a good bunk for shoes and purses, thirty percent off for great Spanish phony Guccis and Diors."

"That my trouble should have come from the good guys." I sigh. "Who would have figured them as swifties?"

"Remember high school days in the AYD?"

"At fourteen we thought Communists were real sexy."

"Not me—my style always was Trotsky."

"You were a Walden kid—more politically sophisticated than us East Side Dalton girls. But no matter how much we *thought* we rebelled against our parents, there was no real split between their culture values and our own. Christ, Inez, your uncle was killed at Teruel. We are merely a continuation of our progressive, liberal, cosmopolitan, intelligent parents—" I yawn sleepily. *Cambio 16* had jokingly referred to Jorge Semprún as *"Rin-Tin-Tin chez les fascistes."* I turn to Inez: "Just a couple of New York progressive-school brats *chez les fascistes."*

When you create a public event, what starts as an idea in your head ceases to belong to you, but becomes transformed and is received as part of other people's lives. The next afternoon, while I am standing in the hall of the Velázquez with Ángel Jasanada and Jorge Edwards, who have flown in from Barcelona as representatives of the publishing house, Seix Barral, I overhear a middle-aged man asking directions from the desk clerk. The man is neatly dressed and mild, he carries an umbrella; it has been raining all day. "Where is the meeting for Paco Benet? A classmate—we all went to grade school together—told me I should come here for the memorial. Is this the right place?"

Although the books are just now arriving from Barcelona, it is already a heavy seller here. Inside the hall, Paco's sister, Marisol, and his mother, Doña Teresa, are talking to Eduardo Chamorro; he has just handed Doña Teresa a copy of *Cambio 16.* "It's a split cover," he explains. "The crisis in the Suárez cabinet couldn't be overlooked—" Doña Teresa, in her eighties, looks wonderful, her hair glossy, her blue eyes intense; she has chosen to wear long fat pearls and a fox collar knotted loosely around her neck. She takes the copy of *Cambio* and studies the photos—she is used to her son, Juan being in the newspapers, but Paco's name, until now, has never been mentioned. She skims the story, rolls up the magazine, and puts it in her black purse, which she quickly snaps shut.

Doña Teresa was the daughter of a Basque industrialist; feisty, she left home in her teens, went to work in a newspaper kiosk in Barcelona, where she met her lawyer husband while selling him postage stamps. They married and moved to Madrid. She promptly divorced him (during the Republic) for having too many mistresses, but after his murky murder in the early days of the Civil War, she became his widow. She was left with three children, one nephew, and no money; opened her own cafeteria, where Paco helped her, and took up with artists and writers like Pío Baroja, and developed a slightly demimondaine reputation.

Eduardo and others cluster around Teresa, point out that now Paco is being acclaimed according to his generation as having been a "sort of young Spanish Malraux" and one of the first Spanish anthropologists. The statement isn't accurate in the sense that there are no second Malrauxs, Faulkners, or Hemingways. But what is true is that both her sons were very talented. Teresa tells Eduardo, Rosa Regás, and myself that she plans to write her own story. Which she does when she is eighty-two. She would call it *A Girl from Villefranche*, and it would be published.

"In the war I risked my life hiding people from both sides in my house. One time, risking being caught in a volley, I tracked down a beautiful whole ham and shared it with everyone who lived there. Do you think, the next day, those whose lives you have saved know your name? Never." She grasped my hand. "Never overhelp—but remember, I'm on your side—"

Before I go to the platform, Rosa Regás stops me; she is convulsed in laughter. "If a Spaniard fails you, a woman is supposed to have the grace to wilt. You're not supposed to show up, happy as a clam, with Norman Mailer in *Cambio* saying you are wonderful."

I glance at the crowded hall, blink at the clicking cameras; the Madrid hum and buzz had worked; young journalists, school pals of Paco and Juan, family, Goya, Josefina, Fernando, Alberto, campaigners from the Toledo trail, politicos, many of the old Paris crowd, Inez, Carlos Vélez and his daughter—all are present. I notice that Isabel (Manolo Lamana's first wife) is leaning against Pepe's shoulder and crying. *Pepe has always been a looker, and Isabel always has had a thing for him . . .* I listen to Juan describe me; suddenly I turn to him and in a small-girl voice complain, "Can't you say I was a first-rate mathematician?"

"Were you really? I don't remember that phase—"

The two of us are sparring, brother-and-sister-fashion; the audience is listening intently. Meanwhile, Nicolás, and finally Rosa Pereda, have picked up the thread. *Say something wonderful about Spain. Something moving, about history and friends and memory and hanging in there. What's this back-at-the-old-stand business of trying to prove you had dibs on being the smartest girl in the class? That's not what your audience came to hear.* GIVE.

When Rosa finishes, there is a silence. I hesitate; in a low voice I mumble that in the future I hope more women will be on the podium, I thank Seix, the audience, and abruptly I shut up. *Not made for great moments.*

Ángel Jasanada tells me we've run out of copies of the book; the young journalists crowd me, they want signed copies for their lovers and cousins, the atmosphere *smells* good; I hear the right Madrid buzz, without that *bzzzz* nothing takes off in this town. Pepe's brought a display with him from Paris of stuff we used in the Resistance. For the first time in thirty years I see the red-and-white FUE student stickers we had pasted on Madrid walls; frequently I felt those stickers had been a figment of my imagination. "Pepe, you kept them. The stickers were real."

A large-eyed, dark-haired, pretty woman patiently waits for the pack of journalists to thin out. It's Bisagra, the widow of Carmelo Soria, Nicolás's friend who was murdered in Chile. We stare at each other for a few seconds; then we embrace. "When it's over," she says, shaping her mouth into a smile, "we will get together."

Afterward a bunch of us go out to dinner; María Hortelano advises me to shut up. "Now that Cuelgamoros, willy-nilly, has become one of the left's legends in Spain, keep it a family secret that you were never a true heroine but just an ambitious American girl. Legends," María insists, "can be nice." She sighs. "Spain's getting too emotionally skinny on our sardonic diet. We need to let some things be."

But Spain is just askew. During dinner, we hear that the Duchess of Alba, a widow in her fifties, has raided the fashionable left; she has announced she is marrying Jesús Aguirre, an ex-priest and cultural figure of the Opposition. Several of us stay on in the restaurant until late; then we walk through Madrid at four in the morning. We keep laughing at the story of the Duchess of Alba and the left. Most people receive their engraved invitations for my book party after the event. Which is the way it is always done in Madrid.

The next morning Inez, Pepe, and Nicolás leave Madrid. I speak briefly to Ángel Jasanada; although he is delighted the book is doing well in Madrid, he avoids giving me a reply when I ask what the plans are for Barcelona. "It's not really necessary for you to make the trip." There is no point in pressing him. He is a good businessman, he seems to like me; whatever is keeping the book from existing in Barcelona is out of his control.

The next day, before leaving for America, I drop over to *El País* and *Cambio* to thank the journalists who helped me. Xavier reaches in his drawer and returns to me the packet of photos. "I filched the honky-tonk one of you and Paco . . ." in the Coney Island snap we are posing behind a cardboard cutout of naked bodies soaping each other. Reprinted in *Cambio*, it looks like real bodies—wacky and wild. Paco and I are laughing at each other.

"I wondered where that snap came from."

"Did you mind? I saw it underneath a pile of other pictures lying on your bed. I wasn't sure you would let me use it—so I just took it."

"No, that's okay, but Norman Mailer said he thought I was cool; he never said anything about my balls being well hung."

Xavier gazes at me. "Cool isn't Spanish—besides, your book is number two on the best-seller list."

I look at him pensively. "Thanks, Xavier—really."

And when I go into a bank to change a small traveler's check, the teller studies me, my signature, then whispers something to the other men behind the cage. "Are you she?" they ask. The next morning I fly home to America.

28

Ninette was right—a year later, spring 1979, in Juan Goytisolo's house in Marrakech, I still feel wounded by his failure to have shown up. Now I irritate easily. I have just finished reading a piece of Juan's in which he describes how Stalin eliminated Trotsky from official memory. In the patio in Marrakech, I harangue him. "Why should I weep for Trotsky? On the road back to Spain, it seems to me, one day it was the two of us together, picketing in front of the UN, signing petitions; then boom, something got turned around. One morning I wake up—you, the revolutionary, the sexual-freedom fighter, are a solid European citizen, while I, with a pile of debts, but for fighting back in the nick of time, am nearly mistaken for the queen of the CIA. Weep for Trotsky? Why should I weep for Trotsky at three in the afternoon when I can weep for me?"

Juan stares at me—it's always hard for me to figure out when he is listening to the rhythms of my speech, to chop it up in fragments for future use, and when he hears me. "You adopt these metaphysical positions—you are pro-marginal," I continue; "hooray for the outsider. So how come you are establishment and me the outsider? I never felt marginal until I met you." I clatter about the patio, wearing a caftan designed by the French to look native Moroccan. "No wonder Sartre was such a big-time success, merchandizing existentialism. Warmed-over Deweyism," I mumble, "causing a sensation on the Left Bank. You become the sum of your acts, rather than your words. Hah, he can say that again. You people make no connection between what you say and what you do—"

Juan shows his anger at me less verbally. He takes off for his Arab world. When I complain about boredom in the gardens of the Casbah, he snaps, Couldn't I read a book or do some writing?

"I didn't come to Marrakech to stare alone at the blood orange trees or to bone up on the world's great books."

Our desire for one another is disintegrating; the excitement, the private world of fantasy, after five years has collapsed. I take my own revenge: before Juan disappears on his long walks, I ask him to drop me off at the Hotel Mamounia. I throw a terry-cloth robe over my bathing suit and carry a beach bag with suntan oil, bathing cap, and goggles. He has no legitimate reason to object to my swimming. Nor can he insist I wait for him alone, in the garden, like a pasha's girl-friend.

His face mottles with sour anger, but he drives me each morning to the hotel and picks me up there in the early afternoon. I dive, the pool becomes a narcotic, and I swim away from him, away from this part of my life, away from his intensity, talent, betrayal, fury, and shy love. I want to be myself again. I am fulfilling his prophetic dream of losing me in the pool of a lush hotel. Now, years later, in this extraordinary place with gardens and fountains inside the pool, I swim away from him, repossessing myself. In behaving like a typical *turista* carrying a tote with sunglasses and Elizabeth Arden sun-block cream, I know I am smashing his—our—fantasy world. I have destroyed my place in his private Morocco.

I stand in front of the hotel, at the appointed hour, my hair drip-ping, wrapped in terry cloth. Juan drives up and yells at me to quick jump into the car. As if the hotel driveway is foul goods. When we drive to Meknès, Juan evens the score by going off with an Arab, and becomes high on kif, which I loathe as much as he hates the Ma-mounia. When Juan collects himself, he realizes that, in our mean volley, I have retaliated by starting up a mild flirtation with a Sorbonne-trained Arab doctor.

Christ, leavetaking is awful. Had I been Juan's wife, I could have moved over, converted hot passion into loyal old shoe. But that slot is filled; Juan hardly needs two eternally loyal old shoes, and I want ballast.

We fought so hard in Meknès; in the old days, I would have abruptly run away. *You and Juan have planned this trip, you are due to visit Tangier, which you have never seen before; then you are driving to Seville. Goya and Fernando are waiting there for you both. You have a speaking engagement in Seville, local feminists, and Juan has an appearance scheduled at the university. When you were a kid and something went wrong, you always ran away, dazed yourself by taking off to strange places, and panicking. Do it differently; wait until the trip is over, wait until you get to Madrid, get hold of yourself. You are middle-aged and not his wife. Can't fight that; you will have to do something else. You planned to spend three summer weeks with Juan. You have spent some part of five years. Juan's nature is no different from what you knew from day one; maybe you've had better times and he has been more stable than you would have imagined, so what are your complaints?*

After Meknès we drive straight to Tangier. At moments we slip into being old friends again, as Juan retraces with me his Tangier, the square with the snake charmer, the place with the singing birds, he takes me to a *Tangerino* restaurant where the Erotic Boy dances for the patrons, and I burst out laughing. At the table to our right is a young American couple, oil company groupies; they are driving up through North Africa after a stint in Libya. On our left is a leather-beaten, old layabout French couple.

Gregarious, they tell us they bed down in the back of their car and travel the world on a small teacher's pension. Certain types of French who are not ratty can be very nice. *Long-in-the-tooth good companions.* God, how I envy them. Our last day in Tangier I ask Juan if we can visit Paul Bowles; American friends have asked me to look him up. Juan is hesitant, but finally, through other friends, we reach Bowles, who asks us over. He lives in a pleasant, medium-sized apartment crowded with books and lots of plants near the living room window. Bowles asks me about publishing in the United States, what I have read of Jane Bowles; her death still seems to upset him. Lean, aquiline-nosed, ascetic, he asks me why American prose now is so bad. "Have they forgotten that good American writing is clean, short, strong sentences? Writers have begun to use so many adjectives, poor stuff—"

Several young Americans are guests that afternoon at Bowles's apartment. The room is soon thick with hashish. Intimidated by Bowles, I am too embarrassed to mention that I am allergic to it. Nervously I jump up, hoping nobody will see what I am doing. I walk over to the windows, pretending to be interested in the view. But they are closed. "Is this the kitchen? How charming." I wander through the small apartment, inhaling whiffs of oxygen when nobody is looking. Out of desperation, I disappear for a moment into a small closet. "Oh, I thought it was a library door . . ." I make a lame excuse about wanting to check the views from the other side of the building, and get a little relief by standing outside in the front hall near the elevator. When I come back into the apartment, Paul Bowles is looking puzzled. Juan seems puzzled. "I think I am allergic to kif." Finally I confess, as I am beginning to look like a restless wacko, "I am asthmatic."

"Oh," says Bowles, "I was wondering . . ."

Juan stands up; we tell Bowles how wonderfully he writes about North Africa, and we leave. As a desert type I am miscast. In the elevator Juan whispers to me, "Every time I looked up, you had disappeared. First your head, near the window; then half of you in that closet, suddenly you vanished into the hall . . ." Juan smiles at the nuttiness of it all—for a moment our old complicity takes over. Downstairs we walk out into the sun; the sea storm has cleared away. The next morning we will be taking the ship to Algeciras.

I lean back against the low-slung wooden deck chair of the S.S. *Cádiz.* We left Tangier at noon. The ship first hugs the African coast. A city mind goes high; the blood thins, spiked by the good effects of quantities of salt air and sun. Always an optimistic dreamer, I tell myself, age, for a woman, isn't the problem it used to be. It's coming into style for a woman to be *seasoned,* no teeny-bopper. So, if age is wonderful, why is Juan eyeing those young Moroccan women who claim to be Marxists? No, the men I have lived with haven't always been my best friends—I try snoozing, stretched out on the deck chair—nor my worst enemies.

Juan, pensive, shoulders hunched in familiar semiarc, stares out at Tangier. His favorite writing city recedes in the distance. He has dibs on the territory, he has staked out and well used his claim; out of a writer's *politesse,* I avert my gaze, not wanting to overknow what will never belong to me. Still, let Juan keep his own hands in his pockets when it comes to Manhattan and Madrid.

In these quick times even a short ship's crossing takes on the adventurous aura of the old sea crossings of the *Île de France* and the *Queen Elizabeth*. In my twenties, had a man wanted sex with me the day I noticed a wild cheek hair in my reflection in the bathroom mirror or a bad monthly smell rising from between my thighs, I would have either savaged myself or the man. In my thirties, if I had found myself on a trip with a lover and the affair had soured, I would have felt impelled to destroy the vacation. Verbally homing in to the ugly essential truths, the mutual failures of character were then what seemed to matter. Now I just want to take. This day, this cream-colored Citroën, Juan, this ship, this voyage, April, North Africa, this Spain. I've already yowled to him my wounds. Now the rest of the deep truths—who loved whom, who betrayed, who botched—will hold until Madrid. Small gains in character? I twist my face to trap the sun's solar rays.

"During World War II Tangier was the biggest spy center in Europe—"

We have had this conversation before. "Like in Hedy Lamarr. Charles Boyer." I sigh. "Endings of films and books that used to appear tragic won't work anymore."

"Like what?"

"Oh, departures. Ship's whistles. When I was a child a ship's voyage could mean leaving forever. Think of the nineteenth-century Russians, the great train-station partings, Anna, the dense fog, the cold, the snow. Potato-famine Irish waving back as they left Ireland. Emigrants leaving Europe for the New World, knowing they would never go back. The shrieks of despair of the old folks left behind. With Apex fares, there are no more permanent good-byes; maybe the late twentieth century isn't as cruel as we think." I look up at Juan; his intense, cobalt eyes appear focused, as though he is trying to catch my wandering thoughts, but he seems to be seeing beyond me, nose-diving into his own past.

"Let's go inside for lunch," he says finally.

Gibraltar comes up on the coast side while we are eating. Suddenly the Spanish municipal campaign election news flashes onto the TV screen in the second-class dining room. The Andalusian waiter insists on serving us leathery fried steaks; a smell of rancid oil rises from the plates. "Why can't we have some of that roast chicken you brought the couple in front of us?" Juan asks.

"They are having the special supplementary menu."

"Can't we?"

"The menu is special."

"Aren't we special?"

"Because no." The waiter is determined to unload his bad steaks on us; he pretends he is obeying the orders of an absolute higher authority.

Soon we see Algeciras on the left. The Spanish coastal landscape is urban; black smoke and anonymous new buildings, a town of cheap tourism and heavy industry. The S.S. *Cádiz* bumps to a halt. We have landed. Juan runs a comb through his hair. We join the line of passengers waiting to go down to the lower deck, where the cars are parked. When we drive past customs, Juan remarks, pointing, "Police dogs—they are drug-addicted on hashish, then starved. Each boatload new batches of tourists get caught."

The S.S. *Cádiz* has taken slightly more than two hours to travel from Africa to the Andalusian coast. Seen that way, the ancient Arab conquest of Spain was inevitable. Juan heads straight for the highway—we want to be in Seville before dark.

In Seville we stay at Goya and Fernando's house, in the old section, on Plaza Elvira. This time, Juan comes with me when I speak to a group of feminists who call themselves Prímula; we hold one small meeting in the Libreria Fullman, on Calle José Antonio. *You notice a middle-aged man seated on one of the benches. He smiles at you. Well, he says, I didn't expect to read in the newspapers that Harold's wife would be giving a talk today in Seville. John Murra, anthropologist, friend of Harold in that time before your time. You introduce him to Juan, and you say, John was one of those kids in the Lincoln Brigade, one of those heroes. John smiles and mumbles, It was part of being young. He is here using the Archive of the Indies, doing anthropological research on Peru. John says in a wild, reckless moment, he thought of retiring in Spain. He smiles his crooked grin, his dark, Rumanian-Chicago eyes look quizzical. A cool country now, he says. I think I prefer America. The feminists come from upper-class, conservative Seville homes. It's hard for them to understand that women have different battles in America. Lack of supports, lack of family, too much mobility. These women cannot imagine a world in which women have no families. When Juan speaks, several days later, at the university, the main auditorium is mobbed.*

You, Goya and Fernando are seated on the platform. Juan causes tremendous excitement; you hear the wild applause, and suddenly the child in you is satisfied. You take walks in Seville with Juan and Fernando, room by room; Fernando explains the Alcazar to both of you. Fernando and another architect in charge of preservation of the Arab palace smell the stones, searching for false repairs, centuries old. They pat, poke, smell. Fernando explains the history of the gardens to Juan, you watch both of them walk ahead. You listen again to the dreamlike story of the caliph who wished to please his bride, who yearned for snow. He built a garden of layered snow blossoms, blanketing the Alcazar in white. You smell the orange, the Arab cement, the snow blossoms. You watch Fernando walk ahead with his arm resting on Juan's shoulder, as he did so many years ago, first with Paco, then with Juan Benet. Paco died and Juan grew away from Fernando, creating a void. When Fernando heard the applause for Juan at the university, he was listening to the applause he had wanted for Paco and Juan. The child in you delights at Juan's applause for the same reason as Fernando: Juan fits into some ancient dream you have concocted, an older dream than you talking to feminists in bookstores. For one day it works, the smart girl hand in hand with the bright boy. Magic, but it changes nothing; you have to leave him because he has already left you, and there are his Arab friends, his wife; you can't sustain the magic.

We spend five special days in Seville, just Juan and me, traveling to nearby seaport towns, then coming home nights to Goya and Fernando. We stay close to the old part of town.

Then we drive to Madrid. The last night before I leave for America, Juan Benet, Juan Goytisolo, and the Madrid poet Antonio Sarrión and I finally have dinner together. Sarrión and I stare at each other; soon the two Juans are feeling each other out, each warding off possible aggression; very mildly, tentatively, they compare notes on their mutual childhoods in Arénys de Mar.

"Was your grandfather's house to the north of the old summer casino?"

"On that fork? We must have been less than five minutes away from each other."

"Which years in the war were you there?"

" 'Thirty-seven. 'Thirty-eight, too."

We walk through the Madrid streets, Sarrión and I behind them; the two Juans are gesturing, explaining the geography of the past.

"Now, why couldn't they have met before?" Sarrión whispers to me. "Spain's two best narrative writers—why did they have to indulge in that elaborate dance?"

Lopsided, Juan Benet meeting Juan Goytisolo, just as you are going home to America. Everything you wanted, but the timing all wrong.

The next morning I talk to Juan Goytisolo. *He has already left you but be prepared, he will never forgive you for accepting his leave-taking; his mother died, Juan can't abide finality.*

We are both dressed, my suitcase is closed, we are having breakfast in my room in the Gran Versailles, a small hotel. "Juan"—I am no good at this—"we took two different bedrooms last night—"

"I was sleepy from driving—"

"No, Juan. I've been replaced"—I hesitate, feeling awkward—"by whomever. You have your Arabs, and whoever new—and in the end, you love your wife."

Juan's blue eyes focus on me; he winces when I say, "It's over, I really have to go back to America."

"But I *stayed* with you—five years—we traveled together, and you weren't easy, scared of deserts—and heat, and being lost—I adjusted to all of it. We could go to Turkey in the fall. Couldn't you find a second lover for Christmases and your birthday?"

"Juan, I can't hack these French solutions. Besides, I got hurt. One minute we were together and you were advocating the free life, then Franco is dead, and you return to Barcelona, a married man. Meanwhile, I get stuck in a nineteenth-century doorjamb, playing this old-fashioned mistress role—and to a man who has Arabs yet. Juan, our lives are a mishmash." *You were impressed when you visited Ahmed in Casablanca this time. Ahmed has taken a second wife, Zineb's younger cousin. She has given Ahmed a son; now he has three sons, some real estate, and two wives, whom he treats equally.*

"When I saw Ahmed's baby, I thought, *Merde,* he *has* built a life. He is—within his own framework—coherent. Okay, we Americans are crazy for divorcing at every sneeze, but in the late twentieth century these French 'arrangements,' consisting of double and triple lives, are equally wacky. Look, Juan, I got *hurt.*"

"*Hurt?* In all relations everyone dishes out hurt and gets hurt," he yells at me. "That's not sufficient reason for—for walking out—"

"We never talk—will you now? I have no one," I yell at him. "Don't think I won't miss you."

"*Tu m'emmerdes.* You discombobulate me; I'll think about it after I get to Paris. Do you hear me? *Tu m'emmerdes!*"

I look at him. His eyes have turned a hard blue, his skin a dark olive. I feel his shyness, fury, and anger. Suddenly I slam the door of my room and run down the single flight of stairs to the lobby of the Gran Versailles. Outside, the morning air in Madrid is still fresh. My plane will be leaving in three hours. I walk rapidly. *Don't panic, don't think about it until New York. You will keep feeling pain; then one day, less, then less, then less. Ahmed had a son, you can't do that, but keep moving, build something new.*

I mean to part elegantly, with panache, class, and so forth. *You are leaving him for behavior that was clear to you the first day you met him, the only difference is that the sexual glue that held you together has come unstuck.* But I yak at him during a year's worth of transatlantic correspondence—attack and counterattack.

29

Then, during another hot New York summer, Clancy comes by; he stays for several weeks in Carla's old room. "Look, love," he says, "we've been through a bloody lot these years; you are my down-to-earth, tea-giving, optimistic friend; now get on with it, get yourself a new bloke." The easiest way to follow Clancy's advice is to eliminate the entire Iberian peninsula.

A Yugoslavian friend puts my name on a list for a writers' conference in Belgrade. The Yugoslavian attaché needs a complete literary dossier: I grumble, but take down old cartons from the top of the hall closet; the man wants reviews of all my work, from the earliest days on. There, stuck among the yellowed newspaper clippings, is the text of a telegram sent by Harold to the UN (and reprinted in the newspapers) asking for the release of eighty lawyers, professionals imprisoned in Spain.

I take the time to read it. December 1959: Signed by Saul Bellow, Ralph Ellison, Francisco García Lorca, Norman Mailer, Carson McCullers, Dorothy Parker, Meyer Shapiro ... Eleanor Roosevelt. *Roosevelt, Roosevelt—have you forgotten your own childhood?* I stare at the yellowed petition, out of another point in time. *Eleanor Roosevelt. You need to keep repeating the name, as though to reassure yourself who you were, no, you never came out of the CIA. One cold afternoon you took the petition yourself down to Washington Square, you were a student then at Columbia; you spoke to her secretary. Please, you said, it's very important, please could you ask her to sign it. Come back, the secretary said, tomorrow morning, and we will have a definite answer for you. The next newspaper clip is your own short piece in the* Reporter *magazine, same subject. You characterize the men arrested as being among the future leaders of Spain.* A name catches my attention. Juan Reventós. I stare at it, I sit down, knees crossed, on the floor near the hall closet, surrounded by dusty yellow clippings. The next piece of paper is a letter I wrote Harold from Paris the following June. I had gone over on the *Queen Elizabeth* with Carla and Maria; Harold was due to join us in July. Christ, the long letters people wrote then.

> Dear Hal
> ... please read letters to my family ... I received Mother's letter, tell her, as I really haven't time to write anybody but you. Now: please call my agent and tell her this. Next week (17 or 18) there is going to be a strike in Madrid and Barcelona, she can mention this, and they are all preparing it from Paris. Benjamin Wells in Spain knows about it, but probably his reports will be censored. I will meet group (Goytisolo in a few days) and I have the whole story, plus all the business about the lawyers, there is plenty going on here now ...

That summer you met Juan Goytisolo for the first time; then you, Harold, and the girls drove down through France and spent the summer in Collioure with Teresa and Pallach. The lawyers were released from prison; when you went with Harold to Barcelona, the lawyers who met with both of you told you the Roosevelt name and publicity in American newspapers had worked. On the floor you find more clippings; the truth is always buried in a box of papers on the top shelf of a hall closet. Letters from Teresa and Pallach from the year before, urging you to help get their friend Reventós out of prison; poor Reventós, Teresa had written. Juan Reventós, Juan Reventós.

I keep staring at the name—I get out my old Spanish address book from that period. There it is: Juan Reventós, 35 Calle Angli, and in parentheses, Giordi Petit, Calle Monterola 4, Saint Gervais. It was Giordi who took Harold and me through Barcelona, introducing us to the lawyers; he was elated with the Roosevelt signature and the attention given the case because Harold had sent it on to the International Jurists in Geneva. Without a hall closet we would lose vast chunks of the past. My memory lively now, I think back to my brief visit with Pallach the first time I was in Barcelona after Franco's death. The visit had been in December; by January 11, before we had again been in touch, Pallach was dead. I leave the musty papers from the past strewn on the floor; then I go to the living room, over to my desk. In the first Barcelona notebook is my daily calendar. *Nov. 25, 1976: Joan Reventós (Ariel) canceled. Luis Goytisolo suggested a long list of people for you to see. "You mustn't miss Joan Reventós," he had said, a very intelligent Socialist, one of the political leaders of Barcelona. You didn't associate Joan Reventós, editor, Barcelona, with Juan Reventós, Paris, and prisons. The publication of your own book and being with Juan was what filled your head. The secretary telephoned you: Mr. Reventós is ill, impossible to receive you. That night you met Miguel Núñez, of the PSUC; the two of you relived your mutual past. No, you weren't thinking then about an editor named Joan Reventós.* I stare at the musty clips and match them with my Barcelona notebook. Then I call Juan Gerona, an old friend, who works at the Spanish desk at the UN. I ask him, "Is Pallach's Joan Reventós, *our* Paris Juan Reventós . . . is he the person they now call Joan Reventós?"

"Of course he is the same—Joan Reventós y Carner. His grandfather was a very important man in Barcelona."

"Are you *sure?*" I persist.

"Joan is the Catalan for Juan."

After I hang up, I telephone Nicolás and again go through the questioning. *It doesn't go through my head. Why would a Spanish Socialist I had once helped get out of prison not receive me in his office? Nicolás says, "Yes, the same Reventós." Maybe he forgot your name, if you didn't make the connection, after so many years, why should he?* I am troubled. A Spanish friend in New York says, Don't just leave the matter in limbo, send him a letter, see what he replies. *I take the newspaper clips and send them to Ángel Jasanada. Reventós is an editor at another branch of Seix Barral. I write Ángel to see that the clippings get to Reventós, as he will probably want Eleanor Roosevelt's signature for his personal files. Ángel writes back: He delivered the letter, and he is sure Reventós will be writing to me personally. No reply. Why? People who have been in prison tend to overremember, overidealize those people responsible for getting them out. You make inquiries and are informed that Pallach and Reventós had split. They had become rival Socialists. Pallach's group didn't want a Socialist-Communist coalition. Was your visit politically inopportune? Would it have been awkward for Reventós then to acknowledge that his former friend, now turned political adversary, had worked to get him released from prison? Awkward to acknowledge the push came from Americans? The collage on the cover of the Spanish edition of your book was made from pieces of Península, with your name and Pallach's name. Reventós had to recognize, when the book came out, his own past. Did he feel guilty? Pallach had falsely been called a Fascist and was dead. Did Reventós think when you got in touch with him you were going to make some claim on him, ask him to acknowledge your book, or whatever? Or did he see Pallach's ghost? Doña Teresa said, You run out in the street in the middle of a war and you bring your neighbors a slice of ham, or hide someone's cousin in your bedroom, and the next day, they don't know your name. What happened to you with Reventós has happened, in some form, to everyone.*

In the winter of 1980, *Arriving Where We Started,* renamed *Los Felices Cuarenta,* wins a literary prize in Barcelona, I am sent a first-class air ticket, put up in the Hotel Majestic near the Ramblas, and in my bedroom are florist's boxes with red roses; two years later, my book is noticed in Barcelona. The publicity man from Seix Barral has arranged many press interviews. He asks if I notice how often I am asked by the press to describe how Pallach helped in the Cuelgamoros escape. They now want to hear about Pallach, he has been rehabilitated. And closed doors have opened for me. It turns out Pallach has now become the great Opposition hero of Catalonia. Everyone talks about his charisma, brilliance, and so forth. When I ask about Reventós, I am told he has fallen from favor. Pallach is the big gun, if he had lived, they say, life would be better now in Catalonia. The dead are always better. And no competition. I find vases for the roses. Teresa Pallach drives in from her home in Palafrugell; she spends the night at the Majestic with me, and she comes with me the night I am given my prize—a modern tubular sculpture with my name engraved on it; it is made of very heavy steel. Nobody but Pallach's aide, a few of his close friends, Amadeo and Teresa seem to remember now the campaign held against him; it now all seems a dream. Teresa and I have dinner together; I watch her slowly, neatly divide her fresh fish, carefully forking it the way Europeans do. Her eyes still have the same clear, somber gaze of an old-fashioned liberal trained to educate, not to shock. She teaches linguistics at the university; she tells me she drives in to Barcelona several days a week; the rest of the time she spends in Palafrugell. Her daughter, her grandchildren have remained in France, but they visit her at summer and Christmas. I look at Teresa, one of my many surrogate mothers. When I was young, and my own family seemed too complicated, too sophisticated, I ran off and wanted to be the good little girl to the pure, sober revolutionaries. But another part of me is more frivolous, eclectic, spendthrift. I make my own peace with the gauche divine, or what now remains of the fancy left in Barcelona. Teresa orders sliced oranges and a decaffeinated coffee. I suffer a stomach attack; Teresa gives me a white antacid pill. Here, she says, you should travel with these, they are useful.

"Teresa," I say firmly, "your own book must be published . . ."

"Oh, you know how they are here—cliques. I'm not what they want," she says, stirring her coffee.

"Pallach's in style now," I point out firmly. *"Carpe diem . . .* And the world is bigger than Barcelona; there's Madrid, which is—more various, and New York. Holocaust subjects are okay in English." I tell her, "Look at what you have—as a young girl you walked across the Pyrénées with your mother and sisters; you spent your adolescence in a French concentration camp; you escaped, went to work as a maid for a French family, then in Toulouse joined an underground smuggling Jews to safety; then you met a leader of the Spanish Resistance—Pallach—who had just escaped from jail and a death sentence in Spain, and the two of you married. Teresa, you have so much material," I remind her; "don't get conned into thinking it's not fashionable, not this year's news—if Spaniards aren't interested in what it was like for a young Spanish girl to grow up in a French concentration camp, then, Teresa, sell it outside of Spain—"

The two of you talk late into the night, you remember the days in Collioure; then Teresa kisses you good-bye. Two Uruguayan women interview you for one of the literary magazines. One of the women says, Spaniards don't like their exiles, do they? "Not overly much," the woman named Ana sighs. "We are political exiles from Uruguay. But I guess no one is ever given a good welcome back. I have had so many fantasies of how wonderful it will be to see my friends in Montevideo, that's a waste of time, isn't it?" The next day you give away the extraordinary red roses, and fly home.

30

When I announce to my friends, I've come home, to New York, the astonished reply is, Have you been away? They are thinking: Is she so nutty she thought that we believed she would stay with a man who had a wife and Arabs, just for starters? In the face of such silence, I add nervously, "Well, but we had an awfully good time." The sentence sounds meek. The flow of Europeans comes in our direction now. Just as I've burned my Spanish—or Catalan—bridges, New York is filled with Catalans. I am wined, dined, and, in the end, forced, by their great efforts in my direction, to love, *in absentia,* Catalonia. I've many new friends from there. Gloria Villardell, Manolo Vázquez Montalbán, Jordi Herraldi, Gorgina, Rosa Regás, the Barrals. Weakminded, I can even be forced to utter a few Catalan phrases, most of which sound like *molch, polch,* a round potato in the Spanish mouth. Well, New York is Paris now.

Juan Benet and Rosa Regás fly in from Madrid. He had been invited by Yale to give a lecture. At Kennedy customs I see a bearded student, a nun, and a well-dressed man protectively steering his wife along, his arms encircling her as though warding off America's blows; the Madrid flight is coming out.

After they come back from Yale, I give a party for Juan and Rosa in New York. We eat leftover Christmas ham in the kitchen and drink lots of wine. Maria joins us, Inez too. A friend of theirs from Madrid, Carmen Martín Gaite, carried away by the view of Central Park and Gardel tangos, wraps a faded aubergine shawl around her bosom, and with cigarette in mouth sings:

> *I dreamed I was a great artist*
> *Who was performing in New York.*
> *I dreamed that they applauded without stopping*
> *. . . me with Mickey, la Betty and Charlot.*
> *I dreamed that in a crystal palace*
> *A young black was playing the saxophone.*
> *I dreamed he came to rape me,*
> *But I escaped while dancing the fox trot . . .*

Juan watches her mimicking the gestures of forgotten Spanish B-movies from the 1940s; his brown, sardonic soft eyes and down-bent nose work well with his tall, tweedy look. A glass of Scotch in hand, he seats himself at the piano at the far end of the living room. "There I was, six years old, playing Schumann; then Franco came up from Africa." Juan looks in surprise at the ivory keys. "No more Schumann, no more musical career, my father was dead . . ."

"Juan, the music went into your novels about the Civil War—There's your Schumann, he's trapped in your writing." Juan smiles, he's thrown the clue and Rosa has caught it. *Los dos Juanes,* shy exhibitionists, play the same game. Gratified, he reaches for Maria, herself a jazz dancer. He whirls her around the room, and Inez claps her hands. The white living room with the view of the park and the black piano at the far end reverberates from the shouts and swift circular motion; Juan and Maria imitate old-fashioned tango dips, Argentine *porteño* music.

When the other Juan shows up a year later for a similar writers' conference, the terms are different. We eye each other like two old warriors, the battle over, just checking out the territory. Juan Goytisolo stalks the apartment that was once one of his many homes; he looks for clues of my present new life, while I avoid finding out who has replaced me. Valerie drops in for a visit, and she sighs, "Just like old times." Juan sheepishly admits to Valerie, who has come dressed in blue jeans and a silk shirt, and bearing halvah, that his wife's daughter is having a baby.

"Juan," Valerie shrieks, "a grandfather!"

"And Ahmed has a whole new family," I add. "Two more sons with the second wife."

"*No me digas*—a real Jewish patriarch," Valerie whistles; "not like us New York Gypsies." Valerie ends by eating the halvah herself. "You don't like it, Juan? I bring pounds of it to my Puerto Rican boyfriend. When I visit Pupi in Puerto Rico, his sisters go for it; oh, I love the islands." Valerie munches, pensive. "But I'm no longer on a straight Spanish track, Juan. Recently I've added Yiddish, very comforting." Valerie chews. "Very new . . . Are you continuing with your Arabic?"

Juan nods. After Valerie leaves, he slowly walks through the apartment, committing it to memory, as though he does not expect to be coming back. He examines and packs his new Nikon FE, which is still encased in white styrofoam; he slips it back in the plastic carrying bag provided by the Forty-seventh Street Camera Shop. "Spain," he says, "is depressing." His blue eyes fix in a private, inward gaze, as though he has already left New York and is absentmindedly thinking other thoughts; the room smells from his Agua Brava. "After the euphoria, nothing that much seems to change . . ."

"In Spain they keep giving names to each period, don't they? First the 'uncorking,' now *el desencanto?*"

"*Gloomy* disenchantment."

"Maybe it happened too quickly. If there was a replay, maybe people would do things differently. I mean, there was never a real break with the past. If you are truly to let something new happen, you must make a real end to what has gone before. Maybe we really need all the traditional rituals of change, of welcoming back the defeated, praising the heroes—even the wrong ones. No *paloma* is going to fly in, carrying a bundle of democracy. You have to make that happen."

"I feel very sad," Juan says. "The Resistance never defeated Franco. He died in bed."

"Juan—you wanted *paradise.*"

He looks up at me, astonished. "You knew that? About paradise?"

"You said you wanted the lot, remember? Men, women, fame, adventure, but, Juan, who do you think lives in paradise, who did you think would be there when you arrived but a bunch of squabbling children?"

He gives you his new novel, Makbara, *and roughly points to the "bara," half apologetic, indicates you had some vague existence in that novel. You search and find maybe a scarf, silk clothing, a gesture, a remark, some scraps of you exist. You want to apologize for not reading it sooner. Does he understand, you are backing off? His hermetic, intense vision overwhelms. You retreat from his enormous talent in order to have room to create your own world. Wait for me, Juan, three years, four years, I am my own Peer Gynt now, going on my own voyage, taking the pieces, rearranging my own puzzle of what Bunny was planning to happen. Oh, Bunny loved her Juan!*

The two of you taxi to Kennedy. You mean to tell him how much you will miss him, you mean to say a rush of last-minute sentences, no words come out. You mean to say, Don't go. He checks in at the TWA counter, you walk to the rotunda where the incoming flights are listed, then Juan goes toward the white tunnel that leads to the 747 for Paris. It is early, abruptly he turns to you and says, When you come into a country, two people should be there, the one taking the trip, the one waiting, when you leave, you leave alone. He pushes you away, then he runs the length of the tunnel, not looking back, carrying his raincoat over his shoulder. You wait a minute, turn, and walk back out to the taxi stand. He has left his Moroccan bedroom slippers in the bathroom. You pick them up, smell them, smell the Agua Brava, the room has his odor, you hesitate, then you take the slippers to the back door and put them in the trash, several minutes later you change your mind, fish them out and throw them in the back of your closet. Final gestures can wait.

From the living room window, snow, melting into the early brown bones of spring, you write your reinvented Spain, you rail, criticize, chastise. But you were also that frivolous, you became part exile, paralyzed after Franco's death; you were giddy, that porno, that narcissistic, that confused. You laughed when you should have cried, were silent when you should have spoken, were fashionably left when you should have been pure.

Spaniards have rotten politics, but they do nice things with the late afternoon. *And you wanted paradise.* Well, Bunny, I whisper to myself over a cup of tea, *what did you expect you'd find? Nobody lives in paradise but a bunch of squabbling children.*

Just when I have written myself out, exhausted at living so long in a dream world I have reinvented with scraps of real names and fake forming a collage, Valerie comes back. She brings me a copy of her and Ann-Jo's recently published *Feminist Women During the Franco Years.* I've endorsed it. Valerie walks into the living room; she pushes her mane of red frizzed hair casually against her back. "I'm into loss," she says. "My mother's dead—you heard the news from Ann-Jo?"

I nod, and rush to bring her some tea.

"And I've left Pupi—I finally told him, No way, José, I need a *mensch*—so, yes, you might say, now I'm definitely into loss—" She walks the length of the room; today she is wearing running sneakers, blue jeans, and a white sweater. "I didn't think I had it in me—she had the big C—but in the end all of us rallied around. Barbara, imagine me, bathing and cleaning my mother. I thought I'd mind, but in the end I did all right." She pauses, and says in a low voice, "She was in Lauren Bacall's class in Julia Richman—"

"Mine was just before Lillian Hellman . . ."

Valerie sits down on a hassock; her legs dangle, grasshopper-style, along the thick wool carpet . . . "Barbara, you are just going to have to *tell* me things, now that she is gone. You've been through this so many times, why, you can remember before the sixties. I'm so mixed up now, I can't get the male-female scene right; when do we share?

Who pays? In my mother's generation, it was so *clear.* She told me, Your heart's not the Bank of America ..."

She keeps hinting I've been through the mill. I catch a glimpse of my face in the mirror, the once deep-greenish pupils of my eyes now lean toward cinnamon; the color's toned down, while my skin—in earlier life, on the pale side—has a ruddier, middle-aged, high hue. "Losing Pupi and my mother at the same time," Valerie sighs, "is heavy. Barbara, does it improve?"

"Look at it this way, Valerie, pieces of your past, with new twists reappear. When my father died, I took it for granted, well, that's it— no more Anthonys. And now Carla has brought home a Yalie—she's marrying him; I see shadows of our past—named Anthony, like my father, a lawyer like Harold, and of Italian descent (I suppose the Latin touch is my part). But it's reshaped into something new." I pause. "Carla's a clinical psychologist, Maria studies languages—Russian, German, Polish ... and Yiddish, like you. She dances too."

"Yiddish is a very new thing—Maria's right on target, both your daughters."

Things change and become other things, many times you think about Ahmed, then you receive, from a very different source, a letter from a student in a south Moroccan prison. Arriving has found a Moroccan reader. Mutatis mutandis. *He writes that he spent two years at the London School of Economics before his political protests landed him in prison for twenty years. His study group is using the Spanish experience as a metaphor for their present situation. Could more books on the same subject be sent? His English is impeccable. While in prison he has had a crisis: Communism is meaningless, the new religious fervor dangerous. He remains anti-capitalist and perhaps will become an ecologist. You wanted Ahmed to be your faithful fan; now, there is this different reader near Essaouira, by the coast. One of the Moroccan women students from Fez sends you a Christmas card, a picture of Christ the infant, and a Merry Christmas from a Muslim to a Jew, maybe the message to Valerie should be that life is goofy.*

Valerie squats on the hassock, waiting for words of wisdom fitting in a woman of my age.

"Oh, Barbara," she wails, "help me, tell me—you've lived through the worst of it—take Pupi, I thought he was a Puerto Rican stray. I gave him halvah and I typed and translated, and fought for his cause. After we split, I realized he was becoming Mr. Fellowship of some bilingual theater with big bucks in Houston. Now, what has been youı attitude to those men? I mean, you knew the pack, it was your generation in Spain who inherited all the anguish." Valerie blows her nose, pauses, meditates. "And the land. How do you manage? I've been through it, their drugs, their revolutions, the Off Off Broadway bilingual theaters; my mother's gone, but now I have her voice in me— Valerie, your heart's not the Bank of America . . ."

Carla brings Anthony to the place, when I come home I find my old wedding album on the floor, they have been studying it. She has brought me double lilacs from Saugatuck; the new owner, she says, sent them. He says he feels he is living in our house. But, Carla, houses belong to the people who live in them—we had Saugatuck in the good days, when it was meant to be. Outside, it is a clear day, the fresh smells of new grass rise in the air. The trees in Saugatuck were also designed by Olmsted. I could see them from my bedroom window, the way I see the park from here. *Mutatis mutandis.* I wait for Maria to walk through the door, her light touch on my shoulder, bringing me news of the day. And set my daughters free. And want them back. Behind Lincoln Center is the Louis Brandeis School. And *Dover Beach.* And Juan, Ahmed, and me in Cambrai. Wildflowers grow near the gulleys of the Atlas Mountains. The day Paco and I met Pepe, just arrived in Paris, in front of Notre Dame, zero kilometers 1948. Well, Nicolás said, we stayed friends thirty years. The Prado Hotel in Chicago. My mother, making her collages, taught me that any shape is on its way to becoming another.

We can catch the last of the sun's heat and have a swift walk in the park before the school kids take over with baseball. While I throw a suede jacket over my shoulders, mentally I am rummaging for some truth I do not possess, something for Valerie to hang on to during her bad period. But nothing comes to mind; just that odd phrase, *Who did you think lives in paradise but a bunch of squabbling children?* I can't let her be overwhelmed by her sorrow—some days it's you lean on me; other times, me on you. In lieu of something better, I firmly steer her toward the open door, for a moment let myself be her mother, and briskly tell her, "So, Valerie baby, improvise."